# Tense, Aspect, and Indexicality

# OXFORD STUDIES IN THEORETICAL LINGUISTICS

GENERAL EDITORS: David Adger, Queen Mary College London; Hagit Borer, University of Southern California

ADVISORY EDITORS: Stephen Anderson, Yale University; Daniel Büring, University of California, Los Angeles; Nomi Erteschik-Shir, Ben-Gurion University; Donka Farkas, University of California, Santa Cruz; Angelika Kratzer, University of Massachusetts, Amherst; Andrew Nevins, Harvard University; Christopher Potts, University of Massachusetts, Amherst; Barry Schein, University of Southern California; Peter Svenonius, University of Tromsø; Moira Yip, University College London

RECENT TITLES

14 Direct Compositionality
   edited by Chris Barker and Pauline Jacobson
15 A Natural History of Infixation
   by Alan C. L. Yu
16 Phi-Theory
   Phi-Features Across Interfaces and Modules
   edited by Daniel Harbour, David Adger, and Susana Béjar
17 French Dislocation: Interpretation, Syntax, Acquisition
   by Cécile De Cat
18 Inflectional Identity
   edited by Asaf Bachrach and Andrew Nevins
19 Lexical Plurals
   by Paolo Acquaviva
20 Adjectives and Adverbs
   Syntax, Semantics, and Discourse
   edited by Louise McNally and Christopher Kennedy
21 InterPhases
   Phase-Theoretic Investigations of Linguistic Interfaces
   edited by Kleanthes Grohmann
22 Negation in Gapping
   by Sophie Repp
23 A Derivational Syntax for Information Structure
   by Luis López
24 Quantification, Definiteness, and Nominalization
   edited by Anastasia Giannakidou and Monika Rathert
25 The Syntax of Sentential Stress
   by Arsalan Kahnemuyipour
26 Tense, Aspect, and Indexicality
   by James Higginbotham
27 Lexical Semantics, Syntax, and Event Structure
   edited by Malka Rappaport Hovav, Edit Doron and Ivy Sichel
28 About the Speaker
   Towards a Syntax of Indexicality
   by Alessandra Giorgi
29 The Sound Patterns of Syntax
   edited by Nomi Erteschik-Shir and Lisa Rochman

For a complete list of titles published and in preparation for the series, see pp 259–60.

# Tense, Aspect, and Indexicality

JAMES HIGGINBOTHAM

OXFORD
UNIVERSITY PRESS

# OXFORD
UNIVERSITY PRESS

Great Clarendon Street, Oxford OX2 6DP

Oxford University Press is a department of the University of Oxford.
It furthers the University's objective of excellence in research, scholarship,
and education by publishing worldwide in

Oxford  New York

Auckland  Cape Town  Dar es Salaam  Hong Kong  Karachi
Kuala Lumpur  Madrid  Melbourne  Mexico City  Nairobi
New Delhi  Shanghai  Taipei  Toronto

With offices in

Argentina  Austria  Brazil  Chile  Czech Republic  France  Greece
Guatemala  Hungary  Italy  Japan  Poland  Portugal  Singapore
South Korea  Switzerland  Thailand  Turkey  Ukraine  Vietnam

Oxford is a registered trade mark of Oxford University Press
in the UK and in certain other countries

Published in the United States
by Oxford University Press Inc., New York

© James Higginbotham 2009

The moral rights of the author have been asserted
Database right Oxford University Press (maker)

First published 2009

All rights reserved. No part of this publication may be reproduced,
stored in a retrieval system, or transmitted, in any form or by any means,
without the prior permission in writing of Oxford University Press,
or as expressly permitted by law, or under terms agreed with the appropriate
reprographics rights organization. Enquiries concerning reproduction
outside the scope of the above should be sent to the Rights Department,
Oxford University Press, at the address above

You must not circulate this book in any other binding or cover
and you must impose the same condition on any acquirer

British Library Cataloguing in Publication Data
Data available

Library of Congress Cataloging in Publication Data
Data available

Typeset by SPI Publisher Services, Pondicherry, India
Printed in Great Britain
on acid-free paper by
the MPG Books Group, Bodmin and King's Lynn

ISBN  978–0–19–923931–3 (Hbk)
       978–0–19–923932–0 (Pbk)

3 5 7 9 10 8 6 4 2

*To my teachers
and particularly to the memory of George Boolos
and Sidney Morgenbesser*

# Contents

| | |
|---|---|
| *Preface* | x |
| *General Preface* | xii |
| *Provenance of the Chapters* | xiii |

| | | |
|---|---|---|
| 1 | Tense, Indexicality, and Consequence | 1 |
| | 1.1 Tense, quantification, and temporal cross-reference | 3 |
| | 1.2 Interpretations of consequence | 8 |
| | 1.3 Some elaborations of tense | 12 |
| 2 | On Events in Linguistic Semantics | 18 |
| | 2.1 General considerations | 18 |
| | 2.2 The visibility of E | 27 |
| | 2.3 Telicity | 36 |
| | 2.4 Can events be negative? | 48 |
| | 2.5 Concluding remarks | 51 |
| 3 | Tensed Thoughts | 53 |
| | 3.1 Tenses and contents | 53 |
| | 3.2 Tenses and truth | 58 |
| | 3.3 Reflexive states | 62 |
| | 3.4 Discards | 67 |
| 4 | Tensed Second Thoughts: Comments on Richard | 76 |
| 5 | Why is Sequence of Tense Obligatory? | 83 |
| | 5.1 Introduction: Relations between tenses | 83 |
| | 5.2 The interpretation of tense | 85 |
| | 5.3 Tense anaphora | 87 |
| | 5.4 A reanalysis | 93 |
| 6 | Anaphoric Tense | 102 |
| | 6.1 Introduction | 102 |
| | 6.2 General outline | 104 |
| | 6.3 Some general questions | 106 |
| | 6.4 Adding the perfect | 110 |
| | 6.5 Rigidity and indexical mismatch | 111 |
| | 6.6 Subjective time | 114 |

viii  *Contents*

7 Accomplishments — 116
  7.1 Introduction — 116
  7.2 Telic pairs — 117
  7.3 Applications to causatives and location-locatum constructions — 120

8 The English Progressive — 126
  8.1 Preliminary remarks — 126
  8.2 Semantic elements — 127
  8.3 Background to the English progressive — 129
  8.4 Counterfactuals: Dowty (1977) — 130
  8.5 An extensional view: Parsons (1990) — 133
  8.6 Counterfactuals again: Landman (1992) — 138
  8.7 Revision I: Making telicity explicit — 139
  8.8 Revision II: Telics and stages — 143
  8.9 Revision III: Defining '*Prog*' with counterfactuals — 146
  8.10 Revision IV: Some influences of context — 147
  8.11 Cross-linguistic questions — 154

9 The English Perfect and the Metaphysics of Events — 157
  9.1 Introduction — 157
  9.2 Metaphysical issues — 160
  9.3 Interactions with sequence of tense — 165
  9.4 Shifted perfects — 169
  9.5 Conclusion — 178

10 Competence with Demonstratives — 179
  10.1 Introduction — 179
  10.2 Normal forms for demonstrative reference and truth — 182
  10.3 Complement clauses — 185
  10.4 Coordinate transformations — 187
  10.5 Puzzles of perspective — 188
  10.6 Perspective and truth — 192
  10.7 Concluding remarks — 193

11 A Plea for Implicit Anaphora — 195
  11.1 Introduction — 195
  11.2 Implicit arguments and control — 198
  11.3 Incorporated anaphora — 204
  11.4 Else — 208
  11.5 Concluding remarks — 211

|    |                                                                          |     |
|----|--------------------------------------------------------------------------|-----|
| 12 | Remembering, Imagining, and the First Person                             | 212 |
|    | 12.1 Introduction                                                        | 212 |
|    | 12.2 Gerundive complements                                               | 215 |
|    | 12.3 The interpretation of (certain) gerundive complements               | 217 |
|    | 12.4 Immunity to error through misidentification: A characteristic of PRO | 221 |
|    | 12.5 Ways of remembering and imagining                                   | 224 |
|    | 12.6 The semantic contribution of PRO                                    | 226 |
|    | 12.7 Alternatives explored                                               | 234 |
|    | 12.8 Links to formalization                                              | 238 |
|    | 12.9 Concluding examples and extensions                                  | 239 |

*References* 246
*Index* 255

# *Preface*

The work brought together in this volume consists of articles in linguistics and philosophy, lightly revised, and with some clarifications and extensions, published between 1995 and 2008. The articles have been loosely grouped, but contain numerous cross-references. I have suppressed a number of repetitions; but I have also retained some, on the grounds that the reader who is not bent on reading every single word that I have written may find it useful for the investigation of the specialized topics to have a quick summary of the background that I assume.

The topics themselves are as in my title: tense, aspect, and indexicality. The last has figured in other work of mine, not represented here. I became interested in tense and aspect only late, spurred in large part by the realization that their semantics was unclear, and hard to think about even at the level of individual examples. It was easy to see that traditional studies were onto something. But capturing that something in a truth-conditional setting, and respecting what was coming to be discovered about the syntactic triggers of tense and aspect, presented, at least to me, a task that was all the more interesting for its inchoateness.

Over the next several years I had occasional opportunities to pursue the subjects of this volume; but these opportunities came interleaved with other duties, both administrative and pedagogical, which slowed me down. In the meantime my topics gained in importance, thanks to work by Dorit Abusch, Alessandra Giorgi and Fabio Pianesi (jointly and singly), Manfred Krifka, Toshi Ogihara, Carol Tenny, and many others; I consider some of their work in the chapters that follow.

The work below is almost entirely English-centered. Sympathetic as I am with Noam Chomsky's thesis that the study of human linguistic competence must be approached from a comparative standpoint, at least if we are to shed light on the acquisition of first languages by normal children, I would have wanted to understand my topics from that perspective. In what follows I do make occasional forays into Italian and Chinese; but mostly I stick with English data that I can intuitively probe in depth. In doing so, I have felt rather like a lawyer arguing the best case for his client, in this case for (my) English; arguing, that is, that despite its hybrid Germanic-Romance status, and its limited morphology, English is after all well constructed, in the sense that its Tenses and Indexicals, and the Progressive and Perfect aspectual heads, contribute definite context-independent conditions on interpretation, to be clarified through the application of modern logic.

A number of my intellectual debts will be apparent from the references to this volume. I am also grateful to Peter Ludlow and an anonymous reviewer for Oxford University Press for their scrutiny and their suggestions. Besides these, especially to be mentioned are the audiences in graduate classes at MIT (some taught jointly with Irene Heim) and the University of Oxford. I am grateful also to the discussants at the Girona Summer School, 1996; the University of Stuttgart, 1997; the European Society for Logic, Language, and Information meetings in Trento, 2002; meetings in Kyoto, Sendai, and Tokyo, Japan in 2005; various conferences in Paris and Lyon, France; lectures at the Scuola Normale, Pisa, Italy; and three Semantics and Linguistic Theory meetings in which I was honored to be an invited speaker.

*University of Southern California*                                               James Higginbotham
*December 2008*

# General Preface

The theoretical focus of this series is on the interfaces between subcomponents of the human grammatical system and the closely related area of the interfaces between the different subdisciplines of linguistics. The notion of 'interface' has become central in grammatical theory (for instance, in Chomsky's recent Minimalist Program) and in linguistic practice: work on the interfaces between syntax and semantics, syntax and morphology, phonology and phonetics, etc., has led to a deeper understanding of particular linguistic phenomena and of the architecture of the linguistic component of the mind/brain.

The series covers interfaces between core components of grammar, including syntax/morphology, syntax/semantics, syntax/phonology, syntax/pragmatics, morphology/phonology, phonology/phonetics, phonetics/speech processing, semantics/pragmatics, intonation/discourse structure as well as issues in the way that the systems of grammar involving these interface areas are acquired and deployed in use (including language acquisition, language dysfunction, and language processing). It demonstrates, we hope, that proper understandings of particular linguistic phenomena, languages, language groups, or inter-language variations all require reference to interfaces.

The series is open to work by linguists of all theoretical persuasions and schools of thought. A main requirement is that authors should write so as to be understood by colleagues in related subfields of linguistics and by scholars in cognate disciplines.

David Adger
Hagit Borer

## *Provenance of the Chapters*

As noted in the Preface above, the chapters of this volume are lightly revised from earlier published work, and cross-references have been adjusted so as to suit their appearance together.

Chapter 1, 'Tense, Indexicality, and Consequence', appeared in Jeremy Butterfield (ed.), *The Arguments of Time*, a British Academy 'Centenary' Monograph. Published for The British Academy by Oxford University Press, Oxford, 1999, 197–215.

Chapter 2, 'On Events in Linguistic Semantics', appeared in James Higginbotham, Fabio Pianesi, and Achille Varzi (eds.), *Speaking of Events*. New York: Oxford University Press, 2000, 49–79.

Chapter 3, 'Tensed Thoughts', appeared in *Mind and Language* 10 (1995), 226–249. The article was reprinted in Wolfgang Künne, Albert Newen, and Martin Anduschus (eds.), *Direct Reference, Indexicality, and Propositional Attitudes*. Stanford, CA: CSLI Publications, 1997, 21–48.

Chapter 4, 'Tensed Second Thoughts: Comments on Richard', appeared in Aleksander Jokič and Quentin Smith (eds.), *Time, Tense, and Reference*. Cambridge, MA: The MIT Press, 2003, 191–197.

Chapter 5, 'Why is Sequence of Tense Obligatory?', appeared in Gerhard Preyer and Georg Peter (eds.), *Logical Form and Language*. Oxford: Clarendon Press, 2002, 207–227.

Chapter 6, 'Anaphoric Tense', appeared as 'The Anaphoric Theory of Tense' in Masayuki Gibson and Jonathan Howell (eds.), *Proceedings From Semantics and Linguistic Theory 16*. CLC Publications, Cornell University, Ithaca, NY, 2006, 59–76.

Chapter 7, 'Accomplishments', appeared in *Proceedings of Glow in Asia II*. Nagoya, Japan: Nanzan University, 2000, 72–82.

Chapter 8, 'The English Progressive', appeared in Jacqueline Guéron and Jacqueline Lecarme (eds.), *The Syntax of Time*. Cambridge, MA: The MIT Press, 2004, 329–358.

Chapter 9, 'The English Perfect and the Metaphysics of Events', appeared in Jacqueline Lecarme and Jacqueline Guéron (eds.), *Time and Modality*. Berlin: Springer Verlag, 2008, 173–193.

Chapter 10, 'Competence With Demonstratives', appeared in *Philosophical Perspectives* 16 (2002), 3–18. The article was published also in Bjørn Ramberg and Martin Hahn (eds.), *Reflections and Replies: Essays on the Philosophy of Tyler Burge*. Cambridge, MA: The MIT Press, 2003, 101–115.

Chapter 11, 'A Plea for Implicit Anaphora', appeared in Hans Bennis, Pierre Pica, and Johann Rooryck (eds.), *Atomism and Binding*. Amsterdam: Foris, 1997, 183–203.

Chapter 12, 'Remembering, Imagining, and the First Person', appeared in Alex Barber (ed.), *Epistemology of Language*. Oxford: Oxford University Press, 2003, 496–533.

# 1

# Tense, Indexicality, and Consequence

The truth value of a predication is relative to time, signalled in some of our simplest utterances by the grammatical tenses. In any systematization of the world as we know and speak about it, this relativity must be made explicit, and our account of the central notions of logic, and of defeasible inference, adjusted accordingly. How, exactly, we do this depends upon our aims. If the aim is to take up our actual and potential utterances in a form suitable for the exposition of the content of science, then temporal relativity is accommodated by viewing those utterances as containing extra places for temporal arguments, whose identity is to be supplied through some system of temporal designators. To paraphrase Quine (1960: 193), if the utterance is of 'the door is open', then we take it up as 'open(the door, $\delta$)', where '$\delta$' is replaced by such a designator. Times, the referents of such designators, are objects. Likewise intervals, and even arbitrary collections of times; and their ordering relations and topological structure will come in by way of axioms governing the temporal order, and so governing implication and reasoning. There is room for much further inquiry, as we move from the more commonsensical realm into contemporary physics, but the basic strategy remains the same: the tenses, such as the present tense of 'the door is open', disappear in favor of relativized predication in explicitly given languages for which the notions of truth and logical consequence are well understood. A mark of this development is that the sentences of those languages are eternal, in Quine's sense: any two utterances of them have the same truth value.

A somewhat different aim, especially prominent in writings on the semantics of natural language, is that of understanding temporal relativity from within the notation offered by those languages themselves. If, as in the case of 'the door is open', these languages abound in sentences with tenses but without temporal designators, then we shall not want to take them, utterance by individual utterance, as if they did. For one thing, that would simply obscure the question how the various utterances of the same tensed sentence mean what they mean, a question that can only be addressed if the notation of this basic part of our languages is studied in its own right. For another, we are precluded from asking about good and bad reasoning within that notation. But more would be lost even than these inquiries, because we should have abstracted away from the question of the basis of our capacity to use language in the way that we do, and the role of our talk of time within such use.

In this chapter, as elsewhere and in other connections in this volume, I intend the second aim: the interpretation of our talk of time and other things within the basic notation, that of ordinary spoken language, in which we talk of it. There is, indeed, an important and growing literature on tense and time reference in natural languages. But I want to concentrate here on two aspects of the issues that have not always been prominent in these discussions. The first of these is the issue of indexicality, and the extension of the notions of logic to indexical languages. The second is the issue of the notation itself. I expand upon these in turn.

Both the inflectional and periphrastic tenses of human languages are expressions of generality involving time.[1] They are indexical, in the technical sense that their contribution to the meaning of utterances that use them depends upon factors external to the sentence uttered. Some conception of the proper form for a semantic theory for languages containing indexical expressions therefore lies in the background of a discussion of tense. Whatever this form is, it will affect the conception of a model for a tensed language, hence the definition of logical consequence for such a language. The issues involved in such a definition constitute the first topic of major concern here.

Second, whereas the notation for temporal relativity, in the case for example of the eternal sentences of Quine's project, is not only familiar but entirely explicit, the notation of natural language is a matter not only for formulation but even for discovery. In particular, the logical syntax of the tenses is a debatable question. Are they unary operators, with the syntax of negation, or perhaps binary or still more complex operators? Do they, or may they, give times or objects related to times as values of variables, and therefore sometimes occupy quantifiable places?

---

[1] A tense is inflectional if it is realized as an affix on a head (in English, a verb), periphrastic if it is realized as an independent word. Thus the English past is inflectional, but the future is periphrastic, co-opting the modal 'will'. Languages differ in how they realize tenses. In the Romance languages the future as well as the past is inflectional; in Yiddish, all tenses are periphrastic; in Chinese, tenses are not overtly realized at all. From the perspective that I adopt below, these differences are not material.

In what follows I shall take up these issues in reverse order, beginning with the logical syntax, and turning from there to possible characterizations of the notion of consequence. I conclude with a discussion of some further semantic phenomena, which if I am right underscore the need to take context and language together.

## 1.1 Tense, quantification, and temporal cross-reference

An important tradition, identified first of all with the work of A.N. Prior (Prior (1957) and (1967)) and continuing to the present day, has examined and elaborated the view that the tenses are operators. This view gains prima facie plausibility from the fact that the tenses, whether inflectional or periphrastic, do not occupy quantifiable places. Of course, we have reference to times in elementary language: 'He went there at that time', 'After some not too distant time I shall return to London', and so forth. But the thought is that there is a fundamental part of our language whose logical syntax does not involve quantification over times, even if, in the metalanguage, the action of the tenses is explained in terms of quantification. The tenses then become a species of modality. Model-theoretic studies, including Kamp (1971), Dowty (1979), and others, assumed this point of view.

It is in my opinion an important result of the studies of recent years that the modal theory of the tenses is inadequate: there is no basic part of our language for which it is correct. Some reasons are given in Kamp and Reyle (1993: chapter 5); Cresswell (1990) gives other examples to similar effect.[2] I concentrate here on one phenomenon among many, that of *sequence of tense*, illustrated by sentences such as (1) (from Ladusaw (1977)):

(1)  Mary said that a unicorn was walking.

Suppose that John makes an assertion by uttering (1) at a temporal location *t*, and let *u* be this utterance. Then whether John speaks truly depends upon whether, amongst Mary's utterances of root (i.e., unembedded) sentences prior to *t* (not necessarily assertions), there is one whose content is, or is sufficiently close to, the content of John's complement clause, as he uttered it at *t*. Only past utterances of Mary's count, because John used the past tense form 'said' in his utterance. And these must be utterances of root sentences rather than utterances that are themselves embedded within longer utterances of Mary's

---

[2] Cresswell (1990) shows how the effect of quantification over time can be achieved by relativizing truth to sequences of times. The method is analogous to the treatment of quantification in cylindrical algebra. See my review of Cresswell (1990) in Higginbotham (1993b).

(a nicety that I will assume but not explicitly mention in what follows). Now, John's utterance of (1) can be verified in two different ways, and that when John said it he must have intended it in just one of those ways: either, when he uttered (1) he intended to assert that Mary had in the past made an utterance that purported to be about the scene as of the time of that utterance; or he intended to assert that Mary had in the past made an utterance that purported to be about the way things were prior to that utterance. Supposing for simplicity that Mary speaks only English, the thought is that, on one interpretation, John speaks truly if and only if amongst Mary's past utterances there is one whose content is that of 'A unicorn is walking', as said then by Mary; and on the other interpretation John speaks truly if and only if amongst Mary's past utterances there is one whose content is that of 'A unicorn was walking', as said then by Mary.

Consider now that part of John's utterance that consists in his saying the complement sentence, 'A unicorn was walking'. Taken in isolation, and taking the past tense as entirely general, its content is unproblematic. That content is verified if, at any (relevant) time prior to $t$, a unicorn walked. But that is not the content that John asserts belongs to some past utterance of Mary's. For it is not the content of any past utterance of Mary's of 'A unicorn is walking', or words to that effect, since any circumstance in which a unicorn walks sometime between the time of Mary's utterance and the time of John's utterance of the complement would verify the complement but would not verify Mary's utterance; nor, for the same reason, is it the content of any past utterance of Mary's of 'A unicorn was walking' or words to that effect.

In sum, we have the following observations with respect to John's utterance of (1):

(i) It is ambiguous as between attribution to Mary of a past utterance about the then past, and a past utterance about the then present.

(ii) The complement cannot be understood as if it were uttered in isolation.

Any theory of the past tense must have both (i) and (ii) as consequences; and it must characterize the interpretations of utterances of (1) and the like in explicit semantic terms.

The example (1) shows two past tenses, a superordinate past on the main verb 'say', and a subordinate past on the complement auxiliary 'be'. Comparing (1) with (2), also taken from Ladusaw (1977), which places a subordinate past within a relative clause contained in the direct object, we see an immediate difference in the possible interpretations of the subordinate tense:

(2) Mary found a unicorn that was walking.

Suppose that John makes an utterance *u* of (2) at *t*. Then we can understand John's utterance as true if Mary found at some time *t'* prior to *t* a unicorn that walked at some time *t"* prior to *t*; so that, possibly, *t"* even lies between *t'* and *t*. A little contextual nudging makes this last possibility evident:

(3)  Last week, Mary found a unicorn that was walking yesterday.

The analogue of (ii) therefore fails: the past tense in the relative clause can be understood just as it would be in an utterance, 'It was walking', said by John at *t*. The analogue of (i) for an utterance of (2) is (iii):

(iii)  The past tense of the relative clause may be taken as ranging, for each time *t* prior to the utterance, over times prior to *t*, or as having its value fixed at *t*; if the former, then the utterance is true if and only if Mary found a unicorn, some walking by which preceded her finding it; if the latter, then it is true if and only if she found a unicorn that was walking at the very time she found it.

(It is, I think, clear that the past tense of the relative clause may be intended in either of the ways indicated in (iii).)

We thus have two questions. The first is the source of the ambiguities of (1) and (2), as specified in (i) and (iii); the second is the proper explanation of (ii), the fact that the embedded clause in (1) cannot be interpreted as if said in isolation. The last is especially significant not only because of the contrast between the two interpretations of (1) and the three of (2), but also because the normal case for indexical expressions is that they have a fixed interpretation, independently of embedding.[3]

I state a simple theory that has the desired consequences.[4] Suppose that tenses express temporal relations between events, understood as attaching to predicates in the manner proposed in Davidson (1967), so that the morphological feature +past is effectively a two-place predicate[5]

$$e < e'$$

A simple past-tense utterance, e.g., of the sentence 'Mary spoke', assigns the utterance *u* itself (or its time) as the value of *e'* and generalizes over *e*, so that the utterance as a whole means

---

[3] This point is made perhaps most forcefully in Kaplan (1977).

[4] In what follows I use some material presented in work, published and unpublished, by Mürvet Enç (1987), Dorit Abusch (1997), Timothy Stowell (1993), Karen Zagona (1992), and Toshiyusi Ogihara (1995), as well as Higginbotham (1995b).

[5] As in Higginbotham (1985b) I extend Davidson's proposal so that every ordinary predicate, even including nominals, carries a position for events; see further Chapter 2 below.

$(\exists e)$ (speak(Mary,$e$) & $e < u$)

Likewise, suppose that the feature −past is a two-place predicate

$e$ temporally overlaps (or: surrounds) $e'$

Abbreviating 'temporally overlaps/surrounds' as '≈', an utterance $u$ of the simple sentence 'Mary is speaking' is taken up as:

$(\exists e)$ (speak(Mary,$e$) & $e \approx u$)

Suppose now that the second argument of the embedded past tense in (1) or (2) can take on the value of the first argument of the superordinate past tense. For (1), that gives (4):

(4) $(\exists e)$ [say(Mary,$\alpha$,$e$) & $e < u$ & $\alpha$=(the proposition that $(\exists e')$ (walk(a unicorn,$e'$) & $e' < e$))]

The embedded proposition that the speaker says that Mary said is a true report of her speech if amongst Mary's past utterances there is one with that content; namely, that a unicorn is walking prior to that very utterance of Mary's itself. It follows that we have captured the truth conditions of one meaning of (1). For the second interpretation, we might follow traditional grammar in taking the embedded past as a 'copy' of the superordinate past. The embedded clause is then −past, but its second argument continues to be anaphoric to the first argument of the superordinate clause. In that case, the proposition said to be the content of one of Mary's past utterances is:

$(\exists e)$ (walk(a unicorn,$e$) & $e' < e$)

The speaker who is reporting Mary then speaks truly if amongst Mary's past utterances there is one whose content would have been expressed then in English by then saying, 'A unicorn is walking'. The interpretations of (1) are then assimilated to well-known features of cross-reference, or in the jargon of linguistic theory *anaphora*. Evidently, the same devices give the two interpretations of (2), as specified in (iii).

We can improve on the formulation of the basis for the interpretation of (1) in which the speaker reports a past, present-tense utterance of Mary's. Michela Ippolito (1998) observes that the single feature +past may in a given language be interpreted in any combination of three different ways: (a) as expressing temporal priority $<$; (b) as requiring that the second coordinate of the tense be anchored in some time prior to the time of utterance, and restricting the event-quantification to that time; (c) as merely facilitating anaphora.[6] Indeed (c) is seen in English in the use of the past perfect, as in discourses such as (5):

(5)  John arrived at seven. He had left at six.

where the perfect is evaluated, not with respect to the utterance or time of speech, but with respect to the antecedently given time of seven.

Or consider the minimal pair due to Hans Kamp (1971):

(6)  A child was born who would be king of the world.

(7)  A child was born who will be king of the world.

In the modal setting within which Kamp was working at the time, (6), which contains an embedded future 'will' (to which past-tense morphology has been added) within the scope of a superordinate past, comes out as expected, say as in (8):

(8)  P [($\exists x$) (child($x$) & born($x$) & F(king($x$)))]

where P and F are the simple past and future operators. But (7) is problematic: if it is true, then some child born in the past comes to be king of the world in the future of the utterance, or time of evaluation, of (7) itself. But the future 'will' is embedded, hence within the scope of the superordinate operator P; and this gives the wrong result. Kamp's own solution in (1971) was to propose that in (7) there is a kind of reference to the time of utterance, in the form of a tacit occurrence of an operator N, read 'Now', whose effect is to carry the formula on which it operates back to the time of evaluation. In detail, this account led to the system of 'double indexing', generalizable to two-dimensional modal logic in the sense of Segerberg (1973).

On the view proposed here, however, it is not (7) that is problematic, but (6). In (7) the tenses are interpreted independently, and we have (9) (anchoring the second coordinate of each tense to the utterance $u$):

(9)  ($\exists e$)($\exists e'$)($\exists x$) [born($x,e$) & $e < u$ & king($x,e'$) & $e > u$][7]

The problem now is to make the future 'would' of (6) relative to the superordinate past. Just here I appeal to the past-tense feature as licensing

---

[6] Amongst other things, Ippolito argues that the Italian *passato remoto* is interpreted as expressing a temporal relation as in (a), whereas the imperfect is a past tense in the sense of property (b), not expressing a temporal relation, but demanding anchoring in a past time. See Ippolito (1996) and (1998).

[7] Here I have reduced clutter: strictly speaking, we should relativize also to an event of $x$'s being a child, and stipulate that it temporally overlaps $x$'s birth.

anaphora, with the effect that the second occurrence of '*u*' in (9) is replaced by '*e*'.

Finally, we need to answer the question why the two past tenses can be interpreted independently in (2), but not in (1); in other words, why the embedded clause in (1) cannot be understood as if spoken in isolation. For the purposes of this section, I shall assume that, by linguistic rule, it is necessary for the quantification over events in the embedded clause to be restricted to events that temporally overlap or surround the superordinate position; some elaborations are given in section 1.3 below.[8]

I have illustrated the interpretation of sequence of tense in English with respect to an isolated example; but even this single example brings out the features of the tense system that bear upon the two issues with which I began. For, if it is right to say that sequence of tense is a phenomenon of cross-reference, then even within sentences lacking any temporal designators whatever, we have determined that they involve objectual reference (to events, and through them to their times) in the object language. Second, if indeed the simple past tense expresses priority to the time of utterance, then the utterance itself (or its time) must be a constituent of the proposition expressed; but that raises the question of the relation of contextual elements to the constituents of the tensed utterance, and the appropriate notion of consequence for such utterances.

## 1.2 Interpretations of consequence

To the foregoing, consider the simple objection: doesn't the conception of truth conditions for tensed utterances as in (9) make it a logical consequence of any utterance of 'the door is open', not only that there are doors, but also that there are utterances? And how could that be? The question is stronger rhetorically than it is in content, but it is not irrelevant. To answer the objections, I turn first to the more general question how truth conditions should be given for indexical and context-dependent languages.

Elsewhere (Higginbotham (1988) and Chapter 10 below) I suggest (following proposals by Scott Weinstein and Tyler Burge) that the theorems of a theory of truth conditions for indexical languages make those truth conditions dependent upon satisfaction of an antecedent, wherein the import of the context-dependent elements is spelled out. Here I render the simplest outlines of the proposal. Consider again an utterance of 'the door is open'. This utterance is to be evaluated as an utterance *u* of a particular syntactic

---

[8] See Ogihara (1995) for an alternative view.

structure Σ, containing various pieces of syntactic information. The utterance contains at least two indexical elements, namely the present tense and the incomplete definite description 'the door' (we may take it for granted that the speaker knows, and knows that everybody else knows, that there are lots of doors). We suppose that the speaker, Tom say, intends to refer to some particular object $d$, which if he is speaking as we expect him to we have the right to assume that he takes to be a door. Again, Tom knows how the present tense of English restricts the range of quantification of the variable ranging over situations. We therefore conclude (10):

(10) If Tom refers to $d$ with his utterance of 'the door' as part of $u$, $d$ is a door, and Tom confines the range $X$ of the quantification over events to those that temporally overlap $u$, then his utterance $u$ of Σ is true ↔ $(\exists e)$ (open($d,e$) & $X(e)$).

If the antecedent of (10) is satisfied, we can go on to evaluate Tom's utterance as true or false, depending upon the state of $d$; if not (e.g., if Tom is mistaken in thinking that $d$ is a door), we cannot detach the consequent, and nothing follows. Whether Tom's utterance has truth conditions is, on this view, conditional upon upon his antecedent proper use of the devices of demonstrative and indexical reference.

There is an obvious relation between the above proposal and Sir Peter Strawson's discussion of definite descriptions in Strawson (1950), and we might on those grounds think of the satisfaction of the antecedent condition '$d$ is a door' as a presupposition of Tom's utterance. For Strawson, however, all definite descriptions (or at least overwhelmingly those in subject position for ordinary predication) carried presuppositions, whereas what we have identified is a special class, arising in connection with demonstrative reference.

The discussion of Tom's particular utterance generalizes to all utterances of that type, by any speaker of English. Thus, what the theory of truth conditions says about the *sentence* 'the door is open' is as in (11):

(11) For all $s$ and $x$, if $s$ refers to $x$ with $s$'s utterance of 'the door' as part of her utterance of $u$ of Σ, $x$ is a door, and $s$ confines the range $X$ of quantification over events to those that temporally overlap/surround $u$, then $u$ is true ↔ $(\exists e)$ (open($x,e$) & $X(e)$).

If we are to have conditional truth conditions as suggested, then there must be some conception of a model for the elements—the utterances $u$ of syntactic structures Σ—that have truth values, of what it is for such a model to be a model of them, and sets of them, and what it is for one of them to be a consequence of a set of others.

There are in fact at least two notions of a model for a language with conditional truth conditions, and these lead to different notions of consequence. Suppose first of all that a full account of the truth conditions of pairs $(u,\Sigma)$ has been given, in a non-indexical formal language. Where $\Sigma$ is a particular syntactic structure, the truth conditions of its utterances will be given by a formula as in (12):

(12) $(\forall u, x^*, X^*) \{A(u, x^*, X^*) \rightarrow [(u,\Sigma) \text{ is true} \leftrightarrow \Phi(u, x^*, X^*)]\}$

where $x^*$ and $X^*$ abbreviate sequences of first- and second-order variables, and $A$ is a family of conditions on their values within $u$. Then a model for $(u,\Sigma)$ can be taken as a model for $\Phi$, together with an assignment of values drawn from the universe of that model to the free variables $u$ and those in $x^*$ and $X^*$. On this conception, a model $(M,a)$ for (a potential utterance of the syntactic structure for) 'the door is open' is simply a model $M$ for

$$\Phi = (\exists e)\,(\text{open}(x,e)\ \&\ X(e))$$

together with an appropriate assignment $a$ of values in the universe of $M$ to $u$, $x$, and $X$; and $(M, a)$ is a model of 'the door is open' just in case $a$ satisfies $\Phi$ in $M$.

I shall call the above conception of a model for $(u, \Sigma)$ the *reduced conception*; reduced, because it discards the information that would be wanted to determine whether the antecedent in (12) for a particular utterance of $\Sigma$ is or is not satisfied (or, in another formulation, retains only the information that is derived by instantiating the right-hand side of the biconditional consequent on the assumption that the antecedent of the whole is satisfied).

The reduced conception can be questioned, e.g. for failing to make 'there are doors' a consequence of 'the door is open'. For if complex demonstratives function as suggested above, then the information that the demonstrated object is a door is present only in the antecedent $A$, and not elsewhere. This and similar circumstances invite another conception of consequence, the *full conception*, according to which (referring to (12)) a model for $(u,\Sigma)$ is a model for the set $\{A,\Phi\}$, together with assignments of values to the free variables. In our example, the antecedent condition $A$ will contain as a conjunct

$$\text{door}(x)$$

or more precisely, if we were right to say that even nominal predicates such as 'door' carry an event position (see note 5 above),

$$(\exists e)\,(\text{door}(x,e)\ \&\ X(e))$$

where the parameter $X$ again represents confinement of the range of the quantification to events overlapping $u$, then, where a potential utterance $u'$, simultaneous with $u$, of the syntactic structure $\Sigma'$ for 'there are doors' will have as its truth condition

$$\Phi' = (\exists y)(\exists e) \, (\text{door}(y,e) \, \& \, X(e))$$

it follows that every model of $\{A,\Phi\}$ (in fact, of $A$ alone) is a model of $\Phi'$, and hence, according to the full conception, that a contemporaneous utterance of 'there are doors' is a logical consequence of an utterance of 'the door is open'.

Consider now a worry due to G.E. Moore (1927: 71): how, using a simple past tense, can you say the same thing twice? To advert to Moore's example, if I say twice, 'Caesar was murdered' I seem to say in the first utterance that he was murdered before that, and in the second that he was murdered before *that*. Moore's question arises whether tenses are taken as operators or as involving temporal points and predicates, since utterances of the same past-tense sentence at different times will have different truth conditions. But if we integrate our understanding of context with the purely semantic exposition, the answer is clear: even if you can't, in a way, say the same thing twice by saying 'Caesar was murdered', we know that if any utterance of 'Caesar was murdered' is true then all subsequent ones are. And where we avow 'Many people have said that Caesar was murdered', we count ourselves as speaking truly despite the difference between the truth conditions of any two non-simultaneous past utterances of 'Caesar was murdered', because we know that the context links them so as to make them true or false together. We don't need identity; closeness of fit is enough.

Our familiar notion of consequence was built for languages without context-dependent elements. For this reason it may be explicated in different ways for different purposes, once such elements are added in the manner suggested above. But are we justified in speaking of the full conception of consequence as *logical* consequence? It is not easy to attach other than a terminological significance to the question, because the consequence relation is explained, on both the reduced and full conceptions (and on intermediate conceptions, which perhaps include some contextual information but omit some as well), in the same terms; at any rate, I shall not consider it here.

In the exposition of examples of sequence of tense above, I allowed material that enters the antecedent $A$ of the canonical or normal form for truth conditions to seep into the formulas that gave the interpretation of main and embedded clauses. The shift is consequential, inasmuch as the inclusion of the contextual material within the scope of higher predicates, operators, or quantifiers, will falsify truth conditions. The *locus classicus* of this observation is Kaplan (1977), who observed that modal operators are insensitive to the way in which the reference of a demonstrative is secured. If I say, 'That might have been green', pointing to a conspicuously red object, I cannot intend to be taken as having spoken truly because I might, after all, have been pointing to a green object. Applying this observation, say, to a modal embedding as in (13):

(13)  There might have been no doors.

it matters whether what gives the truth conditions incorporates reference to the utterance, as in (14), or eschews it in favor of the values of variables determined in context, as in (15):

(14)  $\Diamond \neg (\exists x)(\exists e) \ (\text{door}(x,e) \ \& \ e \approx u)$
(15)  $\Diamond \neg (\exists x)(\exists e) \ (\text{door}(x,e) \ \& \ X(e))$

For, it appears, what follows the modal in (14) will be true in any possible world in which $u$ does not exist; whereas (14) is true only in those containing no doors at the time of speech. Only the official exposition, following (11), gives the right result. In the final section I return to the issue of sequence of tense, asking how it should be expounded in light of these facts.

## 1.3 Some elaborations of tense

I have suggested that the phenomena of sequence of tense involve cross-reference between coordinates, which I have supposed to be events in the sense of Davidson (they could, for the purposes of this discussion, have been the times of those events equally well). Now, such cross-reference is normally understood as conditioned by syntactic structure, and as appearing overtly in interpretation. However, returning to the earlier examples of sequence of tense phenomena, we can see that cross-reference must occur within the antecedents $A$ of the formulas giving canonical truth conditions. For (1), repeated below, we initially gave interpretations as in (16) and (17), the first representing the embedded, anaphoric past, and the second the case where we suggested that the +past feature mediated anaphora, but did not express temporal anteriority:

(1)  Mary said that a unicorn was walking.
(16)  $(\exists e) \ [\text{say}(\text{Mary}, \alpha, e) \ \& \ e < u \ \& \ \alpha = (\text{the proposition that} \ (\exists e') \ (\text{walk}(a \ \text{unicorn}, e') \ \& \ e' < e))]$
(17)  $(\exists e) \ [\text{say}(\text{Mary}, \alpha, e) \ \& \ e < u \ \& \ \alpha = (\text{the proposition that} \ (\exists e') \ (\text{walk}(a \ \text{unicorn}, e') \ \& \ e' \approx e))]$

In these formulations, both the speaker's utterance and the proposition referred to by the embedded clause incorporated the anaphoric information directly; but, as we have observed, that would (in general) give the wrong impression. The point is perhaps most easily shown in reports of past utterances that embed the simple future, as in (18):

(18) John said (last week) that Mary will be here next week.

The future is understood as the speaker's future, so that we would obtain for the reference of the embedded utterance (19):

(19) the proposition that ($\exists e$) (Mary here next week($e$) & $e > u$)

But, barring the unlikely event that, when John spoke, he made explicit reference to the speaker's utterance, (19) gets it wrong, in the sense that although in John's speech the range of quantification was confined to situations following his own utterance, that confinement was not by way of referring to that utterance. It is, I conceive, as legitimate as it was in speaking of 'saying the same thing' by two utterances of 'Caesar was murdered', to report John using the speaker's future tense; for we know from the context that if John said last week, 'Mary will be here in two weeks', then the speaker's report, understood as the speaker said it, will be equivalent to John's original. But we should not put reference to the speaker's own utterance (or its time) into the truth conditions of the speaker's utterance, or the speaker's report of John.

It is not difficult to modify the account so as to reckon with the issues here. For the case of (18), we replace the explicit restrictions on the quantifiers by a predicate variable, whose value will be determined in the context. For (16) and (17), which show anaphora, we require distinct predicate variables, one for the superordinate and one for the subordinate clause; and their values must be linked. Abstracting from the technical details, we can observe a general moral: that what is contextually given in the evaluation of an utterance is not just a matter of setting up appropriate objects and values of predicate variables one at a time, but also a matter of the syntactic and semantic interactions amongst the context-dependent expressions.

In English, a −past subordinate clause cannot be anaphoric to a +past superordinate clause. This fact is already exemplified in the minimal pair from Kamp, repeated here:

(6) A child was born who would be king of the world.
(7) A child was born who will be king of the world.

in that the embedded future of (7) is interpreted with respect to the time of speech only. Likewise, one can say (20) on Friday, not on the following Sunday; but (21) is acceptable on either day:

(20)   John said on Thursday that Mary will be here on Friday.

(21)   John said on Thursday that Mary would be here on Friday.

A further example, much discussed in the literature following Enç (1987), is (22):

(22)   John said that Mary is pregnant.

The judgement here is that the content of (22), if true, implicates not only Mary's current pregnancy, but also her pregnancy as of the time of John's speech. From the fact that the non-past 'is' must be interpreted as if in isolation, it follows that the content is (the proposition that)

$$(\exists e) \ (pregnant(Mary,e) \ \& \ X(e) \ )$$

where the value of $X$ is fixed at periods overlapping or surrounding the time of the speaker's utterance $u$.

Recall now the further restriction, which prevented an interpretation as if in isolation of the past tense in the complement clause in (1), repeated here:

(1)   Mary said that a unicorn was walking.

The restriction was that the quantification over events in the embedded clause be confined to events that overlap the superordinate position; i.e., the time of Mary's speech. With this understanding, we can formulate the truth conditions of (22) as in (23):

(23)   $(\exists e')$ [say(John,$\alpha$,$e'$) & $X'(e')$ & $\alpha$=(the proposition that $(\exists e)$ (pregnant(Mary,e) &$X(e)$))]

where the conditions on '$X$'' and '$X$' are linked, in that '$X$' can be replaced by '$Y(e)$ & $X'(e)$', with the extension of '$Y$' fixed at periods surrounding the utterance $u$ of (22).[9]

In the official notation, there will be linguistic rules such as those given above for the interaction of context-dependent elements, notably the tenses, and further principles governing the combinatorics of other elements. For a properly evaluatable utterance, with the values of the free variables on the right-hand side of the biconditional consequent all filled in, the information that was deployed in assigning those values is lost.

[9] See Chapter 5 below for a fuller account.

Within possible-worlds semantics, however, there is a method, more than occasionally perspicuous, for representing contextual information in the truth conditions such that it may be seen, but all of it removed from the proposition except the extension. This method may be called *rigidification*; i.e., attaching to the context-dependent expressions an operator that, by definition, delivers in each possible world the extension in the actual world of whatever it attaches to. This operator David Kaplan (1977) christened 'dthat'. Using his notation, we might for example render (23) as in (24):

(24)  $(\exists e')$ [say(John,$\alpha$,$e'$) & dthat[ $< u$]($e'$) & $\alpha$=(the proposition that $(\exists e)$ (pregnant(Mary,$e$) & dthat[ $\approx u$]($e$) & dthat[ $\approx e'$]($e$)))]

The analogy would be to an utterance of 'that man wearing sunglasses is a friend of mine', where the linguistic material serves only to fix the value of the subject, and what is expressed is a proposition about him, whose truth conditions can be given by:

> dthat[the man wearing sunglasses] is a friend of mine

But the device of rigidification should not be taken as a serious proposal about the workings of the language; or so I think. For one thing, it makes the rigidity of context-dependent expressions adventitious, whereas it ought to be a matter of principle.[10]

Up to this point I have been free in the use of intensional abstraction, represented by the prefix 'the proposition that...', appealing only to differences amongst propositions as determined by their possible divergence in truth value, but not advancing any conception of propositional identity. It is, I should say, manifest that the latter question cannot be resolved apart from taking the notation of the language seriously, and I will close by remarking, concerning the use of the tenses, two respects in which this is so.

Indirect discourse, which has formed the basis of the examples in this discussion, concerns itself with the question what it is to make a faithful report (or prediction) of what someone has said (or will say). We have seen examples where the fidelity of the report is consistent with a tolerable divergence in truth conditions—that was the point of the discussion of Moore's example. But we may also find (a) cases where provably equivalent truth conditions, even on a reduced conception of these, are not enough to make for a faithful report; and (b) cases where idiosyncratic properties of the language in which the report is made restrict the possible interpretations.

---

[10] As I understand him, Kaplan takes this point of view as well. In any case, I elaborate upon it in Chapter 10 below.

For the first point (a): let John say on Sunday, 'It was raining at noon yesterday', and let Mary say at noon on Saturday, 'It is raining now'. Then John's speech is true if and only if Mary's speech is true, even in all counterfactual situations.[11] Suppose even that Mary is perfectly aware of what John will say on Sunday, and knows that it is noon on Saturday. Still, Mary cannot predict John's speech indirectly by saying (25):

(25) ??John will say tomorrow that it is raining now.

Rather, the past tense must be used, as in (26):

(26) John will say tomorrow that it was raining now.

In keeping with the general case, the past tense licenses anaphora, so that the content of John's speech is represented through (26) (using the 'dthat' shorthand) by

$$(\exists e) \, [\text{rain}(e) \, \& \, \text{dthat}[\, < e'\,](e)]$$

where the value of $e'$ is the event of John's speaking on Sunday. A possible reason, along the lines of Ogihara (1995), is that John's and Mary's temporal perspectives on the same event, rain at noon on Saturday, are different. Whatever the solution may be, the example counts against the idea that for the sake of determining whether a report is faithful we have only to compare direct utterances; see Chapter 5 for some further discussion.

For the second point (b): consider a contrast between our initial example (1) and an example where the embedded clause is not progressive, as in (27):

(1) Mary said that a unicorn was walking.

(27) Mary said that a unicorn walked.

For (1), we said, there were two possibilities: either the (putative) walking was placed as simultaneous with Mary's past utterance, or as lying in its past. But for (27), only the second possibility obtains. If we were right to say that the past tense may serve only to mediate anaphora in (1), then there is no reason it should not do so in (27), giving the content

$$(\exists e) \, [\text{walk}(a \text{ unicorn}, e) \, \& \, \text{dthat}[\, \approx e'\,](e)]$$

where the value of $e'$ is Mary's past utterance.[12]

---

[11] Or at least all those in which time continues through Sunday.

[12] As Irene Heim pointed out to me, the restriction that the past tense in (27) and the like be understood as the genuine anaphoric past, expressing temporal anteriority, is not captured in Enç (1987) or some other treatments of the subject. Enç (1991) suggests that there is a relativization to

The reason seems to lie in a property of English. In contrast with Romance, and even most Germanic languages, English does not permit a simple present-tense, non-progressive sentence to be a report on the current scene.[13] Thus 'a unicorn walks' must, in contemporary speech anyway, be understood as 'generic', stating that it is a general property of unicorns that they walk, and in this respect contrasts with the present progressive 'a unicorn is walking'. But the result of using the past tense as anaphoric merely, and not also as expressing anteriority, yields a content that is indistinguishable, save for the value of the variable $e'$, from what would be the content of 'a unicorn walks', understood as non-generic. The point then is this: (27) cannot report Mary as having said (if she were speaking English) 'a unicorn walks'; but it also cannot report her as having said 'a unicorn is walking', because fidelity to her speech would require the reporter also to use the progressive. Suppose that this hypothesis is correct. Then we have a case where it is not just the proposition expressed but also the interaction of the sentences of the language, together with a refined notion of what it is to report a person's speech faithfully, that drives the interpretive possibilities. Speech in any language can of course be reported in indirect discourse in English. But if there is no direct discourse in English to which the report can be faithful, then it may not be used as an indirect report at all; or so it appears. If so, then we cannot fail to attend to the variety of notation that the home language makes available.

In sum, the theory of tense, including the particular phenomena discussed here, constitutes a semantic inquiry of considerable complexity, the more striking because native speakers use their systems with such sureness and speed. The semantics sketched here is another pointer toward the need for integration of contextual and linguistic material in the interpretation of natural languages. The larger lesson, both for logic and philosophy, is that we should be prepared to elaborate systems and conceptions of truth and of consequence that show context and language working together.

---

events in 'eventive' predicates such as 'walk' in isolation, but not in statives (including the progressive). The suggestion would block the standard uses to which the relativization to events in predicates like 'is walking' may be put, and for that reason alone seems to me very doubtful.

[13] For discussion and much cross-linguistic data, see Giorgi and Pianesi (1997).

# 2

# On Events in Linguistic Semantics

## 2.1 General considerations

There is no doubt that reference to events and states is a pervasive feature of human thought and language. How is such reference made available through the syntactic and lexical resources of human speech, and what is the nature of the objects referred to? In this chapter I will defend and elaborate one view on these questions, derived ultimately from Davidson (1967) but subsequently developed and extended by a number of researchers. The elaboration will lead to a number of interconnected points that I believe deserve further study.

The inquiry pursued here lies within *linguistic* semantics, so that the first interest of the subject is taken to be psychological, not metaphysical (although metaphysical questions inevitably arise). As I will understand it, the aim of linguistic semantics is to determine what native speakers of human languages know about the relations of form to meaning, in virtue of which they are able to speak to others and understand them; and to explain how they came to know these things. If we turn from the question of the semantic competence of the native speaker to the problem of acquisition, then our conceptions of the formal information provided by syntax, and the nature of semantic values and projection rules, must satisfy a requirement of *learnability*: it must be possible for a first-language learner, on the basis of ordinary linguistic experience, to grasp these conceptions. In semantics as in syntax, the learnability requirement can be satisfied only if the theory is sufficiently restrictive; that is, if it does not offer a wide space of alternatives given the data. I will argue below that a signal use of event- and state-reference in semantic theory is precisely to provide a restrictive semantic framework. I begin with some history, and a sketch of alternatives.

### 2.1.1 *Davidson and Montague on events*

In the setting outlined above, the proposal of Davidson (1967), that there is reference to events in human language through the medium of an unapparent argument position in verbal heads, may be introduced as part of a theory of semantic competence. I take Davidson's proposal up here, following terminology I have used elsewhere (Higginbotham (1985)), as the hypothesis that there is a special argument position, the *E-position*, associated with every predicative head, thus with all of V(erb), N(oun), A(djective), and P(reposition).

According to the E-position hypothesis, a head $H$ has, besides the positions $1,2,\ldots,n$ set aside for its arguments, also a position E for events (in a wide sense, thus including states; I use the term *situation* when there is need for an expression that explicitly covers both), and therefore carries with it at least the structure $<1,2,\ldots,n,E>$. $H$ is then an $n+1$-place predicate, whose interpretation is known to the native speaker to be satisfied by an appropriate sequence of objects just in case some condition $C$ holds of that sequence. For expository purposes we may represent this state of knowledge by interpreting $H$ as

$$\Phi(x_1,x_2,\ldots,x_n,e)$$

where $\Phi$ is the appropriate condition on reference.

On the E-position hypothesis as I have stated it there need be no assumption that the things that may appropriately be assigned to it are objects of a metaphysically special sort (except insofar as they are events); on the contrary, one may follow Davidson in taking events to be objects.

Alternatives are possible. For one of the most interesting, I refer back to Richard Montague's article 'On the Nature of Certain Philosophical Entities' (the version of 1967, in Montague (1974)). For Montague, events counted as 'philosophical' entities, at least in the sense that they are routine in language and routinely suspect in metaphysics. Montague proposed that events (together with some other types of things, which will not concern us here) be thought of as properties of moments of time, in the sense of *property* that he himself made familiar through possible-worlds semantics; that is, the intension of a predicate.

If events are properties in Montague's sense then they are a type of universal: Montague called them *generic* events. On Montague's view there is, for instance, a generic event of the sun's rising, which is, for each possible world $i$, the set of moments $t$ such that the sun rises at $t$ in $i$. The predicate 'rises' is understood as 'rises$(x,t)$', expressing a relation between individuals and times. The generic event of $x$'s rising is

$$^\wedge\lambda t\ \mathrm{rises}(x,t)$$

derived by intensional abstraction over times and possible worlds. Montague held that English definite gerunds like 'the rising of the sun' typically referred to generic events.

But besides generic events Montague recognized that there were *particular* events, for example the particular event of the sun's rising that occurred in Manhattan on August 13, 1967. A particular event was again a property of moments of time, but as it were a very restricted property, typically quantified over or referred to by an indefinite gerund or mixed nominal. The nominal 'rising' as it occurs in (1), for example

(1)   (They witnessed) a rising of the sun.

was understood as 'rising($P,x$)', for $P$ the kind of property of moments of time that answers to the individual risings of $x$. Various axioms were proposed to link the two predicates 'rise' and 'rising'.

Montague's view of events and event-reference in semantics was thus fundamentally different from the view encapsulated in the hypothesis of the E-position. The difference between these views affects all of the conceptions that form the substance of a semantic theory. On the hypothesis of the E-position, the arguments of a head must reserve a place for events; Montague's theory does not recognize such a place. Semantic values for nominals must for Montague include higher types, and the combinatorial semantic principles, projecting meaning from parts to wholes, will (even for the simple sentences discussed above) include the application of functions whose arguments are of higher type. But higher types do not appear in connection with the E-position. Moreover, as Davidson noted in part, and as I explain more fully below, with the E-position hypothesis a certain simplification and principled restriction of semantic combination becomes possible; at the cost, of course, of positing the E-position itself.

In a footnote, Montague remarked that he believed his view to be consistent with Davidson's work on action sentences and causal relations; but he added that Davidson did not inquire into the 'ontological status' of individual events (Montague (1974: 178, fn. 18)). The remark is somewhat obscure, since Davidson did in fact have a view about the ontology of events, namely that they were individual objects, rather than universals of any sort. However, the question certainly arises how the contexts that Montague treated should be analyzed in a semantics that assumes the E-position, but not the higher-order apparatus of Montague's article.

To this end, we would need to see how, once the E-position is admitted in ordinary predicates, both generic and particular events are accommodated, and we require a theory of the semantic relation between a root V or VP and its nominalizations, as in (1).

The semantics of nominalization is straightforward. On the E-position hypothesis, the nominalizations that refer to or quantify over events are those that pick out the E-position as the position to be bound by the determiner. Thus 'a rising of the sun' is just an indefinite description as in (2):

(2)   an *e* such that rise(the sun,*e*)

This same semantics goes for derived nominals in their event-interpretation, as in (3):

(3)   an examination (of the students), the murder (of the policeman)

and the like.[1] I will call it *E(vent)-Nominalization*, on a par with the agentive nominalization expressed in English by '-er', as in 'examiner', 'murderer', 'riser', and the nominalizations that select the internal argument of the verbal root, as in 'examinee', 'employee', 'belief', 'gift', etc. Thus the position that Montague recognized for individual events in gerunds and nominals derives immediately from the corresponding position in the head.

Events and states must be associated with time, and in particular must have temporal locations. In a system with the E-position, temporal adjuncts take for their subjects the position in the verb. Thus sentences like (4) express a predicational structure as in (5):

(4)   The sun rose at eight.

(5)   rise(the sun,*e*) & at(eight,*e*)

and temporal adjuncts may relate events to other events, as in (6), whose structure is as in (7):

(6)   The sun rose before I woke.

(7)   rise(the sun,*e*) & before(*e*,*e'*) & wake(I,*e'*)

What now of the generic events? Well, just as we have sorts of *things* whenever we have a predicate that ranges over objects other than events, so we will have sorts of events—really, sorts of things, each member of which is an event—whenever we have a predicate that ranges over events. Suppose, following Montague and using the account of kind-reference developed first in Carlson (1980), that a generic object or kind can be identified with the property of being an object of that kind, so that for example the kind *dinosaur* is

$$^\wedge\lambda x \; dinosaur(x).$$

Then we will identify the generic event that is the rising of the sun with

$$^\wedge\lambda e \; rise(the\; sun,e)$$

---

[1] See Grimshaw (1991) for a discussion of the types of derived-nominal interpretations.

that is, with the property of being a sunrise. Here, then, we have properties, since we are taking kinds to be properties; but they come in, not as part of the fundamental apparatus, but alongside the properties that answer to kinds of objects of all sorts.

It remains to verify that the construction of generic events just suggested will be adequate to the purposes for which Montague invoked them. In this place I will consider two analogic points of comparison.

Following the original discussion in Carlson (1980), reference to kinds coming from nominals for individuals is seen in examples like (8) and (9):

(8) Rabbits are plentiful/widespread.

(9) The dinosaur is extinct.

The predicates 'plentiful', 'widespread', and 'extinct' are truly applied only to kinds. Thus for (9) we will have an interpretation as in (10):

(10) $\text{extinct}(^\wedge \lambda x\, \text{dinosaur}(x))$

We also use derived nominal subjects to refer to kinds of events and states, as in (11) and (12):

(11) Happiness is not widespread.

(12) Murder is far too commonplace.

The subject of (11), for instance, refers to a kind of state, and not the state of any particular individual. The interpretation of (11) should therefore be as in (13):

(13) $\text{widespread}(^\wedge \lambda e\, \text{happy}(e))$

Besides kind-predications, there are other generic sentences involving events that are on a par with generics concerning ordinary objects; thus compare (14) with (15):

(14) Dogs bark.

(15) Barking frightens me.

In Carlson's original discussion, (14) would have involved reference to the kind *dogs*, and (15) presumably to the kind *barking*, a generic event in Montague's sense. However, adopting the (better-supported) 'relational' theory of generics sketched in Carlson (1989), we may see (14) as a conditional (perhaps with a 'generic' quantifier), as in (16):

(16) If $x$ is a dog, $x$ barks.

The quantification in (16) is over individual dogs, not kinds. Applying the same account to (15) we would have (17):

(17)   If *e* is barking, *e* frightens me

(that is, I am prone to be frightened by *e*; and with the usual, ill-understood, provisions for exceptions). The quantification now is over individual events of barking, not the kind. We conclude that generic events are not required for these cases; moreover, the fact that 'barking' is a predicate of events stems directly from the E-position in the root 'bark'.

The philosophical literature on events, especially that defending generic events, or events as universals, has made use of the fact that we often speak of the same event occurring again, or recurring. If events are taken as individuals, following Davidson, then this talk either cannot be taken literally, or if so taken points to a defect in the system. Suppose I have a toothache during the day Saturday, which fades Saturday night, but returns to me on Sunday morning. I can express my condition by saying, 'The toothache is back again', and in fact I did express it by supposing that *it* returned on Sunday. But the Saturday toothache and the Sunday toothache are individual events, each confined to its own temporal location; and the larger event, the toothache of which the Saturday episode is one part and the Sunday episode another, is also a single event, incapable of recurrence. How then can I speak of the same toothache at two different times? The obvious answer is that the notion of sameness employed in these locutions is qualitative, and not numerical, identity, as when we speak of *A* 'owning the same car' as *B*, when all we mean is that they own cars of the same kind. Similarly, when I say that my toothache is 'back again', I mean only that I have another toothache of the same kind as the toothache that I had the day before, perhaps implicating as well that the new toothache shares the etiology of the old. There is certainly more to be said about questions of qualitative identity. But it is sufficient for present purposes to note that arguments for generic events on the grounds that events can recur are fully analogous to arguments for generic objects on the grounds that we speak of different individuals as being 'the same'.

In sum, whereas Montague's approach was to commence with events as universals, and specifically properties of moments of time, and then to construct individual events whose link with the generics could be guaranteed only by special axioms, the approach that suggests itself once Davidson's E-position is adopted is to commence with events as individuals, obtaining generic events as kinds by whatever procedures give names of kinds of objects from predicates of objects of other sorts.

## 2.1.2 Generalizing the E-position

Davidson (1967) proposed the E-position only for action predicates. The extension to statives suggests itself for sentences such as (18):

(18) John's happiness lasted ten years.

(18) is obviously virtually interchangeable with (19):

(19) John was happy for ten years.

and the semantic problem is to explain not only why it is interchangeable, but also why this property is obvious. It is, in fact, an advantage of Montague's approach over Davidson's original that it can associate events (again, in a wide sense) with any predicate having a temporal parameter. A response to Montague therefore requires an E-position, not only in action predicates, but in predicates of all sorts. But pairs such as (18)–(19) provide direct evidence for the position. I consider one by one the steps leading to the full analysis.

In Davidson's original formulation, and in most subsequent work, simple sentences (bearing a tense, but lacking modals or aspectuals) were existentially general with respect to events; that is, a sentence such as 'Caesar died' is true just in case there is some (past) death of Caesar or another, the information that Caesar died but one death being no part of the logical form. In more contemporary terms, and assuming that there is a close connection between INFL (the position where tense is realized) and existential quantification over the E-position, the proposal is that in a structure

$$\text{INFL}' = [[_{\text{INFL}} +\text{past}] \text{ VP}]$$

the interpretation of INFL' is obtained by existential closure as in

$$[\exists e < e'] \; \Phi(e)$$

where $e'$ is anchored to the utterance time or some other time in a narrative, $\Phi$ represents the interpretation of VP, and we assume as in Chapter 1 and elsewhere that the tense expresses a relation between events and/or their times.

Applying the account first of all to simple sentences, 'John was happy' say, we will assume an LF structure

$$\text{INFL}' = [[_{\text{INFL}} +\text{past}] \text{ AP}]^{[2]}$$

---

[2] I am assuming here that the overt subject is generated internally to the AP, and moves to the pre-copular position without semantic effect. In section 2.2.2 below I give an application that depends upon the internality of such subjects.

The AP 'John happy' expresses the condition

$$\text{happy}(\text{John},e)$$

with free variable $e$. The sentence then expresses

$$[\exists e < e'] \; \text{happy}(\text{John},e)$$

For (19) itself, we take up the adjunct 'for ten years' as a predicate of $e$, measuring its temporal duration. The interpretation of the LF-structure for (19) is then as in (20):

(20)  $[\exists e < e']$ [happy(John,$e$) & for ten years($e$)]

For (18), we have first of all to consider the predication (21):

(21)  ——lasted (for) ten years

This predicate expresses a temporal measure of states and activities ('the war', 'the drought'), but also of other objects, where it is often understood that their 'lasting' is with reference to a normal or working state, as is seen in (22)–(23), for example:

(22)  The Chrysler lasted for ten years (before it broke down).

(23)  The apple only lasted a week (before it went rotten).

Of course, the predicate may simply measure the lifetime of an object, as in (24):

(24)  The aftershave lasted a month (then it was all used up).

In (18), the predicate is applied to the E-nominalization of the adjective 'happy'; the subject is definite, and expresses (25):

(25)  (the $e$) happy(John,$e$)

Taking account of the past tense, we have finally (26):

(26)  last ten years((the $e$) happy(John,$e$)) & $e < e'$

where $e'$ anchors the tense, as it does in (20) above.

The predicates of situations 'last (for) ten years' and '(for) ten years' have the same meaning: the word 'last' is vacuous with respect to states and activities, as 'happen' is vacuous with respect to events.[3] But (26) trivially

---

[3] The latter point is observed in Montague (1960).

implies (20); and if we assume that there is (or that the speaker of (20) intends) a unique state *e* (in the past) such that happy(John,*e*), then (20) implies (26). The close semantic relationship between (18) and (19) then follows from the theory.

We have seen that there is strong evidence for the E-position in AP, derived from the properties of nominalizations. Evidence for the E-position in NP is similarly obtained, on the basis of examples like (27); or (28), using the derived nominal 'presidency':

(27)  John was a postman for four years.

(28)  George Bush's presidency lasted four years.

English PP resist derived nominalization (*'the being in London of John'), but arguments from anaphora show that there must be states derivable from ordinary PP predicates. Consider (29):

(29)  John was in the kitchen, but it didn't last long.

The pronominal evidently refers to the state of John's being in the kitchen; that is, to

(the *e*) in the kitchen(John,*e*)

Finally, besides the nominalizations 'happiness', 'presidency', 'examination', etc. licensed by derivational morphology, consider the fully productive construction, which indeed has already been used in explaining the import of these nominalizations, exemplified by complex nominals such as (30)–(31):

(30)  the state of being happy/in the kitchen/a philosopher

(31)  the event of the sun's rising/my going to London

The examples in (31) are evidently definite descriptions, purporting to refer to particular events. The expressions in (30) become somewhat awkward with lexical subjects rather than PRO:

(32)  ??the state of John's being happy/my being in the kitchen/Mary's being a philosopher

(33)  ?John's state of being happy

but this syntactic feature should not obscure the fact that they, too, can be understood as definite descriptions, purporting to refer to particular states, if the subject is realized circumlocutorily, as in for example (34):

(34)  the state of being happy that John is in

We thus conclude that, just as the syntax of the construction shown in (35) always yields a definite description or quantification over events, so that in (36) gives definite descriptions or quantifications over states:

(35) [the/every/some event [of PRO/DP's [V'-ing]]]

(36) [the/every/some state [of PRO$_i$ [being AP/PP/NP (that DP$_i$ is in)]]][4]

Assuming the E-position, these nominals, where the type of state or event in question is given through the gerund, are interpreted as illustrated in (37) (for the second example in (31)):

(37) (the $e$) (event($e$) & go to London(I,$e$))

But statives too, as well as 'I-level' predicates in the sense of Kratzer (1995), will be so interpreted, so that (33)–(34) will have the semantics shown in (38):

(38) (the $e$) (state($e$) & happy(John,$e$))[5]

I conclude that if we agree with Montague that there are events, states, or situations corresponding to all ordinary predicates, or at least all of those involving time, then, having adopted the E-position hypothesis for action predicates, there is no choice but to adopt it for all. But the evidence leads in that direction independently anyway.

## 2.2 The visibility of E

We now take up the E-position hypothesis together with the attendant theory of event-nominalizations, including gerunds and derived nominals, and generic events as described. In simple sentences the E-position is very nearly invisible, being realized only through existential closure. In nominalization and in the construction of generic events on the other hand it performs actual semantic work, or is as I shall say *visible*.

---

[4] The determiner D in these schemata may be filled by articles, quantifiers, or WH-words such as 'which'. Furthermore, although the understood subject PRO in descriptions of states that use bare PRO subjects has the usual property of uncontrolled PRO that it is confined to humans (e.g., 'the state of [PRO being on the hill]' does not plausibly speak of a rock), PRO may be controlled by a non-human DP, as in (i):

(i) the state of [PRO$_i$ being in the frying pan that [the steak]$_i$ is in]

However, I have no account of the awkwardness of lexical DP subjects with the copula.

[5] The proposed semantics therefore has the consequence that the hypothesis of Kratzer (1995) that I-level predicates lack an event argument should be rejected, and that the data that show that this argument is in a number of contexts not available to the semantics should be reanalyzed so that the argument, while present, is in some way, perhaps differently for different contexts, unavailable. For one hypothesis along these lines, see Chierchia (1995), and for discussion of the diversity among the cases, see Higginbotham and Ramchand (1997).

A good bit of the evidence in favor of the E-position hypothesis comes from tracking the environments where it can be supposed to be visible, as for example in mediating the causative-inchoative alternation, following Parsons (1990). There are many other applications. As Davidson remarked at length, recognition of a position for events also permits a simplification of the combinatorics of adverbial modification; and as a number of people have observed, the quantificational adverbs can bind positions for events, as well as other indefinites. Thus the hypothesis of the E-position serves to capture the roles of adverbial modifications by manner adverbs as in (39) or adverbs of quantification as in (40):

(39) John walked slowly.

(40) John usually walks to work.

In (39) the adverb 'slowly', whose interpretation is just the same as that of the adjective 'slow', when predicated of events, is semantically conjoined with 'walk', so that the interpretation of the predicate in (39) (ignoring tense) is as in (41):

(41) walk($e$) & Actor($x,e$) & slow($e$)

In (40) there is quantification over events as contextually determined (for example, John's travels to work), the assertion being to the effect that usually they are walks. We have (42):

(42) [Usually $e$: $C(e)$] walk to work(John,$e$)

where $C$ is the contextually supplied background condition. Besides these well-known applications, I will consider some others involving adverbials. These will constitute further evidence for the E-position.

### 2.2.1 Adverbial interpretation

Consider the ambiguity of (43):

(43) Mary quickly objected.

On the interpretation in which 'quickly' is taken as a manner adverb, (43) has it that Mary's objection was quickly delivered. On the other interpretation, which I will call *thematic*, the objection could have been delivered at any speed, but came quickly after the proposal to which it was an objection. This second interpretation is evidently paraphraseable by (44):

(44) Mary was quick [PRO to object]

Any explanation of the ambiguity of (43) must explain the adequacy of the paraphrase (44) as well. I will show that with the E-position it is straightforward to distinguish these interpretations.

We take the V 'objected' to be as in (45):

(45)  objected(x,e)

where the θ-position marked by 'x' will be assigned to the surface subject. The manner interpretation is derived by taking 'quickly', like 'slowly' above, as a predicate of events, and derives for the modified V the interpretation shown in (46):

(46)  objected(x,e) & quick(e)

For the thematic interpretation we take a cue from the paraphrase (44) above. In that example, 'quick' is a *transitive* adjective, whose complement is an argument. That complement has its own E-position, being an indefinite description of events, so that the interpretation is as in (47):

(47)  quick(Mary,e',e) & object(Mary,e')

But now the very same semantic combination that we see in (44) may be applied to (43), as follows.

We assume that the syntactic structure for (43) shows a VP-internal subject trace, as in (48):

(48)  [Mary [quickly [t objected]]]

The adverb 'quickly' takes the VP as complement. Within that complement the trace $t$ is a free variable, whose value will be fixed as the value of its antecedent when that is encountered in the course of the semantic computation. We compute the interpretation of the predicate as shown in (49):

(49)  quickly: quick(x,e',e)
      t objected: object(y,e'')
      quickly [t objected]: quick(x,e',e) & object(x,e')

The combination represents a kind of unification of θ-positions (E-positions in this case), or θ-identification in the sense of Higginbotham (1985). Notice that on this account the subject 'Mary' is the subject both of 'quick' and of 'object'. Hence the subject trace behaves semantically as if it were PRO, occupying a position of control, a point to which I return in the discussion of subject-oriented adverbs below.

Further support for the above interpretation of the ambiguity of adverbial modification comes from examples such as (50), which like (43) has no clausal complement, and from nominals like (51):

(50)  Mary was quick with her objection.

(51)  Mary's quick objection (was appreciated by everyone).

Both examples are ambiguous, in just the way (43) is. Thus the adjective is the fundamental ambiguous form, with the adverb retaining the same semantics.

Davidson (1967) considered some adverbs that, in the present terminology, are thematic only, such as 'intentionally'. As he ultimately agreed in response to a comment from H.-N. Castañeda, the adjectival form 'intentional' not only takes two arguments, one for the subject and one for the action of which the subject is the agent, but also shows the semantic equivalent of control of the agent by the subject. Thus the context in (52) is referentially opaque with respect to the position of 'Jocasta', but transparent with respect to the subject 'Oedipus':

(52)  Oedipus's marrying Jocasta was intentional (of him).

The same is true of course for (53):

(53)  Oedipus intentionally married Jocasta.

If we pursue the path suggested by these applications of the E-position hypothesis, then two lines of thought present themselves.

The first is that, contrary to what is often assumed, the semantics of human languages contains, insofar as these constructions anyway are concerned, no modifications of higher types. In giving the semantics of any construction the question arises what is the nature of the projection rule that binds the pieces together: the semantic glue, so to speak. In the case of heads and their arguments, it is simply the filling of an argument slot. For overt nominal quantification it is what may be called θ-binding by the determiner or quantifier D of the open position in the head by the determiner: thus 'every' binds the open position in 'dog' in the DP 'every dog'. Simple modifications, including relative clauses, can be understood as conjunctions, hence as glued together by truth functions. But there are modifications that the simple picture does not seem to fit, and for these higher types have often been invoked. Thus one could regard 'leave slowly' as denoting the value of the result of applying the denotation of 'slowly' to the denotation of 'leave', so that the denotation of the adverb is a function whose argument is itself a function. The adverb then has a denotation of higher type than that of predicates. As just noted, however, no such view of the adverb need be taken if we have the E-position, for then 'slowly' falls into place with other modifiers as forming, with its head, a conjunctive predicate. Similarly, I propose that we do not understand 'leave intentionally' as representing the action of the adverb on a verbal denotation; rather, we understand 'intentional' as a relation between an actor and an event (and having its own E-position), so that 'leave intentionally' is interpreted as shown in (54):

(54)  intentionally: intentional($x,p,e$)
      $t$ leave: leave($y,e'$)
      $t$ leave intentionally: intentional($x,{}^{\wedge}$leave($x,e$)) & leave($x,e$)

The θ-grid assigned to 'intentional' in this analysis is supported directly by sentences like (55):

(55)  John's leaving was intentional (of him).

The semantics for (55), or the simpler 'John left intentionally' is ultimately as in (56):

(56)  For $x$=John, $[\exists e]$ [intentional($x,{}^{\wedge}$leave($x,e$)) & leave($x,e$)][6]

The second line of thought has already been illustrated in the semantics of (43) and other examples. It is that one should always seek to understand modifiers as they occur in *simple* sentences, of which they themselves are the main predicates. If, for instance, we want to probe the semantics of an adverb such as 'quickly' or 'intentionally', we should look at cases where the adjective from which these are derived is the main predicate of AP, as in the examples above. Ideally, the θ-structure that is discernible in the simple cases should carry over to the complex.

When the strategy of carrying modifiers back to main predicates is successful it frequently happens that what is from a syntactic point of view an adjunct functions semantically as the head of the expression that it modifies, and conversely that the syntactic head is semantically part of an argument. Comparing the syntactic structure of (43) to the interpretation shown in (47),

---

[6] Notice that, on this view, 'John left intentionally' is stronger than the conjunction, 'John intended to leave, and he left'. To intend to leave is merely to intend that there be such a thing as one's leaving; and one leaves if there is such a thing. But, according to (56), to leave intentionally involves passing from the state of intending to leave to a state where one intends, of a particular thing that one is doing, that it constitute leaving, and for it in fact to be so. I believe this view to be correct, and its correctness even to be manifested in ordinary experience. For example, I can intend to express my displeasure at someone's remark, and be surprised to discover myself already frowning. If such cases are accepted, then I can intend to express my displeasure, and express it, without expressing it intentionally. (For discussion on this point I am indebted to Hans Kamp.)

we see that the main predicate in (43) is 'quickly', not 'objected'. Let us say that the *semantic head* of an expression Z=X-Y is whichever of X and Y is the predicate, the other being the argument. Then we might sum up the situation by saying that the syntactic head of an expression may, but need not, be its semantic head. I will argue for further instances of the divergence of syntactic and semantic headedness below.

### 2.2.2 *Syntactic constraints*

In a right-branching language such as English the licensing positions of adverbs are correlated with their linear position.[7] Following Bowers (1993) I will assume that C licenses the sentential or speech-act adverbs such as 'clearly', 'frankly', and 'apparently'; that INFL licenses the subject-oriented adverbs such as 'reluctantly', 'intentionally' and adverbs of appraisal such as 'probably'; and that V licenses manner adverbs. Within the account proposed here this diversity of positions, with associated correlation in types of meaning, is to be expected.[8]

Consider the hypothesis that, stylistic rearrangement aside, adverbs may θ-mark only their sisters, and may modify, by θ-identification, only as they occur adjoined to nodes where the positions with which they are to be identified remain open. We expect, then, that sentential adverbs must be sisters to whole clauses. Thus (57) has only the (somewhat strange) meaning that John's learning was clear, whereas (58) and (59) both express that it is clear that John learned French:

(57)  John learned French clearly.

(58)  Clearly, John learned French.

(59)  John clearly learned French.

The sisters IP to C and VP to INFL are both clausal structures. Assuming that the subject moves to Spec(IP) or a higher position, we have in both (58) and (59) a structure

[clearly [ ... [Subject-Predicate] ... ]]

---

[7] In recent work following especially the suggestions of Kayne (1994), it may be suggested that these correlations are universal.

[8] Since this chapter was written there has been considerable further study of adverb placement and interpretation, prompted in large measure through the work of Cinque (1999). What follows in the text can be put succinctly as: the interpretation of adverbials is governed (at least for these cases) by *local compositionality* in the sense of Higginbotham (2007), a sense that is intended to express what is commonly assumed in ongoing research.

suitable for θ-marking. If the predicate in (57) is constrained to be generated as

[[learn French] clearly]

(i.e., within the verbal projection) then the relevant structure is not present, and the interpretation of 'clearly' as a sentential adverb is not possible.

Subject-oriented adverbs can be licensed by INFL, and will θ-mark the subject in the position SPEC(IP) to which it raises. Suppose that 'reluctantly', for example, has the θ-grid of the adjective 'reluctant', which is transparent from examples like (60):

(60)  Mary was reluctant [PRO to leave]

The adjective takes two arguments, which in (60) are filled respectively by 'Mary' and the proposition about her that she leave, and it has its own E-position. The adjective is therefore

reluctant(x,p,e)

Suppose then that the (relevant part of the) structure of (61) is as in (62), with t the trace of 'Mary':

(61)  Mary reluctantly left.

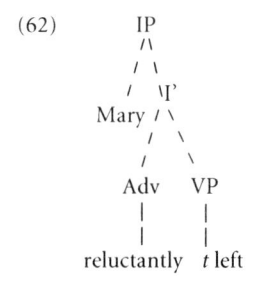

(62)
```
            IP
           /\
          /  \
         /   \I'
     Mary /  \
         /    \
        /      \
      Adv     VP
       |       |
       |       |
   reluctantly t left
```

The trace of the subject is a free variable so that the interpretation of the clausal sister of the adverb is the proposition $^\wedge(\exists e)$ left(x,e) that x left (i.e., there was an event of x's leaving). The adverb takes the clause as an argument. The subject 'Mary' is θ-marked once through the V 'left', but again by INFL through the adverb, an independent θ-marker. The interpretation of the whole is then as in (63):

(63)  For Mary=x, reluctant(x,$^\wedge(\exists e)$ left(x,e))

Semantically, then, the trace behaves exactly as if it were PRO, coindexed with the subject.

We have seen that (60) and (61), despite the syntactic distinction between them, behave similarly from the point of view of semantic projection. They differ, however, in presupposition. The adjective 'reluctant' is not factive, so that (60) is neutral on the question whether Mary left. The adverbial construction, however, does presuppose that Mary left. Negation will normally be understood as applying only to the modifier, so that someone who asserts (64) will under many circumstances implicate that Mary left:

(64)  Mary didn't leave reluctantly.

The presuppositional difference between (60) and (61) is no accident, but characteristic of the constructions themselves. To express it, we must allow that the IP is a conjunction, as in (65):

(65)  For Mary=$x$, ($\exists e$) [reluctant($x$,^($\exists e'$) left($x,e'$)) & left($x,e$)]

(Of course, there is an E-position within 'reluctant' as well; here and elsewhere such positions are understood when they contribute nothing to the purpose.) In this sense, one might say, the adverb really is a 'modifier' in the classic sense: it adds information to the main assertion. But its role as a semantic head must be acknowledged as well.

Consider now the passive (66):

(66)  Mary was reluctantly instructed $t$ (by Joan).

The adverb is by hypothesis free to θ-mark the subject 'Mary', just as it did in (43). It is not free to θ-mark 'Mary' in the corresponding active (67), since it is never a sister of that expression:

(67)  Joan reluctantly instructed Mary.

From this point of view, the semantics of subject-oriented or passive-sensitive adverbs is trivial: they may θ-mark whatever element emerges in the subject position. What is problematic is that the adverb retains its ability to select the agent as its subject, whether the agent is overtly present or not. The latter interpretation may involve θ-identification between the open positions or implicit arguments represented by the agent of the V 'instruct' and the experiencer of 'reluctant'. This interpretation is available even when no 'by'-phrase can be appended, as in (68):

(68)  the reluctantly instructed student (*by Joan)

From a semantic point of view, the verbal passive unsupported by a 'by'-phrase shows a default existential closure, whose scope is below that of the external argument. Assuming a phrase structure for (66) as in (69), with the adverb higher than the passive suffix '-en', we may allow closure to apply freely at the subordinate point Y or the superordinate point X:

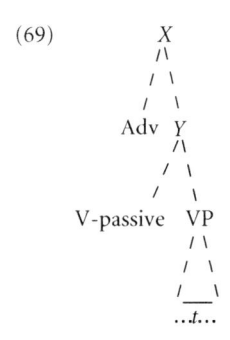

(69)
```
            X
           /\
          /  \
         /    \
        Adv    Y
              /\
             /  \
            /    \
      V-passive  VP
                 /\
                /  \
               /____\
                ...t...
```

with *t* the trace of V. If closure applies 'too soon'—that is, at Y—then the adverb in (68) will lack a subject, violating the θ-criterion; otherwise, its subject may be identified with the subject of V-passive, and closure apply at X. This yields the 'internal' interpretation of (66), where the reluctance belongs to the understood agent rather than the subject.

Finally, for adverbs that are ambiguous between manner and subject-oriented interpretations, e.g. 'clumsily' as in J.L. Austin's pair (70)–(71), positioning disambiguates:

(70)  Clumsily, he trod on the snail.

(71)  He trod on the snail clumsily.

The manner adverb, a predicate of the E-position in 'tread', must appear at a low adjunction site, before that position is bound; hence below INFL, if INFL binds that position. But the sentence-initial adverb must adjoin at INFL or above. So (70) is unambiguous, and cannot mean that the treading was clumsy. Conversely, the subject-oriented adverb must be able to θ-mark a clause, and so cannot appear in an adjunction site lower than INFL.

The semantics I have suggested for subject-oriented adverbs, in fact for all thematic adverbs including 'intentionally' and the thematic interpretation of 'quickly', discussed above, raises a question for application of the θ-criterion. In the syntactic structure (66) we must allow the subject 'Joan' to be simultaneously (a) the head of the chain ('Joan',*t*), θ-marked by 'instructed', and (b) the head of the trivial chain ('Joan'), θ-marked by the complex 'reluctantly instructed', through the adverb. In this sense we must allow the subject position in SPEC(IP) to be a θ-position, at least in the sense that it can receive from the adverb a 'secondary θ-role' in the sense of Zubizarretta (1982).

How should the θ-criterion be revised so as to allow the analysis given above, while retaining the usual consequences of its application to syntactic structures? Turning from adverbs to other elements with similar effect, consider the pair (72)–(73), cited in Higginbotham (1989b):

(72) John seems to be a nice fellow.

(73) John is seeming to be a nice fellow.

As noted there, the assertion of (73) carries the implication, not shared by (72), that John is actively engaged in giving off the appearance of being a nice fellow. Suppose (now extending the discussion in the article cited) that the Progressive, a functional head *Prog*, is acting in (73) as a secondary θ-marker of the subject 'John', also θ-marked through the chain ('John',*t*) by the predicate nominal '(a) nice fellow'. We then have the syntax shown in (74), with the semantics computed as for the adverbial cases:

(74) [John [*Prog* [seem [*t* to be a nice fellow]]]]

Examples of this type may iterate, so that in (75), for example, the subject will be θ-marked in three distinct ways, namely through the thematic adverb; the progressive; and the lower predicate:

(75) John quickly appeared [*t* to be seeming [*t* to be a nice fellow]]

The examples suggest that where $C=(A_1,\ldots, A_n)$ is a maximal A-chain, the sister $\sigma$ of an element $A_i$ may θ-mark the initial segment $(A_1,\ldots, A_i)$ of $C$, provided only that the head of $\sigma$ does not θ-mark any element immediately containing a θ-marker of a larger segment $(A_1,\ldots, A_j,\ldots, A_m)$ of $C$.

(This last proviso, or some conditions implying it, is necessary to rule out the existence of heads having the syntactic properties of raising, but the semantic properties of control.)

## 2.3 Telicity

In the last section we saw the E-position as visible for adverbial modification, including syntactic and semantic aspects. In this section I will argue for a greater complexity within the E-position itself, whose visibility explains some puzzling aspects of the telic–atelic distinction in English (see also Higginbotham (1995a)).

Recall that a predication is *telic* if it appropriately indicates an 'end' of activity, and *atelic* otherwise. The temporal adverbials 'for such-and-such period of time' and 'in such-and-such period of time' distinguish telic from atelic predicates, inasmuch as the 'for'-phrase, uncontroversial with atelics, forces telics into the 'activity' mode (as explained more fully below), and the 'in'-phrase, uncontroversial with telics, forces atelics to be interpreted as incomplete expressions. I propose that the reason is that the 'for'-phrase, 'for an hour' for instance, merely has the function of measuring the duration of an event or state, whereas the 'in'-phrase requires *two* arguments, given either as times *simpliciter*, or as the times of situations, and measures the temporal distance between them. Thus in (76) the meaning is: John will run in an hour from now.

(76)   John will run in an hour.

That is, an hour will elapse between now and the onset of John's running. And in a sentence like (77):

(77)   The patient walked in an hour.

we have the interpretation that the onset of the patient's walking took place in an hour from some unspecified earlier point. In the case of an achievement predicate, as in (78):

(78)   The patient died in an hour

the earlier point can and typically will be taken as the onset of the process that led to the patient's death, so that the first temporal point is given in terms of an event. For accomplishment predicates, it is natural to suppose that both process and telos are supplied, so that (79):

(79)   John solved the problem in an hour

contains both elements, the work on the problem, and the arrival at the solution, within the θ-grid of the head 'solve'.

Simple durational adverbs like 'for an hour' combine with verbal complexes through conjunction (θ-identification). For the case of 'in an hour' we may suppose either (i) that the thematic structure of the V 'solve' shows two E-positions, or else (ii) that it shows only one, but from these it is possible to extract both process and telos. Adopting the first hypothesis, if the distinction between adverbials like 'in an hour' and 'for an hour' is as stated, then the E-position may itself be satisfied by events represented as complex; that is, as made up of two parts, of which the second is the *terminus ad quem* or telos of the first. For (79), then, we take the V 'solve' as having an E-position that is in turn broken down into two positions forming an ordered pair $(e,e')$. The semantics for (79) is then as shown in (80):

(80)   solve(John,the problem, $(e,e')$) & in an hour$(e,e')$]

## 2.3.1 *Argument parameters*

Consider now the problem of explaining why quantificational or singular-term internal arguments make for telic predications, whilst bare plural internal arguments, and incorporated nouns, do not. The contrast is exemplified in (81)–(82):

(81)   Mary drew a circle in/for an hour.

(82)   Mary drew circles in/for an hour.

(81), with 'in', has the expected meaning that an hour elapsed between Mary's commencing to draw and her completion of a circle; with 'for' the sentence is obviously false, since a circle once drawn cannot be drawn again. Compare (83):

(83)   Mary drew John's face for an hour.

Here we have the 'over and over' reading: Mary drew for an hour, producing some number of representations of John's face. In (82) with 'for' we can also derive an 'over and over' reading, with the difference that the individual acts of drawing are then said merely to have various representations as their objects, and nothing is said about what they represent.[9] In (82) with 'in' there is a natural interpretation, discussed in Higginbotham (1995a), where Mary's circle-drawing is regarded as the telos or final state coming to be following some unspecified process, so that the meaning is, roughly, that it took an hour for Mary to get to drawing circles. Passing over this phenomenon, the problem is to explain why (82) with 'in' cannot be an ordinary telic, and inversely why it can be an atelic, taking 'for'.

Telic interpretations are derived under rather specific circumstances, namely where the arguments are singular terms or certain other quantificational expressions, and the predicate headed by V, which involves a telos, is also taken as singular (I will justify the talk of singularity in a moment). Singular terms include not only names of objects and definite descriptions with count-noun heads, but also individual variables. Thus Verkuyl (1993: 20) is right to say that a sentence like (84):

(84)   Judith ate no sandwich.

is (in his terminology) 'non-terminative', despite the fact that in (85):

(85)   Judith ate no sandwich in an hour.

---

[9] In the most natural interpretation, that is: a circle can also be what is represented in a drawing of a circle, and in this case one can draw what is represented—the sacred circle, say—for an hour.

we have an ordinary telic. The point is that (85) is taken as (86):

(86)  For no sandwich $x$ did (Judith eat $x$ in an hour)

where the parenthetical clause is telic, so that the interpretation (in relevant respects) is as in (87):

(87)  [No $x$: sandwich($x$)] ($\exists(e,e')$) [eat(Judith,$x$, $(e,e')$) & in an hour($(e,e')$)]

What is excluded is the (somewhat strained) reading: there is a situation of Judith's eating no sandwich that lasted an hour (but see the discussion of 'negative events' below).

By speaking of the singularity of the predicate I mean to exclude the case where the existential closure over the E-position either is a plural quantification, seen in the salient interpretation of (88):

(88)  John shot ducks for an hour.

which we give as (89):

(89)  $(\exists \Sigma)$ {$[\forall(e,e') \in \Sigma]$ [$\exists x$: duck $x$] shoot(John,$x$,$(e,e')$) & for an hour($\Sigma$)}

Even though each $(e,e')$ in $\Sigma$ has a process and a telos, the family $\Sigma$ itself does not; hence (88) is atelic, like (83). In general, the 'over and over' readings represent a pluralization of the E-position of the predicate, independent of the nature of the arguments of the head.

Tenny (1994) argues that telic interpretation is restricted to what I am calling singular-term internal arguments because only in this way can the verbal head *measure out* the change in objects that it indicates. Thus when one draws a circle, there is a measuring out of the process of creating the circle up to the point of its completion. Similarly, in an example like (90), the internal argument *the apple* supplies the object relative to which the measuring out is taken:

(90)  John ate the apple in an hour.

I will redirect this proposal so that what Tenny calls 'measuring out' is a consequence of telicity, and not a basis for it. If the event $e$ satisfying the verbal projection 'eat the apple' is separable into a process $e$ and telos $e'$, then the sense of measuring out that Tenny rightly discerns derives from the fact that, at least normally, attainment of the telos (the apple's being consumed) through the process (taking one bite after another from the apple) is an affair involving a systematic change in the apple, such that the attainment of the telos is brought closer and closer.

Returning now to our earlier question, what prevents a telic interpretation in cases where the internal argument is a mass noun or bare plural, as in (91)–(92)?

(91)  John ate apples/chicken in an hour.

(92)  Mary drew circles/clothing in an hour.[10]

Bach (1986), among others, has called attention to the fact that (in the terms we are employing here) the events that would make it true that John ate apples for an hour, or Mary drew circles or clothing for an hour, are in a sense *homogeneous*. Roughly, an event of apple-eating is made up of subevents of the same type, an event of repeated circle-drawing is made up of subevents that are also circle-drawings. Moreover, sums of events of the type are again events of the type. The analogy, as Bach especially points out, is to the homogeneity (as far as it goes) of mass terms, the intuition that parts of gold—down to molecules anyway—are gold, and that a substance whose parts are gold is again gold.[11]

However, the notion of a 'subevent' is a technical one, requiring interpretation. To fix ideas, let us suppose that, where an event $e$ has for its time $\tau(e)$ some interval $I=(t_1,t_2)$ of real numbers, possibly closed at either extremity, and possibly trivial, a subevent of $e'$ of $e$ is determined by selecting any subinterval of $I'$ of $I$ (again, possibly closed at either or both extremities, and possibly trivial).[12] Then we may say that the subevents of an apple-eating, or at least all of those that are describable as eating at all, are events of apple-eating.

Let $x$ be an apple. Why is an event of eating $x$ *not* homogeneous? We cannot say that it is not homogeneous because its proper subevents cannot be described as *eating an apple*; for our question was why this is so. The answer suggested by the analysis of the verb in terms of process and telos is that an event $e$ of eating $x$ is not homogeneous because (none of) its proper subevents—the event of eating half of it, say—are such that the telos of eating $x$ is attained. If so, then it is telicity that is responsible for inhomogeneity, and not conversely.

---

[10] These examples are of course fully acceptable when another coordinate for the adjunct *in an hour* is given, say by adding the phrase *from when he/she finished work*. In that case, as remarked above, the onset of the event classified by the V acts as the final state, the difference between which and the supplied coordinate the temporal adjunct measures.

[11] This point of view is heavily exploited in Krifka (1992).

[12] The subevents of $e$ need not be *parts* of $e$ in any natural sense, since they may cross the boundaries that we regard as delimiting the parts.

But now we have the result that homogeneity implies atelicity. If a verbal projection has the property that the subevents of an event $e$ that it classifies are of the same type as $e$, then the E-position in that projection cannot be $(e,e')$: the subevents in question, for instance the initial segments of $e$, are not both (a) telic and (b) of the same type as that classified by the verbal projection. Where the projection, for instance, is that of 'eat $x$', the telos is, say, the onset of the state of $x$'s being in the agent's stomach (in virtue of having ingested $x$ through the mouth).[13] Subevents of the process can well be telic (e.g., an event of taking a bite of the apple), but will not in general have a telos satisfying the condition on $e'$.[14]

The above argument, if correct, shows why homogeneity should be a sufficient condition for atelicity, but does not make it also a necessary condition. This result is perhaps fortunate, since it is unclear, for example, how homogeneous an event of apple-eating really is when it consists of taking only one bite. To avoid the distraction of implicatures with plurals, consider a case with a mass-noun object and the reduced determiner usually written as 'sm', as in (93):

(93)  John ate sm apple.

If we regard the event as (purportedly) described in an assertion of (93) as homogeneous, then we must take the V 'ate' as having a simplex E-position, not an ordered pair. But what if it need not be regarded as homogeneous, and we insert the complex 'ate', whose E-position is broken down as $(e,e')$? We have to say that the (denotation of the) bare mass noun is incapable of being involved in the telos.

The telos of (93), by parity of reasoning, would be the onset of the state of having some (sm) apple in one's stomach, ingested through the mouth. But this state must exist if the process comes off at all. Hence the bare mass noun cannot give a telos: attainment of that telos is *inseparable* from the occurrence of the process itself; that is, the telos comes about if the process does.[15]

Thus far I have considered object quantifications in construction with telic heads only inasmuch as these quantifications are taken as binding variables in the object position, and appear outside the scope of the quantification over

---

[13] Of course, the open texture of language makes determination of the telos (and for that matter the process) somewhat elastic; but stereotypical cases are sufficient to illustrate the grammatical point.

[14] Again, open texture plays a role here. Suppose an organism that can only (finish) eating something by ingesting it three times. Such an organism might be said to have to eat an apple three times in order to eat it. Even so, when this organism eats an apple there will be atelic subevents, properly describable as apple-eating, but not as eating an apple.

[15] This suggestion is perhaps related to, but the inverse of, one that I have heard presented by David Dowty, that in cases like (93) no unique final state can be specified.

events. We can now extend the analysis to inner quantifications, in which the quantification over events is primary. Consider, for example, (94):

(94)  I examined three pictures in an hour (each).

With the distributive 'each', the interpretation is given by (95):

(95)  [3x: picture(x)] ($\exists(e,e')$) [examine(I,x, $(e,e')$) & in an hour$(e,e')$]

But without 'each' the most natural, and perhaps the only, interpretation is that there was an examination of pictures that took an hour, in the course of which three pictures were examined. Under this inner quantification, in part following Schein (1993), (94) is as in (96):

(96)  ($\exists(e,e')$) {examine$(e,e')$ & Agent(I, $(e,e')$) & ($\exists X$) [3(X) &
      ($\forall y$) (X(y) → picture(y)) & ($\forall z$) θ(z, $(e,e')$) ↔ X(z)] & in an hour$(e,e')$]}

where θ expresses the thematic relation between the event, or ordered pair of events, and its internal argument. The sense may be paraphrased by:

> There is a process and telos $(e,e')$ constituting an examination, of which I was the agent, and to which there were in the relation θ three objects, all of which were pictures, and the temporal distance between the onset of the process and the onset of the telos is one hour.

It remains to discuss the nature of the telos for this case. Analogous to (94) are examples with measure phrases in construction with mass nouns, which give telic predicates as in (97):

(97)  John ate a box of chocolates/a pint of ice cream.

Atelicity reappears when the measure is a bare plural, as in (98):

(98)  John ate boxes of chocolates/pints of ice cream.

so that these examples fall under the general point of view given above; that is, they involve plural quantification, like (88). Phrases like 'a box of chocolates' are ambiguous, denoting on one interpretation the chocolates in some box or other, and on the other a *measure* of an amount of chocolates; similarly for 'a glass of wine', etc. It is the measure interpretation that calls for further analysis. Following the conception and the notation in Higginbotham (1994b), the predicate 'a pint of ice cream' is interpreted as

$$\text{ice cream}(X) \ \& \ \mu_{pint}(X)=1$$

that is, X is ice cream, and its pint measure is the number one (corresponding to the indefinite article, which in this case functions as a numeral).

To bring out the peculiarity of the situation, consider that 'eat', taken as a telic, applies to a pair $(e,e')$ just in case (99) holds:

(99)  For some $x$:
      $e$ is a process of eating directed toward $x$;
      $e'$ is the state of $x$'s being properly inside the agent.

(The terms 'directed toward' and 'having been consumed' should be understood as conveying the thematic relations that $e$ bears toward the reference of the internal argument $x$ of the V.) Now, in the typical event of eating a pint of ice cream $X$, $e$ is directed toward $X$; but the telos is not $X$'s being properly inside the agent, but rather that the measure of eaten $X$ should be a pint. Nor is it true in general that $X$ should be a pint: when one eats a pint of ice cream from a quart container, intending to and succeeding in eating a pint, there is no particular pint measure of stuff $X$ that one intended to eat; one may have just intended to eat from the container until a pint had been consumed.

It follows that the characterization 'eat' as a telic is somewhat different for measure-phrase objects.[16]

We may propose (100), in analogy with (99):

(100) For some $X$:
      $e$ is a process of eating directed toward $X$;
      $e'$ is the state of measure $\mu_K(X)$ being properly inside the agent

where the object must supply both the value of $K$ and the identity of the measure.

In closing this section, I compare briefly the suggestions in the text to the construction in Krifka (1992). Whereas I have supposed that a V like 'eat' is systematically ambiguous between the atelic 'eat$(e)$', with a single E-position, and the telic 'eat$(e,e')$' with two, Krifka takes V to be univocal, with a single E-position. Predicates then become telic through the nature of the arguments with which V is in construction. Krifka gives a metaphysical argument for this view, namely that conditions on event-identity suggest that telicity is a matter of event-descriptions, rather than events themselves, as follows. Suppose I eat a pint of ice cream, and thereby eat ice cream. Then my eating of a pint of ice cream is identical with a certain event of my eating ice cream; but then the event of eating cannot be telic or atelic in itself, but only as described.

---

[16] As noted in Higginbotham (1994b: 478), these objects are not quantificational, since they observe a definiteness effect.

On the construction I have suggested, however, Krifka's argument does not go through. My eating of a pint of ice cream is a complex $(e,e')$ with the properties stated. But the events of my eating ice cream (of which there will be many when I eat a pint of ice cream) are none of them identical to this complex; in particular, $e$ is only the first coordinate of the complex, and not $(e,e')$ itself.

A similar case, involving individual objects rather than measures of amount: suppose I walk around the Trevi fountain, making one complete revolution, and suppose that this project takes ten minutes. Then both (101) and (102) are true:

(101)   I walked around the fountain in ten minutes.

(102)   I walked around the fountain for ten minutes.

There is an implication of (101) that (102) lacks, namely that I made one complete revolution of the fountain; (102) can be true if I made no revolutions at all, or many. In the case I have described, however, there is just one ten-minute walk, whose trajectory makes (101) and (102) both true; or so it would seem. So it appears that the same event makes both (101) and (102) true. But if an event considered in itself either has or does not have a telos, and what we have assumed about temporal adverbials is correct, then one or the other of (101) and (102) should not be satisfied by the event in question, contrary to fact.

But the argument is not decisive, because of an ambiguity in the preposition 'around'. In one meaning, 'around' means *go all the way around*, and 'walk around' means *circumambulate*; that is, go all the way around by walking. In the other meaning, 'around' is simply a predicate of the path of the walking itself. Only on the second, atelic, interpretation is the PP 'around the fountain' a true adjunct, or modifier, of V. On the telic interpretation, this PP is itself the main predicate, semantically speaking, and the V serves merely as the modifier, giving the means of locomotion.[17]

The puzzles of event-identity known to me admit solution in the above or other ways; if they are generally soluble as suggested, then we need not say with Krifka that it is only event-descriptions, and not events themselves, that may be classified as telic or atelic.

There are predicates that can be understood as telic or atelic without appeal to 'over and over' interpretations, as in (103):

(103)   I ran upstairs in/for 10 minutes.

[17] For elaboration on this theme, see Higginbotham (1995a).

The predicate 'run upstairs' must therefore be ambiguous, evidently between (a) an atelic predicate true of running events $e$ that go in the upstairs direction, and (b) a telic predicate whose use with 'in' in (103) implies that the top of the stairs was reached. Krifka's construction would require elaboration to deal with these cases, especially since the expression 'upstairs' is not a singular-term argument of 'run'. The proposal above would take the atelic interpretation as in (104), and the telic as in (105):

(104) run($e$) & upstairs($e$) & for an hour($e$)

(105) run($e,e'$) & upstairs($e$) & in an hour($e,e'$)

The ambiguity is then located in the ambiguity of the word 'upstairs', between a predicate true of motions, giving their direction, and a predicate true of states, giving the location of an object involved in them. The latter predicate is independently found in statives, as in 'your bedroom is upstairs'.

### 2.3.2 *Purpose clauses: The visibility of the telos*

Above I have discussed several cases where the E-position is visible to syntactic and semantic processes, and have proposed that accomplishment predicates should be thought of as containing two positions within E, one each for process and telos. This proposal, if correct, establishes that the telos in particular is syntactically represented, and not merely supplied by the semantics of the verbal projection. I will argue in this subsection that to capture the distribution of purpose clauses in English we must also suppose that teli are syntactically represented: it is not sufficient that they be supplied through entailments or common-sense understanding.

The English purpose clause is exemplified by the bracketed constituent in (106) and similar examples:

(106)  I bought bones [to give to the dog].

I will assume the syntactic account of Chomsky (1977), where the purpose clause 'gap' is taken to reflect *wh*-movement of an empty operator O (the important analysis in Jones (1991) notwithstanding). We then have (107):

(107)  I bought bones [O [PRO to give *t* to the dog]]

where O, or the chain (O,*t*), is linked to the antecedent 'bones'.

As observed in Bach (1982), acceptability of a purpose clause not only requires linking the gap to some matrix argument, usually the theme, but also requires that the fulfillment of the purpose in question be consequent upon some state that is in turn consequent upon the truth of the main clause.

In (106), the state is that of the bones' coming to be in my possession; it is because they are in my possession that I am in a position to give them to the dog. The consequent state is therefore the state whose onset is the telos of the main clause 'I bought bones'. I will argue first that this identity is no accident.

We can make Bach's proposal more explicit by filling in a semantics for the purpose clause along the lines suggested in Whelpton (1995). Whelpton proposes that the operator in a purpose clause expresses λ-abstraction, and that its argument structure is as in (108):

(108)  C(x,e,P)

where $x$ is an individual, $P$ is a property (in the sense of Montague, noted above), and $e$ is the consequent state. The meaning of $C$ is to a first approximation as in (109):

(109)  $e$ is a state that is (or is intended to be) causally efficacious in bringing it about that $P(x)$.

The predicate (108) applies in turn to the property, expressed by the purpose clause; the consequent state; and the argument to which the operator is linked.

Atelic matrix clauses can host purpose clauses, as in (110) and (111):

(110)  The sign hung in the window [for people/PRO to read]
(111)  John pushed the cart along the road [for the crowd to see]/[PRO to show to the crowd]

But some pure activities disallow purpose clauses:

(112)  *I wiped the table [for Mary/PRO to impress the guests with]

Compare (113), where the consequent state is manifest:

(113)  I wiped the table clean/free of dirt [PRO to impress the guests with]

What is the distinction between (110)–(111) on the one hand, and (112) on the other? Following Whelpton's semantic analysis, we would conclude that, whereas the event in the main clause (110)–(111) is causally efficacious in bringing about the accomplishment of the purpose—the sign's hanging in the window is what brings it about that people read it, the pushing of the cart along the road is what gets the crowd to see it, or gets me to show it to the crowd—the event of wiping the table (that is, going through the movements of wiping) is not of itself efficacious in getting the guests impressed with it. In (113), on the other hand, the consequent state following on the wiping, namely the cleanliness of the table, is causally efficacious in impressing the guests with it. The efficacy of the wiping derives from the fact that it brought about the consequent state, whose onset was the telos of the wiping.

We can now ask more generally whether purpose clauses are licensed whenever it is a matter of common knowledge that there is a consequent state of a particular kind that will inevitably follow upon the successful completion of a given activity, or whether specifically linguistic information is required. The answer suggested by the contrast (112)–(113) is that common knowledge of a consequent state is not sufficient. Thus we do not have examples like (114) or (115):

(114)  *They deprived the prisoner of food [to starve].

(115)  *The pitcher threw at the batter [to knock down].

We know that starvation is the consequence of food deprivation, and that the pitcher's purpose in throwing at the batter was to knock him down. Nevertheless, the examples are unacceptable.

From these examples, we may tentatively conclude that the formulation (109) of the interpretation of the nexus in the purpose clause should be supplemented by the condition that $e$ not merely be causally efficacious, but that it be the *immediate* cause of the object $x$'s having the property $P$; that is, that it not cause $x$ to have $P$ only because it caused some intermediate event $e'$ that in turn caused $x$ to have $P$. The events described in the atelics (110)–(111) have this property with respect to their purpose clauses. In (112), however, the state (of cleanliness) into which the table is to be put by the wiping action, which is something that the action causes and in turn causes or is intended to cause the guests to be impressed, is left implicit. In (114)–(115), similarly, the consequent states (the prisoner lacks food, the ball strikes the batter), although matters of common knowledge, are not linguistically present. We thus conclude that in the formulation of the nexus of the purpose clause in (108), repeated here, the position marked by $e$ must be in the linguistic material:

(108)  $C(x,e,P)$

with $C$ now being understood to involve immediacy of causation.

If this is correct, we have strong evidence that the telos of a telic predicate not realized by any overt secondary predicate such as the resultative 'clean' of (113), is available to be the second argument of the purpose-clause nexus only because that telos is after all syntactically present. Our first example 'I bought bones' already illustrates the general theme, since the telos, the bones' being in my possession, can only be made available through thematic information in the predicate 'buy'.

The capacity of a verbal projection to license a purpose clause may depend upon the specifically lexical information that is a part of what is understood when its meaning is fully grasped. Compare, for example, (116) to (117):

(116)   *I pounded the meat [to improve the taste of].

(117)   I pounded the meat [to fit into the pan].

Although it is known that tenderization of the meat is a state that is a causal consequence of pounding it; that putting the meat into that state is salient among the reasons for doing so; and that its being in the tender state improves its taste, (116) is unacceptable. The intermediate state, the meat's being tenderized, is not explicit in the sentence. If it is explicit then the purpose clause is acceptable, or at any rate more acceptable:

(118)   (?)I pounded the meat tender [to improve the taste of].

On the other hand, (117) is acceptable as it stands, so that the state that consists in the meat's having a certain shape mediates between the activity, pounding, and the purpose for which it is intended. These and similar examples invite the conclusion that the V 'pound' is in fact ambiguous, having on the one hand a pure activity meaning, and on the other a meaning that incorporates the telos of putting the patient, the object pounded upon, into some shape.

## 2.4 Can events be negative?

Supposing there can be events such as John's playing golf last Saturday, can there also be events such as John's not playing golf last Saturday? If there are events such as my turning off the light, can there also be events such as my not turning off the light? If there are contexts for negative events, then this question looms large for any account of events and states in which they are taken to be individuals, and larger still if events lack a structure of complementation; but conversely if these contexts are restricted then the liberality that complementation would give is itself suspect. In this section, I will defend a limited account of negative events within the Davidsonian framework, and contrast it with what would be available for Montague, and for any account of events that endows them with an intrinsic Boolean structure.

We are concerned here with contexts in which negation is understood *in propria persona*, and therefore put aside the contexts in which it is otherwise interpreted. I argued in Higginbotham (1983a) that naked infinitive complements to verbs of perception expressed existential quantification over events, as given by the E-position of the verbal head. If events could be negative, we would expect reference to them, or quantification over them, in such complements with overt negation 'not'. But I argued also that in fact the word 'not' within these complements does not express negation, but a kind of contrariness. Consider the perception-verb context (119):

(119)   Mary saw John not play golf last Saturday.

The acceptability of (119) depends upon conceiving the complement as expressing something stronger than negation, and contributing to the complement as a whole a meaning such as: John pointedly refrained from playing golf; or, John didn't play golf when he might have been expected to; or, more figuratively, John played golf so poorly that he could hardly be said to have been playing the game; or something similar. What Mary saw, if my assertion of (119) is true, is an event *suspending* the prospect of John's playing golf, or interfering with his playing it properly: what sort of event must be gleaned from the context. If this is right, then cases like (119) should not be understood in terms of negative events.

Negative events also, and more obviously, do not come into the picture in connection with propositional or factive complements, no matter how these may be syntactically realized. However, there are arguments for negative events stemming from causal contexts, and from the behavior of temporal adverbials. Thus in contexts like (120) we seem to make reference to a negative event with causal consequences:

(120)   I kept the child awake by not turning out the light.

and the ambiguity of sentences like (121) suggests that negation can receive internal as well as external scope:

(121)   John didn't play golf until noon.

On the external reading, the speaker of (121) denies that John's golf-playing went on until noon; on the internal reading, the speaker asserts that until noon there was no golf-playing by John. I take these cases in turn.

The case for negative events in (20) cannot be dismissed by saying that, if my not turning out the light kept the child awake, then there is some event non-negatively described, *viz.*, the light's continuing to burn, that was actually responsible for the child's being awake; for there are many cases where we do not know what events of that kind there are, or even whether there are any. Notice furthermore that my not turning out the light may not have been a refrainment on my part, but simply an omission; hence negation in cases like (120) cannot be assimilated to the antonymic negation of naked infinitive complements.

A system that, as in Montague's work, took events as universals, and could in principle construct them from any predicate with a free temporal variable, will admit negative events of all sorts (although the issue is not discussed in Montague (1974)). Thus there is a property of moments of time which holds (in a given possible world) of those moments $t$ such that the light is not turned off at $t$; and the set of moments instantiating this property in the actual world might be said to be causally responsible for the child's being awake. Similarly, if the property of being a moment $t$ such that John does not play golf at $t$ is one that each moment before noon has in the actual world, then, identifying the event John's not playing golf with this property, we can say that as things are it lasted until noon. In this way, locutions such as (120) and (121) are admitted, describing negative events.

To accommodate negative events within the Davidsonian setting adopted in section 2.1.1, we must think of some situations as given to us merely through the family of moments of time that belong to them. Situations of all sorts are in time, and we postulate that for each situation $e$ there is a unique set of moments of time $\tau(e)$ that constitute the *time* of $e$. Where $H$ is an ordinary predicate classifying situations $e$, and $(t_1,t_2)$ is a temporal interval (open, closed, or neither, where we allow the possibility that $t_1=t_2$), if there is no event $e$ of kind $H$ whose time overlaps $(t_1,t_2)$, then we may posit the existence of a unique *H-complement* event $e'$, whose time $\tau(e')$ is $(t_1,t_2)$. Relative to the given interval, $e'$ is an event of non-$H$-ing. Thus the situation of my not turning off the light (between 7:00 and 10:00 p.m., say) exists and has the interval in question as its time, provided that there is no situation of my turning off the light within the interval. More formally, given $H$ we introduce a predicate $H^*$ and the axiom (122):

(122) $(\forall I) \{\neg(\exists e) [\tau(e) \text{ overlaps } I \& H(e)] \rightarrow (\exists e') [H^*(e') \& \tau(e')=I]\}$

Our assumption is that overt negation may express the operation yielding $H^*$ from (at least certain) $H$, thus giving rise to what are intuitively negative events.

The construction just given posits negative events $e'$ of kind $H^*$ only for antecedently given event-classifiers $H$, and only relative to temporal intervals $I$; it goes, therefore, only part way toward a full complementarity that would be realized, for instance, in a Boolean structure. Nevertheless, it is adequate for examples like (120), and also for negation within derived nominals, as in (123)–(124):

(123)  the non-explosion of the gases

(124)  Bill's non-departure

Moreover, the generosity toward negative events that would follow on Montague's theory (and on any theory that endowed events with an intrinsic structure of complementarity) seems not only unnecessary but even profligate. Recall that on Montague's view nominals such as (125) refer to generic events:

(125)  the rising of the sun

The adjective admits negation, so that we have (126):

(126)  the non-rising of the sun

which would presumably denote the generic event that is the property of moments of time $t$ such that the sun does not rise at $t$. There will also be existential quantifiers ranging over particular events, non-risings of the sun. In allowing complementarity at all we have pulled closer to Montague's point of view; but we do not have full complementarity from the beginning.

Consider now the second type of example, (121), repeated here:

(121)  John didn't play golf until noon.

A state of John's not playing golf is any state $s$ whose time $\tau(s)$ does not overlap with any $\tau(e)$ such that $e$ is an event of John's playing golf. On the internal reading of the negation in (121), there is said to be such a state throughout the period ending at noon. Invoking complementarity so as to allow this reading, we are not far from Montague's construal of events as properties of moments of time. The construals nevertheless differ in what they take to be given and what must be constructed from the basic apparatus.

## 2.5 Concluding remarks

In this discussion I have endeavored to explain part of the scientific background that seems to me operative in linguistic semantics, guiding the psychological inquiry, and to give some examples of applications of the hypothesis of the E-position within that theory. The arguments in favor of the hypothesis point toward a restricted theory of linguistic organization: events enter semantic computation only as they are linguistically represented through thematic grids, and discharge of open positions takes place only under structurally controlled conditions. The theory pays in ontology for what it buys semantically; that is, the cost, if it is a cost, of the combinatorial simplification is the positing of objects reference to which is not immediately manifest in linguistic structures. The formalization of the theory, and its application to a greater variety of human languages, is a matter for the future; in the meantime, the theory receives some support from the fact that it makes many of what we take to be obvious implications really obvious, and from the degree to which it fits a reasonable conception of what is learned in mastering a language.[18]

[18] A version of this chapter, itself descended from versions given in various venues since 1993, was read at the Trento conference on events, 1995. I have profited from comments and questions both there and at subsequent presentations at the University of California, Los Angeles, and at the founding meeting of the Society for Semantics, Tübingen, Germany. Even though for want of space I have not been able to take account of all of these, I should like particularly to thank Kit Fine, Hans Kamp, David Kaplan, Anna Szabolcsi, and Ede Zimmermann for their remarks and discussion.

# 3

# Tensed Thoughts

## 3.1 Tenses and contents

When we have thoughts about the present, our temporal reference may be merely to the present time, or to the present conceived as such. The nature of the temporal reference sometimes matters. To adapt a famous example due to Arthur N. Prior, and recently discussed by John Campbell,[1] suppose that I am leaving the dentist's office after undergoing a root canal. I may think, 'Thank goodness *that's* over', referring to the painful operation I have just endured. My thought (1):

(1)   My root canal is over.

is the object of my feeling of relief. Supposing it is 4:00 p.m. on October 31, 1994, the thought (2):

(2)   My root canal is over as of 4:00 p.m., October 31, 1994.

would not bring relief. If I knew independently that it was now 4:00 p.m. on October 31, I would feel relief, but only because I think the thought indicated in (1), not because I think (2). My thought (2) makes reference to the present, in the sense that it speaks of my root canal's being over as of what is in fact the present time. But it does not make reference to the present as being present. Unlike my thought that the root canal is over it does not bring relief. It is therefore a different thought.

The sentence (2) has the designator '4:00 p.m., October 31, 1994' as a constituent. Suppose that the thought indicated by that sentence has a constituent corresponding to that designator; that is, a constituent that refers to the time according to the conventional system that determines the reference of the English words. Suppose further that, besides designators of this sort, thoughts can have for their constituents objects as well: persons, rocks, or in particular times. Then there is another thought, which I shall represent as in

---

[1] Contribution to a symposium, Foundations of Autobiography, at the meeting of the European Society for Philosophy and Psychology, Paris, August 1994.

(3), that is like that indicated in (2) but has the time itself, 4:00 p.m., October 31, 1994, in place of something corresponding to a designator of that time:

(3)  My root canal is over as of $t_{\text{4:00 p.m., 31 October, 1994}}$

This thought is true if the time in question is something of which the rest of the thought is true. In my example, that time is the present, the time at which I think that my root canal is over. I do not secure reference to the present time via a designator, which as it happens refers to it, but think about the present as it were immediately, or in a familiar but perhaps misleading terminology *de re*. The thought indicated by (3) therefore seems a better candidate than that indicated by (2) for being the object of my feeling of relief.

Perhaps it is a better candidate; but the formulation (3) is still inadequate. I had of course always wanted the root canal to be over as soon as possible, and in thinking that it is over as of $t_{\text{4:00 p.m., 31 October, 1994}}$ I think that things have turned out better than they might have. But I could have firmly believed long before I went to the dentist that my root canal would be over by $t_{\text{4:00 p.m., 31 October, 1994}}$. I would be pleased then, and at other times, that it were over then and not later; but I would not then feel relief.

The thoughts indicated in (2) and (3) are tenseless, whereas that in (1) is tensed. In this chapter I will consider the question how tensed thoughts differ from tenseless ones, and I will cite certain parallels between tense in thought and tense in language, with consequences for semantic theory. On some proposals for the semantics of tense and temporal indexicals (words like 'now' and 'then') the difference between tensed thoughts and tenseless thoughts either cannot be made out or, if it does come in, requires special attention. These proposals have their rationale in the behavior of tense and temporal indexicals in conjunction with modality, as discussed most prominently in David Kaplan (1977). I will argue that the behavior of modals should be reevaluated in the light of the distinction between tensed thoughts and tenseless thoughts. If I am right then what requires explaining is not how tensed thoughts are to be constructed, but rather the peculiar behavior of modality, in that it may efface distinctions among thoughts. First, however, I state the account to be defended here.

Suppose that the tenses and temporal indexicals, as they are used in reporting thoughts, may contain as constituents the episodes or states of thought whose content they indicate. Tensed thoughts can then be reflexive in the sense that some of their constituents are episodes or states in the life of the thinking subject. If *e* is the episode of my affirming to myself with a sense of relief, 'My root canal is over' (or: 'over now'), then the thought that I think is indicated in (4):

(4)  (∃s) *s* is the situation of my root canal's being over & (the time of) *s* includes (the time of) *e*

With or without the parenthetical 'the time of', this is a thought that, even as I affirm it, locates my root canal's being over in my own present, and my root canal itself in my own past. (The status of the parenthetical will be considered below.)

What goes for the present and the indexical 'now' goes also for the past and the future, and for at least certain interpretations of the indexical 'then'. For me to have the thought that I once ate risotto in Milan can be for me to think that there is a situation of my eating risotto in Milan before that very episode, which is present to me, or before I came to be in that very state; for me to anticipate with pleasure that I will eat risotto in Milan can be for me to think that there will be such a situation after that very episode; and so on. What goes for thoughts understood as episodes of internal affirmation or states of belief goes also for desires, wishes, regrets, knowledge, and so forth.

If tensed thoughts are distinguished from tenseless ones in the way I have suggested, then certain of the differences between them that matter to us follow immediately. I am relieved when I think, 'My root canal is over', because in so thinking I locate my root canal in my past; I look forward to visiting Milan because I desire something conceived of as in the future of that desire, and I believe I am going to get it. The passion of relief and the attitude of anticipation, like the state of regret, can only be directed toward thoughts that are themselves tensed or else supported by tensed thoughts, which locate the time reference of the untensed thoughts with respect to the thinker's present state.

I have said that the content of a state of relief is a tensed thought. To be more accurate, this restriction on the state holds only for one sense of the notion of relief, the one that surfaces when one locates a painful episode in one's past. There is another sense of this notion, which may arise with respect to any content whatever. Preferring the content *p*, and believing that *p*, one can become apprehensive about whether in fact *p*; and upon being reassured that, indeed, *p*, one feels relief. In this sense of the notion, I can feel relieved that, say, quantum mechanics is not internally contradictory, a content that has nothing to do with time and does not involve my state as a constituent. The notion of relief here examined is quite different. I was, we may suppose, never apprehensive about whether my root canal would be over at 4:00 p.m.; but I am relieved that it is over just the same.

The thought that I have when I affirm with a sense of relief that my root canal is over is a thought whose very existence depends upon the existence of a certain episode of my mental life: it contains that episode as a constituent, and could not exist without it. It does not follow, however, that the thought is not available to me to think except when I am undergoing that episode. I might have anticipated when I got up in the morning that my root canal would be over by 4:00 p.m., and that I would then feel relieved. I then anticipate the episode of thinking whose content is that my root canal is over by the time of that episode. However, I locate the episode in my future; i.e., as following my present anticipation. I am, therefore, not relieved at the content in question.

The formulation (3) was rejected as representing the content of my feeling of relief on the ground that it was possible to believe this content without feeling relieved. But (4) has the same property, provided at least that one can anticipate one's own mental states and think about them. The point of reflexivity emerges when we consider that the thought that I would express by saying (5) essentially involves cross-reference between (the time of) my state and (the time of) the presence of a situation:

(5) I think that my root canal is over.

We thus distinguish between (6):

(6) the thought that $e$ is a state of my thinking that my root canal is over as of $e$

which is cross-referential, and (7):

(7) the thought that $e$ is a state of my thinking that my root canal is over as of $e'$

which is not cross-referential, even where $e=e'$. When I am relieved that my root canal is over, I think (6). Part of the point of tense, I will argue, is that it makes possible the kind of cross-reference that is typical of reflexive thoughts, and essential to such states as the feeling of relief.

The sketch I have just presented is, I am aware, at once too technical and too informal. It is technical in the sense that it uses various background assumptions about thoughts and the sentences that express them, and in that it brings in a conception of tense as mediated by relations between individual events, which I intend in the sense advanced by Donald Davidson. It is informal in that I have not given a semantics for the sentences that I have used to indicate the various thoughts I discuss, and in particular have not given any account of the content of an episode or state of mind, or of objects as constituents of such contents. For such an account one looks to the technical apparatus developed especially by David Kaplan (1977), that identifies contents with propositions in the sense of possible worlds semantics, and for which the notion of an object as a constituent of a content can be given a precise interpretation (even if, as Kaplan remarks at length, the philosophical point of having objects as constituents of thoughts is not captured by the semantic apparatus). But I am partly concerned here to move away from the conception of content that possible worlds semantics gives, and because of that cannot argue straightforwardly that the contents of two sentences coincide when they are true in the same possible worlds, or even that they are different if they diverge in some possible world; for it may be that the divergence stems from the nature of modality rather than the contents of the sentences considered in isolation.

A sentence, or an utterance of a sentence, even if it is completely unambiguous, need not have a unique thing that is its content. John Perry (1993) has canvassed various things that could be called the content of a sentence, or the information conveyed by it, and has pointed out that sometimes we speak of its content in one or another of these different ways. This being so, there are certain degrees of freedom in possible overall accounts of the nature of thoughts, the semantics of sentences or their potential utterances, and the relations between them. I shall in fact maintain that the semantics of English assigns as the content of my speech, 'The root canal is over (thank goodness)', the very thought that is the object of my sense of relief. However, the argument that what I have called the tensed thought about the present is not simply a thought in which the present time figures, either via something corresponding to a designator for the time in question or more directly as a constituent of the thought itself, does not depend on this or any other special correspondence between thoughts and the contents of sentences.

I have suggested that my thought that my root canal is over is a reflexive thought, containing as a constituent the episode of thinking it. The corresponding notion of reflexivity in language is due to Hans Reichenbach (1947), for whom a token *t* of an indexical or demonstrative expression had for its reference an object *f(t)*, where *f* was determined by the meaning of the expression of which *t* was a token. A simple example of the theory is that of tokens of the first-person singular pronoun 'I'. If I say, 'I have got through my root canal', then the semantics of that whole utterance delivers the meaning that the speaker of *t*, namely me, has got through his root canal, where **t** is the very token of the first-person pronoun that I uttered, the function *speaker of* playing the role of *f*. It is possible to construct a token-reflexive theory of tense along these lines as well. The account that I will give below is similar to such a Reichenbachian theory, but is better described as event-reflexive rather than token-reflexive. With this much by way of statement and setting, I turn now to some semantic issues with tense, only afterwards taking up again the question of tensed thoughts.

## 3.2 Tenses and truth

The tenses of English and other languages are expressions of generality involving time. Partly because the tenses do not occupy quantifiable places, it is attractive to take the logic peculiar to tenses as intensional, so that sentences of natural languages can be evaluated as true or false only relative to moments of intervals of time, over which the tenses quantify, as in the tense logics of Prior and later authors. Alternatively and more directly, one could propose that the predicates of natural language are themselves explicitly time-relative. In either case the question arises how one should think of the truth conditions of potential utterances of tensed sentences.

Consider then an utterance $u$ of (8) by an English speaker $x$ at a time $t$:

(8)  John was (once) happy.

(The parenthetical 'once' in (8) is inserted for clarification: I intend (8) to be understood in full generality with respect to the past.) The utterance $u$ is either true or false absolutely. What should semantic theory establish about its truth conditions? On the intensional theory, the logical form of (8) is (9):

(9)  P(happy(John))

with $P$ the past-tense operator, and the utterance is true if and only if (10) holds:

(10)  $(\exists t' < t)$ 'happy($x$)' is true of John at $t'$

and so if and only if (11):

(11)  $(\exists t' < t)$ Happy(John,$t'$)

where 'Happy', with a capital 'H', is a new, binary, predicate of the metalanguage. On a theory that takes tenses to be explicit quantifiers over time, however, there is no bifurcation of predicates: the adjective 'happy' is uniformly a two-place predicate, true of ordered pairs of things and times. The logical form of the utterance has at least the structure shown in (12), where the variable $t'$ ranges over times prior to $u$, or times prior to the time of $u$:

(12)  $(\exists t')$ happy(John,$t'$)

The question now arises whether the restriction on the range of $t'$ is, as I will put it, implicit or explicit in the logical form, and, if it is explicit, how it is spelled out. Understanding the utterance (8) of course requires that the restriction be comprehended. But it may be only implicit, in the sense that

(12) constitutes the whole of the logical form, the restriction being brought in so to speak from the outside, or contextually. The restriction is explicit if it occurs also in the logical form; and here there are at least two ways to proceed. One is to regard the past tense as an indexical predicate *Past*, utterances of which are true of times prior to the given utterance. In that case, the logical form is more fully as in (13):

(13)  $(\exists t')$ [happy(John,$t'$) & **Past**($t'$)]

The other, still more refined, is to incorporate as part of the form the formula that gives the meaning of the predicate *Past*, that it ranges over times prior to the utterance, or prior to its time. In this case the result is (14):

(14)  $(\exists t')$ [happy(John,$t'$) & $t'<$(the time of) $u$]

I am going to argue that the most refined method is wanted for capturing the phenomenon known in linguistic semantics as sequence of tense. But I will first shift the terminology somewhat, so as to speak directly of events, and of times only derivatively, as indeed I did in my statement above of the tensed thought that my root canal is over. The shift will make no essential difference to the analysis of sequence of tense, but will become critical later on.

I will assume that ordinary predicates, besides the positions that are filled by overt arguments, have also a position for individual events in the sense of Davidson (1967) and elsewhere. I extend Davidson's original proposal as in Higginbotham (1985) to include positions in stative predicates such as 'happy'. I will call this position the E-position, although the general term 'event' sits uncomfortably, since events are changes in objects rather than states. To cover both, I use the term 'situation'. With this extension, the predicate 'happy' as it occurs in (8) becomes a two-place predicate, 'happy($x,s$)', true of an object and a situation if the situation is one of that object's being happy. The temporal argument positions that one is practically compelled to put into predicates conceived as not including the E-position can now give way to predicates that locate situations in time; and it is natural to regard the tenses as such predicates. Situations themselves are essentially in time, and I will assume that for each situation $s$ there is a unique set of moments of time $\tau(s)$ that belong to it, the times, as one says, when it obtains or is going on. Temporal order between situations is taken to mirror order among sets of moments of time, so that $s$ precedes $s'$ if and only if every time in $\tau(s)$ precedes every time in $\tau(s')$, and $s$ follows $s'$ if and only if every time in $\tau(s)$ follows every time in $\tau(s')$. Matters are somewhat more complicated if neither of two situations precedes the other. The notion that will be needed in what follows is that of inclusion, where $s$ includes $s'$ if every time in $s'$ is in $s$.

Our example (8) now has at least the logical form (15):

(15)  ($\exists s$) happy(John,$s$)

(15) corresponds to the minimal logical form (12) that was proposed when we used temporal positions rather than E-positions, and we have options in correspondence with that case. One possibility is to confine the past tense to an implicit role, so that although it must be understood that the variable $s$ ranges only over situations prior to the speaker's utterance, that information is not part of the logical form. The more refined option is to understand the past tense as giving an indexical predicate of situations, true of those that precede the utterance; and the still more refined option is to put the utterance itself in the logical form. These options amount to (16) and (17), respectively:

(16)  ($\exists s$) [happy(John,$s$) & *Past*($s$)]

(17)  ($\exists s$) [happy(John,$s$) & $s<u$]

With the above possibilities in mind, I turn now to some of the phenomena of sequence of tense.

In English and many other languages sentences such as (18) are ambiguous:

(18)  Mary said that a unicorn was walking.

What is said to be the content of Mary's speech is either: a unicorn was walking prior to the time of that speech, or: a unicorn is walking as of the time of that speech. Use of the superordinate verb 'say' is inessential, since the same ambiguity is seen in (19):

(19)  Mary thought/hoped/knew that a unicorn was walking.

Indirect discourse helps sharpen things up, however, because speech is behavior, and therefore hypotheses about the interpretation of (18) can be checked against concrete scenarios where Mary is thought of as uttering this or that linguistic form. Our first question must be: what allows either of the interpretations given to arise at all? Suppose I am the speaker of (18). In the complement clause I have used a past tense, which taken in isolation confines events to those that occurred prior to my utterance. But in (18) it is not possible so to understand the past tense; rather, it functions so as to impute to Mary an utterance whose content is confined to times prior to it, or else to contents contemporaneous with it.

We can put the problem this way. Generally speaking, when I say, 'Mary said that so-and-so', I say that Mary produced some time prior to my utterance an utterance of her own whose content matched that of my own sentence so-and-so, understood as it would be were I then to utter it in isolation. Often, contents will match only if there are compensatory adjustments in perspective so as to secure the same reference. So if Mary said yesterday to me, 'You were in Oxford yesterday', I will report her today by saying, 'Mary said I was in Oxford two days ago'. But now the tense in my sentence, 'A unicorn was walking' is understood not as it would be were I to say it in isolation, but with cross-reference to Mary's speech; moreover, it must be so understood. What makes such cross-reference possible? And necessary?

The answer to the first question that comes from traditional grammar, and has been sharpened in recent work by Mürvet Enç (1987), Dorit Abusch (1994), and Timothy Stowell (1993), among others, is that the cross-reference flows from a conception of tense as encoding temporal relations. I shall put the account in terms of temporal relations between events. When I say, 'Mary said that so-and-so', the logical form of the superordinate clause is (20):

(20)  $(\exists e)$ [say(Mary,$\alpha$,$e$) & $e < u$]

where $u$ is my utterance, and $\alpha$ holds a place for the content of the speech that I attribute to Mary. The logical form of the complement clause is at least (21):

(21)  $(\exists e')$ [walking(a unicorn,$e'$) & $e' < e^*$]

where, were the complement said by itself, $e^*$ would hold a place for the utterance $u$. Now, if this second argument of the past tense in the subordinate clause takes on the value of the first argument of the past tense of the superordinate clause, the logical form becomes (22):

(22)  $(\exists e')$ [walking(a unicorn,$e'$) & $e' < e$]

Finally, let us indicate in the sparest way how this logical form figures in (18), by preceding it with 'that', giving (23):

(23)  $(\exists e)$ [say(Mary,that $(\exists e')$ (walking(a unicorn,$e'$) & $e' < e$),$e$) & $e < u$]

The bracketed constituent is to be understood as if its interior were uttered in isolation by the speaker. So I speak truly in saying (18) if for some utterance $u$ of Mary's that constituent, with $u'$ as value of $e$, matches the content of my sentence as potentially uttered. That takes care of one of the interpretations of (18), the one where she is alleged to have said: a unicorn was walking prior to the time of that speech.

Let us sum up the account just given as a principle, (I), governing sequence of tense:

(I) An immediately embedded past tense may draw the reference of its second temporal coordinate by anaphora, referring back to the first temporal coordinate of the superordinate tense.[2]

For the other interpretation we can invoke the classical principle of *consecutio temporum*, much studied in Latin. According to this principle the appearance of the past tense in a complement clause can be an appearance merely; cross-reference takes place as in the first case, but the tense of the complement is present, not past. We then have (24):

(24) $(\exists e)$ [say(Mary,that $(\exists e')$ (walking(a unicorn,$e'$) & $e'$ includes $e$),$e$) & $e<u$]

That gives us the other interpretation of (18), where Mary is alleged to have said: a unicorn is walking as of the time of that speech.

## 3.3 Reflexive states

With the evidence gathered from the sequence of tense phenomena, we are in a position to parlay the account suggested in section 3.1 of the nature of my thought when I think with a sense of relief that my root canal is over into an account of the semantics of the utterance with which I would express the thought, or refer to it as I do when I say, 'I am so relieved that my root canal is over'.

The predicate 'over' is a predicate true of a situation $e'$ and a state $s$ just in case $s$ is the state of $e'$'s being over, where $s$ is bounded below by the last moment $t$ that is in $\tau(e')$, and unbounded above. Thus, for example, the state of the American Civil War's being over is one that commenced with the signing of the surrender at Appomattox, and will continue for always. Precisification of the relations between $s$ and $e'$ calls for a certain amount of fussing around the edges. If $\tau(e')$ does not include its own futuremost accumulation point, so that it contains no last moment, then $s$ will commence with that accumulation point rather than the last moment in $\tau(e')$; if time is not linear then special provision may be required to guarantee that no time of $s$ is also a time of $e'$; and so forth. I believe that none of these details matters to the concerns of this chapter, and so I will continue to assume a simple picture, where time is modeled by the real numbers with the usual ordering, and where $\tau(e')$ for each event $e'$ is a closed interval, generally finite.

---

[2] Similar examples occur with non-past clauses, as in one interpretation of (i):

(i) Mary will say that a unicorn is walking.

The present tense is taken up explicitly as the predicate 'includes $u$', where $u$ is my utterance; and it is predicated of the state. So when I say, 'My root canal is over', what I say has the logical form (25):

(25)  $(\exists s)$ [over(my root canal,$s$) & $s$ includes $u$]

The proposal with which I began this chapter, presented now in a more streamlined notation following the discussion of the last section, was that my thought that my root canal was over was the thought indicated in (26):

(26)  $(\exists s)$ [over(my root canal,$s$) & $s$ includes $e$]

where $e$ is my episode of thinking. Under the circumstances, what I say may be said to express what I think, even though what I think makes no reference to any utterance of mine; for I know that $e$ is contemporaneous with $u$; that $e$ is present, since I am in it; and that $u$ is present, since I am making it. Suppose now that I say (27):

(27)  I am relieved that my root canal is over.

The predicate 'relieved' is true of an experiencer $x$, a thought $\alpha$, and a state $s'$ if $s'$ is a state of $x$'s being relieved at the thought $\alpha$. The present tense in (27) is interpreted as usual, so that if my utterance is $u'$ then the logical form is as in (28):

(28)  $(\exists s')$ [relieved(I,$\alpha$,$s'$) & $s'$ includes $u'$]

The thought to which I refer by saying the complement clause in saying (27) need not be the thought that I express were I to say that clause in isolation; for it is possible to adjust the embedded present tense according to the sequence of tense rule (I), replacing what would otherwise be reference to my utterance of that clause with reference to the superordinate state $s'$. The logical form of the whole is then (29):

(29)  $(\exists s')$ [relieved(I,that $(\exists s)$ (over(my root canal,$s$) & $s$ includes $s'$),$s'$) & $s'$ includes $u'$]

The semantics proposed here thus delivers exactly the thought that, according to my proposal, I am relieved at.

Let us distinguish, among states of mind that comprise relations between thinking agents and thoughts, those that have the property that the state of mind is a constituent of the thought that is the object of the state. I will call such mental states *reflexive*. It seems that any mental state whose object is a thought can be reflexive; for what is there to prevent it? Besides being in the non-reflexive state of believing that I heard a dog bark, I can be in the reflexive state of believing that I heard a dog bark just prior to being in that state.

Besides being in the state of thinking that there are states it is bad to be in, I can be in the state of thinking that there are states that it is worse to be in than that state; and so forth. My chief interest, however, is in states that cannot fail to be reflexive, among which is my state of relief that my root canal is over, and so far as I can see the state of relief quite generally.

Besides relief, anticipation is a necessarily reflexive state, because one can only anticipate what is conceived to lie in one's own future; and according to the scheme in place here that means that the thought whose truth one anticipates is to the effect that there is a situation of some kind that lies in the future of the state itself. There seem to be other such states: remorse, shame, at least most cases of regret, memory of one's own past, etc. It is not to be supposed that the capacity to have reflexive states is all that is required to be capable of being in the particular reflexive states that we are sometimes in, still less that nothing more than reflexivity is required to knit a set of reflexive states into an autobiography; but the capacity for reflexive states is a necessary condition for human emotional and cognitive life.[3]

Reflexivity is essential to some states because they must be ordered in time with respect to one's state. But a state could be reflexive even if the role of the state as a constituent of its object, the thought, was not to order it in time but to place it in relation to other elements of the thought. Intentions to act may well be reflexive in this way. Thus if I intend and desire to fetch a beer from the refrigerator, I may intend that my present state (perhaps my intention itself, but certainly my desire) be causally efficacious in getting the beer fetched.

But perhaps we have been too swift in declaring that the peculiar properties of states such as relief and anticipation can only be captured if these states are necessarily reflexive. In section 3.2 above I contrasted three possible views of the semantics of utterances and thoughts about the past, present, and future, and having presented these alternatives within a framework that took predicates as temporal I switched to one where the temporal dimension of sentences and thoughts came in only by way of the situations that figured in predication. In giving the semantics of sequence of tense and in expounding the conception of certain states as reflexive I have settled upon the alternative, within a theory that takes situations as primitive and brings time in as relating situations, that is the most refined of all. The question now is whether this step was really essential.

Suppose we return to the view that would take time as primitive. Then the candidates for the thought to which I refer when I say that I am relieved that my root canal is over are the following three, (30)–(32):

(30)  $(\exists t)$ over(my root canal, $t$)

---

[3] Perry (1993: 52) briefly suggests that the diagonal proposition be seen as reflexive.

(31)    ($\exists t$) [over(my root canal,$t$) & **Present**($t$)]

(32)    ($\exists t$) [over(my root canal,$t$) & $t$ includes $t'$]

where in (30) there is a (tacit) restriction to temporal intervals that include the time of my thinking; in (31) my thought has for a constituent the indexical **Present**, which as it figures there is true only of intervals that include the time of my thinking; and in (32) it has for constituents the concept of inclusion and the time $t'$ of my thinking itself. Of these alternatives the first may now be dismissed as giving the semantics of the sentence I use in saying, 'I am relieved that my root canal is over'; for since it is a purely contextual theory of tense it makes no room for the sequence of tense phenomena. The last alternative does accommodate these phenomena, and in fact the account of sequence of tense that I have sketched could be recast entirely in terms of relations purely between times rather than relations between situations in time; for the formal apparatus runs along the same tracks. Assuming that sequence of tense is an anaphoric phenomenon, one could still advance the middle alternative (31) provided that indexical predicates were specially constructed for each case. Thus consider again the example (18):

(18)    Mary said that a unicorn was walking.

To obtain the possible temporal placements of Mary's utterance we first apply one of the sequence of tense rules, and then suppress the information provided by temporal relations in favor of a special unstructured indexical predicate. For example, for the case where rule (I) applied, giving the content of Mary's speech as in (33) below, we would replace '$<t'$' with the special predicate '**Past**$_{t'}$', which is true of times prior to $t'$, giving (34):

(33)    ($\exists t$) [a unicorn walks at $t$ & $t<t'$]
(34)    ($\exists t$) [a unicorn walks at $t$ & **Past**$_{t'}$ ($t$)]

Just why the information that is used in giving interpretations following sequence of tense should be thus cast aside is mysterious, although I will consider in the next section, not conclusively, contexts where it is clear that comparable information is indeed cast aside.

    Suppose that on waking in the morning I contemplated the awful day that lay before me, and suppose that I consoled myself with the reflection, which in the event was to be borne out, that my dentist worked swiftly and on schedule, so that my root canal would be over by 4:00 p.m. I think (35):

(35)    Well, anyway, my root canal will be over then.

referring to 4:00 p.m. On the conception of content derived from possible-worlds semantics, it is not possible to distinguish the content of (35) from the content at which I am at 4:00 p.m. relieved, where the latter is as in (31) or (32). Let $t_0$ be the time of my waking in the morning, and let $t'$ be 4:00 p.m. Then for the content of (35) we could have (36):

(36)  $(\exists t)$ [over(my root canal,$t$) & $t$ includes $t'$ & $t'>t_0$]

But given the model structure we are assuming, with a simple linear ordering of time, (36) cannot differ in truth value from (31) or (32); for $t'$ follows $t_0$ in all possible worlds. But I am not relieved when I think (35).

Cases of this sort are notorious, and were discussed at length in Kaplan (1977). I am mildly amused when I think, 'His pants are on fire', but horrified when I realize, 'My pants are on fire', having discovered the legs I was looking at were my own. My thoughts cannot be distinguished by possible-worlds content.

Within possible-worlds semantics, however, there is an interesting construction, due to Robert Stalnaker, that can be brought to bear on this kind of issue. Stalnaker (1981) and (1987) points out that in all utterances and thoughts, whether they are got at by demonstratives or by some other means, we may consider not just the content but also what the content would be if circumstances were different. In this case, the circumstances in question are times (in the actual world). The construction proceeds as follows. First, replace the constant $t'$ in (32) by a variable $x$, obtaining (37):

(37)  $(\exists t)$ [over(my root canal,$t$) & $t$ includes $x$]

We now consider (a) the truth values that result from (37) by setting the variable $x$ in turn to each of various times $t^*$; then (b) the result of projecting these truth values across the same set of times $t^*$, now viewed as times of thinking; then (c) that content consisting of the set of those times $t\$$ such that (37) is true when $x$ takes the value $t\$$, and $t\$$ is the time of thinking. This content, which Stalnaker dubs the *diagonal proposition*, is a fair choice for being the content at which I am relieved.

Let $t_0$ be the time of my getting up in the morning; let $t'$ be 4:00 p.m. as before; and let $t_1$ be sometime later than that. Then my potential thought or utterance, 'My root canal is over', has following the execution of (a) and (b) the array of truth values shown in (38) below:

(38)

|     | $t_0$ | $t'$ | $t_1$ |
|-----|-------|------|-------|
| $t_0$ | F | F | F |
| $t'$ | F | T | F |
| $t_1$ | F | T | T |

The diagonal proposition shown in the ellipse is then the one that is false at $t_0$, and true at $t'$ and $t_1$. If I am thinking at $t_0$ that my root canal is over at $t'$ I am not relieved, because the diagonal proposition that is the object of my thought is not true there. At $t'$ and at least some not too late later times it is true, and I am therefore relieved.

Notice that the truth of the diagonal proposition at a point $t_2$ is only a necessary condition for my being relieved at $t_2$. If $t_2$ is long after my root canal, it would be mere hypersensitivity if I claimed to be relieved. I am not now relieved that my root canal of last year is over. On the other hand, how long after the event one can reasonably be relieved that it is over is a contextual matter. The Cold War has been over for a few years; but I am now relieved and expect for some time yet to be relieved that it is over.

Stalnaker's construction restores the extra structure that the inadequate simple account of content obliterates. It does this by providing that the object of the feeling of relief is the diagonal proposition (or diagonal thought), and not the ordinary content of the sentence that expresses it. The basis for the construction is hidden in the technical apparatus; I suggest that it succeeds because it mimics the reflexive nature of the thought. If we begin with reflexivity, then the diagonal construction is otiose. Thus my sentence, 'My root canal's being over includes the state $e$', where $e$ is the state of my being relieved at that content, and my thought to the same effect, is not to be viewed in two different ways, once as having ordinary content and once as having the content that arises from the diagonal construction. The content is fixed, and can be thought or said at any time. But it brings relief only when I am in the state in question.[4]

## 3.4 Discards

I have argued that the thoughts that are the objects of certain emotional states, and are referred to in speaking of them, contain those states themselves as

---

[4] The case for the reflexivity of anticipation can be made out as follows. Consider the utterance (i):

(i) Harry will land in London at 3:00 a.m.

and suppose that it expresses the proposition that is true in those possible worlds where Harry lands in London at 3:00 a.m., provided that this time in fact follows the time of my thought. Suppose I wake up in the middle of the night, when for all I know it might be anytime between 1:00 and 5:00 a.m. I believe and affirm then that Harry lands in London at 3:00 a.m. If it is 2:00 a.m. am I anticipating that he will land in London at 3:00 a.m.? It seems to me that the answer is no, but at the very least it follows that I do not know whether I am anticipating or not. But then to express my state when I know that I am anticipating we should view the whole sentence (ii) about the future on the analogy with relief at one's present state; that is, as in (iii):

(ii) I anticipate that Harry will land at 3:00 a.m.

(iii) $(\exists s')$ [anticipate(I,that $(\exists e)$ (land(Harry,$e$) & 3:00 a.m.($e$) & $e > s'$),$s'$) & $s'$ includes $u'$]

The state of anticipation then figures in the thought, locating what I affirm in my own future, and is therefore reflexive. (I am grateful to an anonymous reviewer for raising this point.)

constituents, and that language heeds this requirement on the thoughts that it expresses by making available cross-reference between superordinate and subordinate clauses. As we have seen, this conclusion in turn implies that language makes use of the most refined of the methods that I have canvassed for the relativization of utterances to time, that in which the tenses, poor affixed morphemes that they are, function as full predicates expressing temporal relations. In many contexts, part of the information that the tenses give can be thrown away, since it will not matter to truth value. In these contexts one may hold to a less refined view, where indexical predicates are used in place of full temporal relations; and can even throw away the predicates themselves, provided that one takes the range of the situational variable to be temporally restricted. Special interest then attaches to contexts where full information is required, and to contexts where, although it might have been expected to be present, it must nevertheless be discarded.

A context of the first kind, if I am right, is that of a verb that is true only of reflexive states. A context of the second kind—notoriously, one might say, following David Kaplan's work—is that of metaphysical modality. Suppose I think the thought (39), which is the object of my reflexive state $s'$:

(39) $(\exists s)$ [over(my root canal,$s$) & $s$ includes $s'$]

We have no reason to deny that this thought is expressed also by my utterance, 'My root canal is over'. But consider the utterance (40):

(40) My root canal might not have been over (now).

This utterance should be capable of expressing the thought (41):

(41) $\Diamond \neg (\exists s)$ [over(my root canal,$s$) & $s$ includes $s'$]

Well, there are the following two ways in which the interior of (41) could be true. The first is that my dentist commenced working on me later than scheduled, or anyway went on past 4:00 p.m. In that case the state of my root canal's being over would not include my present state. The second is that my state of relief didn't occur at all. But neither is a way that supports the truth of (40). Indeed, whether I ever happened to think anything ever again, and if so what, is irrelevant to (40), which is true or false depending only upon when the state of my root canal's being over began. What may we conclude from this fact?

Notice that there is no question that I may think the thought indicated in (39), and no basis upon which to withdraw the thesis that my feeling of relief is a reflexive state. On the contrary, just as I may say explicitly, 'My root canal is over as of my so thinking', so I may say explicitly (42):

(42) My root canal might not have been over as of my (hereby) so thinking.

and this utterance will be true if it is possible that, following the root canal, I never so think. In Kaplan's terms, where the contents of two pieces of speech must be distinguished if they differ in truth value counterfactually, or in John Perry's terminology where the 'what is said' by two utterances diverges if they diverge under modal embedding, the above familiar observations constitute a demonstration that when I say, 'My root canal is over', I cannot express the thought (39). The conclusion evidently depends upon the assumption that embedding under modality does not discard information. But it may be that it does, and even necessarily so, though of course we would want to know why.

A person who knows a language can utter sentences with definite truth conditions and thereby express thoughts. What the person who knows a language knows is, I suppose, a theory that associates (among other things) truth conditions with potential utterances of sentences. The sentences are understood as carrying significant syntactic structure, so that the deductive consequences of the speaker's theory will have the form (43):

(43)  If $u$ is an utterance of syntactic structure $s$, then $u$ is true if and only if $p$.

where '$s$' is replaced by a proper description of a syntactic structure $\Sigma$, and '$p$' by a sentence of the metalanguage. The speaker will not of course know all of the deductive consequences of the theory that she knows, and for any particular $\Sigma$ will know many things of the form shown, some of which will be more or less or differently informative than others. We may, however, suppose that among the things that are known about a particular $\Sigma$ there are some that are particularly informative and, moreover, required to be known.[5] Idealizing, suppose that, for each syntactic structure $\Sigma$, exactly what a speaker is required to know about the truth conditions of potential utterances of $\Sigma$ may be summed up in a particular choice $T(\Sigma)$ of sentence replacing '$p$'. In this case, it will be both necessary and sufficient for linguistic mastery with respect to $\Sigma$ that we have (44):

(44)  The speaker knows that: if $u$ is an utterance of $s$, then $u$ is true if and only if $p$.

where '$s$' is replaced by the proper description of $\Sigma$, and '$p$' by $T(\Sigma)$. Adapting a terminology of Davidson's, I will say that the $T(\Sigma)$ that sum up the speaker's knowledge are the *targets* of the theory.

Suppose now that $u$ is an utterance of $\Sigma$. Then I suppose that the thought expressed by $u$ is the thought that $p$, where again '$p$' is replaced by $T(\Sigma)$. Under this identification, properties identified as belonging to the thought will enter semantic theory, and conversely what appears in the semantics will be implicated in the thought.

[5] I discuss these background assumptions in Higginbotham (1991b).

The identification just suggested is a version of Frege's link between sense and truth conditions. If we assume another characteristic Fregean view, that thoughts are the reference of oblique occurrences of sentences, then we derive the familiar conception that one can pass freely between what is referred to by complement clauses, the thoughts, and what is expressed and therefore required for the semantics of those same clauses taken in isolation.

Consider now the question of the target statements to be associated with potential utterances of sentences containing demonstratives and other context-dependent elements, such as (45):

(45)  This is red.

Ignoring tense for the moment, I concentrate on the role of the demonstrative 'this'. In other work, substantially following Burge (1974), I argued that the target statements put the parameter, the use of the demonstrative to refer to an object, in the antecedent of the target statement, and on the right-hand side of the biconditional consequent. Up to the relevant level of detail, the target statement for (45) is as in (46):

(46)  If $u$ is an utterance of (45), and the speaker of $u$ refers with the utterance of the demonstrative 'this' therein to $x$, then:
$u$ is true if and only if red($x$).

A particular utterance of (45), whose speaker refers to $x$, will then according to the assumptions stated above express the thought about $x$ that it is red; and that will also be the thought that such a speaker who says (47) attributes to the beliefs of the person to whom he refers:

(47)  She thinks that this is red.

The example generalizes in ways that I pass over here: to personal pronouns and other indexical devices; to second-order variables that contextually restrict domains of quantification, and so forth. The target statements of truth conditions for a whole language are to be consequences of other statements applying to the parts of sentences; that is, to lexical items and to the ways in which they may be combined. Consider again (45), and take for granted the combinatorics of predication and the interpretation of the word 'red' as a one-place predicate, in simplified form as in (48)–(49):

(48)  'is red' is a Copula + adjective, utterances of which are true of $x$ if and only if red($x$).

(49)  An utterance of a construction consisting of a subject NP and a grammatical predicate Copula + adjective is true if and only if the grammatical predicate is true of the reference of the subject.

To complete the picture we must give the semantics of the demonstrative 'this' itself, its lexical entry. I will suppose that the lexical entry takes the form of a *rule of use*, as in (50):

(50)  'this' is to be used to refer to proximate, salient objects.

As Kaplan (1995) observes, the rule of use does not give the word a meaning, in the sense in which a non-demonstrative singular term has a meaning; rather, it describes what type of reference speakers are to make with it.

There is no reason why the content of an application of a rule of use should not be a constituent of what is expressed by the utterance using it. We can perfectly well conceive a demonstrative, call it 'this*', for which that was so. The rule of use for 'this*' is identical to the rule for 'this', but utterances $u$ of 'this* is red' will have the truth conditions shown in (51):

(51)  $u$ is true if and only if $x$ is red, proximate, and salient.

Now, David Kaplan at least at the time of writing *Demonstratives* appears to suggest that 'this*' could not exist. He writes (Kaplan 1977: 510) that operators that allowed demonstratives and indexicals to contribute other than their reference to the content of what was said in utterances of sentences containing them not only do not exist in English but even '*could not be added to it*' (italics in the original). In such a strong form Kaplan's thesis is in my view false, and the phenomena of sequence of tense already show this. If the embedded past tense always carried the meaning that it has in isolation, no shifts of temporal reference would be possible. There are other troublesome examples, not involving tense. Thus the English 'come', used in isolation, is normally appropriate only for motion toward the speaker. There are exceptions, but anyway I cannot out of the blue in Oxford announce, 'I am coming to Egypt for vacation'. But if we are laying plans to vacation in Egypt I can say, 'I'm going to Egypt today, and I would like you to come tomorrow'. I can use 'come' in this shifted context, because your motion tomorrow will be toward where I then will be. (That we have here a genuine shift of interpretation and not a pragmatic phenomenon is supported by data from languages like Chinese, where the common words corresponding to English 'come' and 'go' cannot shift in this way.)

Nevertheless, it remains a fact that English 'this' is not 'this∗', and that a general explanation of this fact is lacking. It is no explanation to be told that the reference of demonstratives (or other words) is 'direct' (whatever that turns out to mean), since we would want to know why it is direct and not otherwise, given that constructions that, like the tenses, are otherwise are so easily devised.

As a first step, consider a simpler case. The dentist knows as well as I do that my root canal is over. The dentist may be presumed not to know (and for that matter not to care) whether I happen to be thinking anything at the moment, so that what the dentist knows does not make reference to my thinking; but then if the dentist and I know numerically the same thing, my thought considered as the common knowledge of me and the dentist cannot make reference to it either. On the other hand, the dentist may be presumed to know the elementary psychology of dental patients, and may know, thinking of me (52):

(52)   The patient is doubtless relieved that his root canal is over.

The dentist then attributes to me a thought my belief in whose truth he believes will bring me relief. In this case the extra information cannot be discarded.

Again, consider adverbial quantification into contexts like those we have been discussing, as in (53):

(53)   I have often been relieved that a root canal was over.

Quantification over the situations of relief (or their times) cannot be confined to the main clause: we have to bring out the fact that my occasions of relief can involve different root canal operations, each of which I located in my then past.

Such examples suggest the following picture. Many of our thoughts, and at least if we assume the relational account of tenses virtually all of the contents of our utterances, are reflexive: they contain the state or the utterance itself as constituents. Their reflexivity is often suppressed, however, when these thoughts are viewed as the objects of other thoughts or utterances; for thoughts that are common knowledge, or knowledge that one can carry through time, will not in general be reflexive. It is perfectly in order to consider a thought denuded of reflexivity: most mental states are not intrinsically reflexive, and one can be in them with respect to contents of all sorts. However, there are intrinsically reflexive mental states, and in such cases reflexivity shows through.

Reflexivity can show through, though it usually doesn't, even in connection with metaphysical modality. To construct the appropriate cases, consider first the nominalizations of predicates, including as a special case predicates involving mental states. One of the attractive features of an account of ordinary predicates that attributes to them an E-position is that it yields automatically an account of nominalizations that themselves refer to events. Predicates like 'examine' admit the nominalizing suffix '-er', whose effect is to pick out the agent of the predicate: obviously, an examiner is a thing that does some examining; also, less productively in general, the suffix '-ee', which picks out the position filled by the argument of the V: an examinee is a person who gets examined. Besides these nominals there is 'examination', with the suffix '-tion', which systematically picks out events in which there is examining going on. The suffix gives rise also to idiosyncratic meanings (so an examination can be, for instance, a certain content on which the examination in the primary sense is to be conducted), and besides '-tion' there are other suffixes that pick out events. In general, however, one can construct from any predicate a nominalization that refers to situations of the type that the predicate classifies. With the E-position at our disposal, the semantics of this operation is trivial: from a classifier 'V($e$)' of situations $e$ one constructs the definite description 'the $e$ V($e$)'. The nominalizations can themselves take complements, as in 'the examination of the candidates', which now by hypothesis refers to the situation $e$ such that examine($e$,the candidates); and these complements can themselves be clauses, as in 'my realization that the Cold War is over', which refers to the $e$ such that realize(I,that the Cold war is over, $e$), a specific episode in my mental life.

Consider now the nominalization (54):

(54) my (feeling of) relief that my root canal is over

I take it for granted that mental states, and for that matter situations in general, ordinarily have their temporal locations only contingently. Suppose that immediately following my root canal I am distracted by the work I have to do and rush back to the office hardly thinking of it. Later, after I have tackled some of the work, the feeling of relief creeps in. Recognizing as I do that I might not have had to rush through all that work, I can say (55):

(55) Had I not been distracted by work, my feeling of relief that my root canal is over would have occurred earlier than it did.

If we take (55) at face value, and assume that the nominalization (54) proceeds by picking up the E-position, then the temporal reference in the complement of the nominal is to the time of my feeling of relief in the counterfactual situation. It is not sufficient to allow it to pick out a time. This can be seen indirectly by noting that the addition of the normally redundant 'now' radically changes the counterfactual:

(56) Had I not been distracted by work, my feeling of relief that my root canal is over now would have occurred earlier than it did.

(56) is false, even necessarily so. The indexical 'now', true to form, picks out the actual time of the content of my feeling of relief, even in the counterfactual

situation. What we want, however, is variation in the time, and this is achieved in (55) by allowing cross-reference between my feeling of relief, or its time, and the temporal reference in the complement.[6]

A crucial point about reflexive states, which has been used repeatedly in this chapter, is that the presentness of the time of the state, as it figures as a constituent of the thought that is the object of the state, follows (in a sense to be explained, but not here!) from the fact that the thinker of the thought is in the state. To adapt to my purposes a terminology that has been used in discussions of the first person (due to Sydney Shoemaker 1968), the presentness of a present mental state is 'immune to error through misidentification'. It is true also, I believe, that the presentness of the time designated by 'now' is immune to error through misidentification. But unless it could be shown (what seems very doubtful) that the latter immunity derives from an interpretation of 'now' as *the time of this mental state*, or something of that order, we have no reason to suppose that the immunity as it attaches to the presentness of a present mental state is more than a special case of the immunity to error through misidentification of the point that is the centre

---

[6] More formally: assume that the counterfactual (55) is as in (i):

(i)  If $p$, then my feeling of relief that my root canal is over$<t_{inf}$

where $t_{inf}$ is the least time of my actual feeling $e$ that my root canal is over. The definite description is (ii)

(ii)  (the $e'$) relieved(I,that ($\exists s$)[Over(my root canal,$s$) & $s$ includes $e'$],$e'$)

This description may be understood with wide or narrow scope; in either case the counterfactual is sensible and possibly true. Crucially, the content of the clause 'that my root canal is over', as it occurs in (55), is not tied to the time of the context of that utterance.

How can one explain the falsehood of (56)? The definite description is like (ii) with the addition of 'now($e'$)' to the complement clause. Suppose that it takes narrow scope, and consider the evaluation of the consequent of the conditional in a possible world $w$. The description then refers in $w$ to a unique feeling of relief $e\$$, and its object, the complement clause, is therefore true in $w$ (the verb 'relieve', like 'regret' and the others discussed above as expressing reflexive states, is factive). But then 'now($e\$$)' holds in $w$, so that, following Kaplan, $e\$$ occupies in $w$ the time period it occupies in the actual world, namely the time of the context of the utterance of (56). Its earliest time is then $t_{inf}$, and the consequent of the counterfactual is false in $w$. Suppose on the other hand that the description takes wide scope. Then the counterfactual is true just in case (iii):

(iii)  If $p$, then $e<t_{inf}$

where $e$ is my actual feeling of relief that my root canal is over now. Let $w$ be a possible world in which $e\$<t_{inf}$, where $e\$$ is some feeling of relief of mine. It is natural to suppose that, if $e\$=e$ then their objects are the same; i.e., they are feelings of relief with the same content. But if so, then $e\$$ must have the content of (iv):

(iv)  My root canal is over now

where the temporal indexical is evaluated as it was as I uttered it in uttering (56); and that content must be true in $w$, again because relief is factive. But then, as in the first case, $e\$$ cannot precede $t_{inf}$.

of one's temporal frame of reference (on these points see Evans (1982: 180 ff.)). Partly for this reason, one can get rather far from a technical point of view in pinning down the reflexivity of feelings such as that of relief by making them reflexive with respect to time alone, and not also with respect to mental state, though even here one must acknowledge the necessity of a construction such as Stalnaker's to get at what can plausibly be counted as the content of one's thought. Ultimately, however, the situation is mixed: we have cases such as the metaphysical modalities that typically obliterate distinctions among thoughts; but also examples like (55) that show the need for the temporal reference in the thought to be given as the time of a mental state.

In this section I have endeavored to reopen certain questions about the contribution to content of indexicals and demonstratives. Theories that, like Kaplan's, do not incorporate the content of rules of use into what is said face serious difficulties, of a sort that is exemplified in the objects of what I have identified as intrinsically reflexive mental states. On the other hand, it is quite clear that contexts of common knowledge and the metaphysical modalities generally obliterate the contribution of rules of use, leaving only the reference that they determine. I have no definitive answer to why this should be so, although one can, I believe, see that it is at least reasonable that it should often be so. In any case, the quirks of modality should not in my opinion be allowed to undermine the thesis that what we say and think is literally and robustly expressed by the words that we use.

# 4

# Tensed Second Thoughts: Comments on Richard

In Chapter 3 above I discussed an issue raised by A.N. Prior, concerning the objects of states such as relief, regret, and anticipation, as expressed by ordinary English tensed sentences. For a subject to be in any of these states involves having a conception of the position of other states or events in one's temporal experience. In the case, for example, of relief that some painful episode is concluded, it is crucial that one conceive the episode as lying, not merely in a time that is in fact past, but in one's own past, or its being over and done within one's own present. To bring out this feature of the state of relief, I proposed that it necessarily involved cross-reference between the state and a constituent of its object, thus making relief what I called a *reflexive state*. On the view I suggested, what the semantics for English delivers as the truth conditions of my utterance $u$ of 'I am relieved that my root canal is over' is (1):

(1) $(\exists s')$ [relieved(I,that $(\exists s)$ (over(my root canal,$s$) & $s$ includes $s'$),$s'$) & $s'$ includes $u$}

or in paraphrase, there is a state of my being relieved, whose time includes that of my utterance $u$, and whose content is that my root canal's being over includes that state. The reflexivity of the state of relief is thus shown in the cross-reference marked by '$s'$.' Since the time of my root canal's being over includes that of my state, which in turn includes the time of my speech, my root canal itself precedes that time, and thus lies in my own past.

In a critical discussion of the article on which this chapter is based, Mark Richard (2003) proposes as one interpretation of my view that, disliking as I do root canals, his (9'), reproduced below as (2), should express a sufficient condition for me to be relieved:

(2) $(\exists s')$ [believe(I,$s'$,that $(\exists s)$ (over(my root canal,$s$) & $s$ includes $s'$)]

that is, it should be sufficient that I am in a state of belief whose content is that my root canal is over as of my being in that state. Relief should follow that belief. But Richard then constructs a scenario on which (2) appears true, indeed one in which I might even be said to know its content, but I am not relieved, being at the time in the dentist's chair and actually undergoing the root canal.

Now, (2) exhibits the kind of cross-reference that I conjectured was essential to states such as relief and anticipation. But neither its truth, nor, where $s^*$ is a state, the truth of (3), is a sufficient condition for me to be relieved; even obviously so, because the object $s^*$ has not been located with respect to my position in time:

(3)  Believe(I,that ($\exists s$) (over(my root canal,$s$) & $s$ includes $s^*$),$s^*$)

Hence any commitment to the sufficiency of (2) or (3) to bring about the state of relief that my root canal is over would constitute a fatal defect for my account. As it turns out, there is no such commitment; but the discussion helps to emphasize the critical features of my or any similar cross-referential account of the content of some of our states and attitudes.

To his objection Richard conjectures one response that he finds implausible, and then a more complex view, which involves a considerable elaboration of the rather elementary apparatus that I gave. I think that the issue to which Richard calls attention begins farther back. Distinguish first of all the thought at which one is relieved (that a painful or distasteful episode lies in one's past) from the emotional state of relief, which has that thought for its object. Having the thought, or believing or knowing it, is insufficient for the emotional state, as Richard rightly observes. But then what state of belief or cognition would be sufficient? Evidently, one that locates that state itself in one's present, and so locates the state of the painful episode's being over also in one's present, and the painful episode therefore in one's past. On the assumptions in force, for the case of *saying*, 'I believe that my root canal is over', the location of the state is given by its relation to (simultaneity with, or temporal inclusion of) the utterance itself. Belief is then sufficient for relief. But for the case of merely *thinking* that my root canal is over, the location is not automatic; or so I take Richard as suggesting. Thus he gives his (9), reproduced below as (4), as sufficient for being in the state of relief:

(4)  ($\exists s'$) [believe(I,that ($\exists s$) (over(my root canal,$s$) & $s$ includes $s'$),$s'$) & $s'$ includes $u$]

But he then proposes that 'since I might have the belief without speaking', his (9') (=(2) above) alone should be sufficient (Richard 2003), which it isn't.

What Richard's considerations bring out, I think, is that there must, in the occurrence of the belief or cognition that is sufficient for relief, be an element that plays the role of the utterance *u* in the avowal of that state. In my article I had glossed over this point, remarking only that the presentness of a present mental state was, in Shoemaker's formulation, 'immune to error through misidentification', so that given (5) in analogy to (4), where *e* is a mental particular, there was no question of the falsehood of '*s'* includes *e*':

(5) (∃*s'*) [believe(I,that (∃*s*) (over(my root canal,*s*) & *s* includes *s'*),*s'*) & *s'* includes *e*]

What then is *e*? By analogy to the case of asserting, 'I think my root canal is over', where my own consciousness of myself as making the assertion through the utterance *u* locates my state of belief in my present, we may take *e* to be the event of my affirming the content of (5) itself. Then the thesis becomes: although the content of (2) is not sufficient for relief, that of (5) is sufficient. In affirming (2) I merely affirm, in effect, 'There is such a thing as my believing that my root canal is over'; but in (5) that there is such a thing temporally coincident with my affirmation. The latter implicates the feeling of relief, the former not.

If only (5), which incorporates tense in the clause '*s'* includes *e*', will suffice, does it follow that we cannot but think in tenses, or as Richard puts it are incapable of untensed thoughts? No; but it does follow that the feeling of relief presupposes an element of self-consciousness, an element that is masked when one considers only public utterances, which are by their nature necessarily self-conscious acts. Evidently, the states of relief, anticipation, and regret presuppose belief if not knowledge. If I am right, however, they presuppose more than this, namely the capacity to locate one's own belief states with respect to one's current affirmations or other mental events.

I have argued above that the account of the truth conditions of utterances expressing relief that some painful episode lies in one's past carries over to the thought itself, that one is relieved. The state of being relieved involves the state itself as a constituent of the object of relief, and demands also the location of that state as present; that is, as coincident with one's own self-consciousness of the state. But now that the latter point has been made explicit, it may be questioned whether the apparatus of cross-reference was essential to begin with. Why not say simply that the object when I am relieved is just (6):

(6) My root canal is over now.

rendered as (7):

(7) (∃*s*) [over(my root canal,*s*) & *s* includes now]?

The word 'now' contributes to (7) nothing but its reference, the time of utterance or, in the scenario lately envisaged, of inner affirmation. If, however, I am affirming it, then we can let that affirmation $e$, or its time $\tau(e)$, serve without cross-reference between the state of belief and its object, obtaining instead of (5) the formulation (8):

(8)  ($\exists s'$) [believe(I,that ($\exists s$) (over(my root canal,$s$) & $s$ includes $e$),$s'$) & $s'$ includes $e$)

For the particular case of present avowals, indeed, there is nothing much to choose between (5) and (8): on either rendition, we have the time of the critical state including that of my avowal, directly in the case of (8), by swift implication in the case of (5). But notice that, even if (8) is chosen, my state of belief, hence of relief, continues to be reflexive, although so to speak at second remove, through the cross-reference marked by '$e$' between my affirmation and the object of my belief.

When we turn to embeddings under the past tense, however, the situation changes. For interpretations in which a subordinate past tense is taken as expressing the past relative to the past state in the superordinate tense, or where as in classical *consecutio temporum* it is taken as non-past but expressing simultaneity with the superordinate state, there is an anaphoric relation between the state arguments, or so I suppose. Thus (9) may be taken either as (10) (asserting the existence of a past belief state whose content was that my root canal's being over preceded that state), or as (11) (asserting the existence of a past belief state whose content was that my root canal's being over included that state):

(9)   I believed (then) that my root canal was over.

(10)  ($\exists s'$) [believe(I,that ($\exists s$) (over(my root canal,$s$) & $s<s'$),$s'$) & $s'<u$]

(11)  ($\exists s'$) [relieved(I,that ($\exists s$) (over(my root canal,$s$) & $s$ includes $s'$),$s'$) & $s'<u$]

If so, then we should recognize as a general principle that the anaphoric connections run from the coordinate $s'$, the first coordinate of the superordinate tense, to the second coordinate of the subordinate tense, as in the original formulation (5). The crucial case is that represented in (11), where (9) is taken as asserting the existence of a past, intuitively present-tensed, state, my belief in which was sufficient for me to have then felt relieved.

Throughout this chapter I have assumed that indexical words contribute to what is expressed nothing but their reference; but it may be proposed (as by Mark Balaguer (1997), in his contribution to the Santa Barbara conference) that since (12) and (13) below may differ, in that assertions of the latter, but not the former, will be accompanied by the feeling of relief, their objects express different thoughts, even under circumstances guaranteeing that they will be true or false together:

(12)  I believe that my root canal will be over then.

(13)  I believe that my root canal is over now.

These examples are useful in expounding more fully the view I defend here. If $u_1$ and $u_2$ are my utterances of (12) and (13) respectively, then (12) is as in (14), and (13) is as in (15):

(14)  $(\exists s')$ [believe(I,that $(\exists s)$ (over(my root canal,$s$) & $s > u_1$ & then($s$)),$s'$) & $s'$ includes $u_1$]

(15)  $(\exists s')$ [believe(I,that $(\exists s)$ (over(my root canal,$s$) & $s$ includes $s'$ & now($s$)],$s'$) & $s'$ includes $u_2$]

If $s^*$ is a state that satisfies what follows the outer existential quantifier in (15), then the objects of belief, namely the contents

(16)  that $(\exists s)$ (over(my root canal,$s$) & $s > u_1$ & then($s$))

of (14), and

(17)  that $(\exists s)$ (over(my root canal,$s$) & $s$ includes $s^*$ & now($s$))

of (15) respectively, are certainly going to be different in their structure. That my belief in the content of (16) does not bring relief follows at once from the fact that the state $s$ follows my self-conscious utterance $u_1$; but to bring out that (17) does suffice, the information that $s$ is located in my present must be recoverable from my use of 'now'. How is this to be done? Evidently, the adverb or the present-tense morpheme in (13) must not only refer to the time of my speech, but also place the state of my root canal's being over in temporal coincidence with it. Let this be so.

But then the modal statement (18):

(18)  My root canal might not have been over now.

must ignore this very feature of the adverb and the tense; for its truth is obviously independent of what I may happen to utter or to think. Could there be a conception of indexical meanings or concepts that can look both ways, on the one hand incorporating information about the agent's temporal position, on the other allowing the simple semantics for the modal statement, to which this information is irrelevant? It is not clear that there could: explication of 'now' as *the present time* simply pushes the problem back a step, and indeed (19), like (18), is indifferent to all but the value of that time, and so indifferent to whether the speaker thinks of it as 'present':

(19)   My root canal might not have been over as of the present time.

In my original article I left the dual behavior of indexical expressions, as sometimes importing into content the principles that govern their use, but sometimes banishing those very principles from content, in the indeterminate state where the data seemed to place it. More recently (Chapter 10 below) I have elaborated the possibility that the proper form of a theory of truth for indexical expressions will systematically imply the banishment of the content-determining rules from content. On this view, indexicals are governed by rules of use, whose content figures in the antecedents of conditional truth conditions of whole sentences. The rule of use for 'now', for instance, is that it is to be deployed as a predicate expressing the simultaneity or inclusion of one's own utterance (or its time) in another state as given by the sentence. As applied to (6), this account gives conditional truth conditions in (20):

(20)   If $u$ is an utterance of (19), and the speaker $s$ of $u$ uses the utterance of 'now' therein as a predicate $P$ true of just those states that temporally include $u$, then $u$ is true iff: $(\exists s) [A(s) \& P(s)]$.

where '$A$' abbreviates the contribution of the linguistic material apart from the adverb (and for simplicity I have abstracted away from the first person and the present tense). Given an utterance of (6) satisfying the antecedent of (20), and instantiating so as to detach the biconditional consequent

$$u \text{ is true iff } (\exists s) [A(s) \& P(s)]$$

the right-hand side contains nothing of the application of the rule of use for 'now' but the value of the predicate $P$. Thus we capture the modal behavior of (6), or the proper truth conditions of (19), but lose the information necessary to set up a content that, apprehended by the speaker, becomes an object of relief.

Suppose that, as far as semantics goes, the relevant parts of the whole story about (6) are as in (20). What consequences are there for a general account of the relations between the words we utter and the thoughts that we express? If I am right about the general form that semantic theory should take, and also about the structure of thought that is necessary to bring out the circumstances under which we are in states such as relief, then we should construe the representations of thought expressed as extending beyond the narrowest truth-conditional conception of semantics, to include the circumstances of our deployment of indexical concepts. The words we use do robustly express our thoughts; but to see them as so doing, we should take account of the principles that set up our assertions, and not just what we assert.

# 5

# Why is Sequence of Tense Obligatory?

## 5.1 Introduction: Relations between tenses

The tenses of human languages are indexical expressions in the sense of Yehoshua Bar-Hillel (1954), in that repetitions of the same sentence may differ in truth value simply because of tense. They are not indexical, however, in the sense of the context-dependent temporal adverbials *now, yesterday,* and others. These are always interpreted with respect to the speaker's current temporal position. The interpretation of the tenses is not so fixed. In particular, a relative-clause or complement-clause tense may be interpreted as if the speaker had used it at a position in time different from the one she actually occupies. Thus the Italian (1), with the complement clause in the Imperfect, can, like the English below it with the complement in the past, constitute a past-tense report of a past, present-oriented utterance:

(1) Gianni ha detto che Maria era malata.
    Gianni said that Maria was ill.

What would make an utterance of (1) true, if it is true, is that Gianni, somewhere in the past, said something to the effect that Maria was ill at the time. The English in (1) can also constitute a report of a past, past-oriented utterance. For Italian, this latter interpretation is available when, contextually or in virtue of further linguistic information, the complement clause is firmly anchored to a prior time, as for example in (2):

(2) L'anno scorso, Gianni ha detto che Maria era malata due anni fa.
    Last year, Gianni said that Maria was ill two years ago.

Research from various points of view has converged on the conclusion that the reason for these phenomena is that the tenses may be anaphoric in some or all of their uses. Sequence of tense, insofar as it has semantic effects, obtains them through anaphora.

There is an important difference, however, between the interpretation of tenses in complement clauses and their interpretation in object relative clauses. Compare (1) with (3):

(3)  Gianni saw [a woman who was ill].
     Gianni ha visto [una donna che era malata].

An English speaker may say the English (3) intending to assert that Gianni saw a woman who was ill at the time he saw her; or intending to assert that Gianni saw a woman who was ill some time before he saw her; or intending to assert neither of these, but merely that Gianni saw a woman who was, at some previous time, ill; and similarly for the Italian. The existence of the last intention, for both Italian and English, is underscored by the acceptability, e.g., of (4):

(4)  Two years ago, Gianni saw a woman who was ill last year.
     Due anni fa, Gianni ha visto una donna che era malata l'anno scorso.

The difference between complement clauses and object relative clauses shows up when we contrast (4) with (5):

(5)  *Due anni fa, Gianni ha detto che Maria era malata l'anno scorso.
     *Two years ago, Gianni said that Maria was ill last year.

Interpreting sequence of tense as an anaphoric phenomenon, we may put the contrast this way: the tenses of the object relative clauses in (3) and (4) may be taken independently, and no particular relation between them intended; but the tenses of the complement relative clauses in (1) and (5) may not be taken independently, or as ranging over arbitrary past times, for if they could then we would expect (1) to be three ways ambiguous, and (5) to be fully grammatical. Thus sequence of tense is obligatory in (1), but optional in (3); and the question is why.

This chapter proposes an explanation for the contrast between (1) and (3), and similar cases. There is also a contrast between the English past tense and the Italian Imperfect, illustrated by the fact that the Italian (1) apparently requires a contextual or linguistic background such as that provided in (2) to be taken as a report of an utterance about the then past, whereas the English does not; but this contrast will not figure in what follows.

My subject has been the target of considerable contemporary research, going back (for English) at least to Ladusaw (1977). I will refer to other, more recent material as I proceed.

Some work is required to set up the background against which I propose to formulate and test hypotheses, and section 5.2 below is devoted in part to that. I then show how, given very simple semantic principles, the basic semantic phenomena associated with sequence of tense will follow. In section 5.3 I take up the fundamental question of this chapter, the asymmetry between complement clauses and object relatives, and argue that an answer that I have proposed off and on since 1993, indebted to the proposal of Ogihara (1989) (later sharpened in Ogihara (1995)), is not correct. Section 5.4, finally, provides an alternative answer, and remarks some questions that remain open.

## 5.2 The interpretation of tense

The inflectional and periphrastic tenses of human languages are expressions of generality involving time. An important tradition, identified first of all with the work of Arthur Prior (Prior (1957) and (1967)), but continuing to the present day, has examined and elaborated the view that the tenses are operators, and truth relative to time. This view gains prima facie plausibility from the fact that the tenses, whether inflectional or periphrastic, do not occupy quantifiable places. Of course, we have reference to times in elementary language: 'He went there at that time', 'After some not too distant time I shall return to London', and so forth. But the thought is that there is a fundamental part of our language whose logical syntax does not involve quantification over times, even if, in the metalanguage, the action of the tenses is explained in terms of quantification. The tenses then become a species of modality. Model-theoretic studies, including Dowty (1982) and much later work, assumed this point of view.

However, an important result of the research of recent years is that the modal theory of the tenses is inadequate: there is no basic part of our language for which it is correct. The reason is that modal theories are unable to express temporal cross-reference: see, for example, Ogihara (1995: 20 ff.), Kamp and Reyle (1993: chapter 5), and references cited there. If so, then we may locate temporal reference and temporal relations within the tenses themselves. In English, these will be associated with the inflectional feature $\pm$ past, the periphrastic 'will', and others.

Going a step further, I will suppose that temporal relations and reference as expressed in the tenses are relations between events, in a sense of that notion derived from Donald Davidson (1967). A position for events (in a general sense, thus including states; I will sometimes use the word *situation* as covering both) is to be found in every ordinary predicative head, or so I assume. An utterance of a sentence is itself an event, and I will suppose that in an utterance of a simple sentence, say (6), one says that there is an event $e$ prior to one's own utterance which is a journey to London by Gianni:

(6)   Gianni went to London.

The semantics indicated may be derived in elementary steps as follows. We associate with the head 'go' two argument positions, one of which will ultimately be filled by the reference of the subject and the other, the event position, a target of existential quantification. The adjunct 'to London' is a predicate of the event position of the head. The inflection, or inflectional feature, +past, expressing the relation < of temporal anteriority between events, has two argument positions, the first of which is again identified with the event position of the head, and the second of which is filled by the speaker's utterance itself. As we build the sentence syntactically the argument positions enter into the relations indicated. There is also syntactic movement, bringing the tense affix into construction with the verb; and, if the 'VP-internal subject' hypothesis is correct, syntactic movement of the subject 'Gianni' to a position to the left of and higher than the tense. These movements are semantically vacuous.

Abstracting from syntactic movement, we may depict the construction of (6) as shown in (7):

(7) [ +past <1,2> [go(Gianni,$e$) & to(London,$e$)]]

where the open positions in the tense are as indicated by the numerals and letters within angled brackets. These open positions, the elements of what is customarily called the 'θ-grid' of the expressions to which they belong, are akin to free variables, but must be sharply distinguished from the free variables '$x$', '$y$', etc. of logical theory. The latter are expressions of a language, in fact terms, whereas open positions are not expressions at all, but simply information about the number, sequence, and nature of their predicates. Following customary usage, I will call them *implicit arguments*. In computing the interpretation of (7), we speak of the conditions on satisfaction of these implicit arguments by assignments of values to them, and give the conditions on complex expressions in terms of the conditions on their parts.

Eventually, we have a theorem giving what the native speaker of English knows about the truth conditions of a potential utterance of (6), as follows:

(8) If $u$ is an utterance of (6) by speaker $s$, then $u$ is true if and only if [∃$e$<$u$] [go(Gianni,$e$) & to(London,$e$)].

We can go much farther with the formalization of the semantics whose basic ingredients I have just sketched; but the formalization would add nothing to the purpose. What is critical is that the semantics aims for an account of the native speaker's knowledge of truth conditions, something that is evidently necessary if the theory is to be one that actually applies to human beings. (There is no 'translation' into an auxiliary language, for which anyway a theory of truth would have to be provided.) Also, the account eschews the use of higher types and the lambda-calculus, confining itself to the simple notion of satisfaction; there may be uses for these other devices, but the semantics of these examples is not one of them.

For the purposes of this chapter, the crucial feature of the semantics sketched above is that it takes the tenses, like other predicative heads, as expressing properties of, or relations between, implicit arguments. We can now propose that implicit arguments can enter into anaphoric relations; i.e., the relation of anaphor to antecedent, with the usual interpretation, that the value of the anaphor is constrained to be the value of the antecedent. The relation between the event position of the PP and the event position of the verb in (6) is already an example of such a relation.

The proposal that there are anaphoric relations between implicit arguments goes back to Thomas Roeper (1987), and has been pursued in Williams (1994), among others; see also Chapter 11 below. Simple examples include the relation between the implicit argument of passive forms and the subjects of certain adverbials, as in (9):

(9) The books were thrown away intentionally.

where the semantics must have the outcome that whoever threw the books away intended to do so. Also, there are anaphoric relations between implicit arguments and actual formatives, what we might call *mixed* anaphora, as in one interpretation of (10), that in which each participant is an *x* who is required to defeat an enemy of *x*.

(10) Each participant is required to defeat an enemy.

Ippolito (1998) argues that the Italian Imperfect shows mixed anaphora, from the implicit argument to an explicit antecedent.

## 5.3 Tense anaphora

Supposing that the tenses express relations between implicit arguments, consider how the principles of sequence of tense, assumed to involve anaphoric relations between these arguments, will operate in the syntax and deliver appropriate semantic interpretations. For the object relative clauses as in (3), reproduced here, the operative parts of the structure will be as in (11):

(3) Gianni saw [a woman who was ill].
    Gianni ha visto [una donna che era malata].
(11) [...[+past <1,2>]...[$_{NP}$...[+past <3,4>]]]...

We suppose that position 2 is 'anchored' (to use the terminology of Enç (1987)) to the utterance itself, and that 1 and 3 are targets of existential quantification, so that an assertion of (3) is an assertion of the existence of a state of illness, and of an event of Gianni's seeing the woman who suffered from that state. The position 4 might then be taken in either of two ways: (i) as anchored, like 2, to the utterance, or (ii) as anaphoric to 1, hence bound to the quantifier that binds it. Assuming that the embedded past expresses temporal anteriority, we have two interpretations of (3), as shown in (12):

(12)  [∃e<u] [∃e′<u/e] [∃x: woman(x) & ill(x,e′)] see(John,x,e)

For the third interpretation, where John's seeing the woman in question occurred when she was ill, we adopt the suggestion of Ippolito (1998), that the feature +past has only the role of facilitating anaphora, and that the relative clause is in fact −past, expressing temporal overlap ≈ or inclusion of the time of the seeing *e* in the time of the being ill *e′*. (This suggestion does the work, in the present connection, of a rule of tense deletion as in Ogihara (1995), but it is not a deletion rule; in fact, tense deletion is incompatible with the system proposed here.) That yields the third interpretation of (3), represented by (13):

(13)  [∃e<u] [∃e′ ≈ e] [∃x: woman(x) & ill(x,e′)] see(John,x,e)

Returning to (1), our problem will be why the interpretation in which the embedded past tense is not anaphoric is impossible. The exact rendition of the semantics of (1), on any interpretation, requires us to adopt a view of the semantics of indirect discourse, and of complement clauses generally. For indirect discourse I will assume, but will not argue here, that the relevant notion is that of the speaker's *matching in content* an utterance of the person whose speech is reported (or predicted). I do not assume that the parameters of content matching can be settled in any notation-free way; rather, it seems to me that indirect discourse, and other contexts, are to be understood in terms of our reporting practice, and that embedded clauses have for their reference themselves, understood as they would be if uttered in isolation by the speaker. This last statement (in a formulation I take from Tyler Burge (1978)), about how embedded clauses are to be understood, guarantees that the reference of 'today', 'now', and the like will be fixed, the tenses being exceptional in that they may undergo anaphora. With this much said, I will mark the exceptional reference of embedded clauses with the familiar '^' of intensional abstraction, but only as a notational device. With this convention, the data concerning (1) are as in (14):

(14)  [∃e<u] say(Gianni,^[∃e′<e/≈ e/* ≈ u] ill(Mary,e′),e)

where the asterisk on ' ≈ u' records the obligatoriness of anaphora.

We could, perhaps, simply record the distinction between (1) and (3) if it were sometimes the case that tense anaphora were obligatory in other contexts. One possibility, suggested by Abusch (1988) and (1991), and Ogihara (1994), is that the English present tense, which must be interpreted relative to the speech time (or, in our terms, always expresses that an event of some kind overlaps the utterance $u$), is deleted within the immediate scope of a higher present tense. As noted above, the system proposed here cannot literally incorporate tense deletion. But it can deploy an empirical equivalent, namely the obligatoriness of present-tense anaphora whenever possible. There are, then, two possibilities for (15) below: either the indefinite description 'a woman who is ill' takes wide scope, in which case there is no anaphora; or it stays within the scope of the auxiliary 'will', which carries the −past tense feature, in which case anaphora are forced, so that the speaker is predicting that Gianni will meet a woman whose illness temporally coincides with the time of meeting.

(15)   Gianni will meet a woman who is ill.

This proposal faces counterexamples, however, of which (16) is a typical instance:

(16)   Gianni will often meet someone who studies with him.

Besides the interpretation with the object NP taking wide scope, meaning that someone who (now) studies with Gianni is an $x$ such that Gianni will often meet $x$, there are two interpretations in which it is within the scope of the adverbial quantifier *often*. These interpretations are rendered by:

[Often $e$: $e>u$] [$\exists x$: [$\exists e'$: ... $e'$ ... ] studies with John($x,e'$)] meets(John,$x,e$)

where the restriction '... $e'$ ...' on $e'$ may be '$e' \approx u$' (non-anaphoric) or '$e' \approx e$' (anaphoric). The non-anaphoric interpretation, which allows that Gianni will have frequent future individual meetings, each of which is with one or another of his current students, each of whom however he meets only infrequently, will not be available if anaphora are obligatory. The point that is brought out by (16), and any number of similar examples, is that, unlike the existentials in (15), the quantifiers 'often' and 'someone' do not commute. Inversely, the thesis that anaphora are obligatory if the object in (15) takes narrow scope survives that example only because the quantifiers (over time or events on the one hand, and using the indefinite description on the other) are both existential, hence do commute. I conclude that tense-deletion, or anaphora, cannot be obligatory.

Ogihara (1989, 1995) and myself in unpublished work (Higginbotham (1993a)) suggested in different ways that the asymmetry between complement clauses and object relatives follows from a restriction to the effect that the temporal orientation of a complement clause must match that of the content that it conveys with respect to the predicate whose complement it is. Thus a speaker cannot use (1) to report speech of Gianni's whose content lay in Gianni's future at the time he made it, but now lies in the speaker's past. Suppose Gianni in February utters words translatable as 'Maria will be ill in March', and the speaker says the following April, 'Maria was ill in March'. Gianni's words and the speaker's match in truth conditions, but not in orientation. Hence the speaker cannot report Gianni's speech by saying 'Gianni said that Maria was ill in March'. The obligatoriness of anaphora in complement clauses then reflects the fact that the temporal orientation of the content said by Gianni must match that of the speaker. And, under anaphora, it does match. In the interpretation of (1) as reporting a past, past-oriented utterance, the orientations are both past (i.e., prior to Gianni's utterance), and in the interpretation as reporting a past, present-oriented utterance, they are both non-past, since as we have seen the +past feature only serves to license anaphora, and the embedded clause carries a present tense.

I have put the above account in my own terminology, rather than Ogihara's, which diverges (and is in fact more adequate) in various respects. We may also follow Ogihara, with some adjustments, in observing that the condition (the 'Temporal Directionality Isomorphism' condition of Ogihara (1995: 210)) applies to the so-called 'double-access' cases, as in (17):

(17) Gianni ha detto che Maria è incinta.
Gianni said that Maria is pregnant.

Since the non-past (in English or Italian) cannot be anaphoric to the past, the complement clause is interpreted as if the speaker had said it, that is, as in (18):

(18) $[\exists e \approx u]$ pregnant(Maria,$e$)

where $u$ is the speaker's utterance. But this clause cannot match in content any speech of Gianni's in which the (alleged) situation of Maria's pregnancy is future to that speech: for in that case Gianni's speech, but not the speaker's, would be future-oriented. It follows that Gianni's speech must have been present-oriented; and since the speaker has said something that is present-oriented also with respect to her, it must be that in Gianni's speech the range of the situation-variable '$e$' takes in the time of the speaker's report as well. Such is the deduction of the properties of the 'double-access' sentences.

How, then, is the speaker to report from her later perspective Gianni's past prediction? The answer is that the future-orientation of Gianni's speech is preserved by using the periphrastic future, combined with a +past affix whose role is to allow the anaphora that would not otherwise be possible, as in (19):

(19)  Gianni said that Maria would be pregnant.

(Italian deploys the conditional to the same effect.) Again, to omit the +past affix, leaving a present-tensed 'will', is to disallow anaphora, as in (20):

(20)  Gianni said that Maria will be pregnant.
      Gianni ha detto che Maria sara incinta.

There is no problem about temporal orientation, since what is future to the speaker must also be future to Gianni as of the time of his past speech.

In sum, the account of sequence of tense in both object relatives and complement clauses in English and Italian is derived from the following premisses:

 (i) −past cannot be anaphoric to +past; all other combinations are allowed;
 (ii) the +past feature can be interpreted either as expressing anteriority <, or as merely triggering anaphora;
 (iii) the temporal orientation of a complement said by a speaker must match that of the content it conveys with respect to the predicate whose complement it is.

It is (iii) that explains the asymmetry for instance between (1) and (3), and the fact that it applies also to the double-access cases is further evidence for this premiss.

I turn now to difficulties for this account. There are two, more nearly conceptual, problems that do not threaten its empirical adequacy, but make it difficult to support on the intuitive basis to which we have so far helped ourselves, using reported speech. The first is that the prohibition in (iii) is global, applying to all complements whatever. The second is that the interpretation of what I have called future-orientation is obscure, and it seems to be restricted to certain morphemes. Thus compare the examples in (21):

(21)  (a)  Last week, they predicted rain today.
      (b)  Last week, they predicted that it is raining.

(21)(b) shows double access, hence makes for an absurd assertion, since the prediction must have been future-oriented. But (21)(a) is fine. Also, notice that (22) can be a faithful report on Sunday of Gianni's saying on Friday, 'Maria will be in London tomorrow':

(22)  Gianni said that Maria was to be in London yesterday.

These examples suggest that the restriction on temporal orientations, whatever it is, is tied to the feature −past, and that it should not be expressed in the metaphysical terms of (iii). But besides these more conceptual issues, there are severe empirical difficulties as well.

Giorgi and Pianesi (1998b) have shown that the possibility of double-access interpretations in Italian is correlated with the presence of a higher complementizer, and that in those cases where the complementizer is omitted (as in some dialects) one has, not double access, but ungrammaticality. This observation suggests that, after all, the double-access interpretations are syntactically represented. But more than this, investigation of some more complex cases reveals that temporal restrictions apply even independently of the question of future-orientation. The simplest examples are somewhat complex, but the evidence seems clear enough. Consider (23) and (24):

(23)  Maria will say on Sunday that Mario was here on Saturday [said on Friday].

(24)  Gianni will say on Sunday that Maria said on Saturday that Mario *is/was here today [said on Friday].

In (23) Maria's speech is past-oriented, but the speaker's complement is not. (24) has the same property. That (24) with present-tense 'is' represents a case of (failed) double-access is shown by the acceptable (25):

(25)  Gianni will say on Sunday that Maria said on Saturday that Mario is here these days [said on Friday].

As I understand him, Ogihara would treat (24) by deleting the past tense in the most deeply embedded complement clause, making it tenseless. The embedded present tense would not delete, with the result that the past-orientation of Maria's speech would conflict with the formal tense information in the innermost clause. (Ogihara does not actually consider these cases in (1995).)

I have already noted that literal tense deletion is not possible on the system that I am assuming. In a system where it is possible, something further must be said to derive the conclusion, for example, that in saying (1) the speaker may report Gianni as having said something that is true just in case Maria was ill at the time he, Gianni, spoke. With tense deletion, moreover, we do not obtain what could be thought a requirement, namely that the belief that

Gianni expressed when he said, 'Maria is ill', or 'Maria è malata', is the very belief that I attribute to him when I say, 'Gianni believed that Maria was ill'. However the technical discussion may go, I am inclined to think that the sacrifice here is very great.

## 5.4 A reanalysis

Having rejected as a basis for the asymmetry between object relative clauses and complement clauses any account along the lines of (iii), we may as a last resort simply stipulate the obligatoriness of tense anaphora for complements, thus abandoning the solution to the double-access cases discussed above. There is another way to view matters, however. Consider (17), repeated here, and what we obtained at the first pass, namely (18):

(17) Gianni ha detto che Maria è incinta.
Gianni said that Maria is pregnant.

(18) $[\exists e \approx u]$ pregnant(Maria,$e$)

The data are that, besides the restriction on the quantifier given as '$e \approx u$' in (18), there is a further restriction, namely that the (alleged) state of Maria's being pregnant overlap Gianni's speech $e'$, or its time. The full interpretation incorporates both restrictions, and may be written as (26):

(26) $[\exists e: e \approx u \ \& \ e \approx e']$ pregnant(Maria,$e$)

But this suggests that what is peculiar about the English (or Italian) present tense is not that it cannot be anaphoric at all, but rather that, even when anaphoric, it cannot abandon its link to the speaker's utterance; in other words, that it is interpreted twice over, once as anaphoric and once as it would have been used by the speaker alone. (This suggestion, and part of its implementation below, I owe to Tim Stowell, from a remark of his at the Bergamo conference, 1998.)

To make this suggestion effective in syntactic representation and attendant semantics, we require a conception where the tense is represented twice. Now, such a conception is available on the assumption that (a) tenses may move at the level LF of Logical Form, and (b) movement is copying. Recall Giorgi and Pianesi's observation that double access is mediated by a complementizer, and suppose, what is commonly assumed for example for Verb-Second phenomena, that there is movement of inflection I into the complementizer position C. Then if, as Giorgi and Pianesi too suggest, one copy of I relates the alleged pregnancy $e$ to the utterance $u$, and the other copy relates it to the event $e'$ of Gianni's speaking, the semantics being obtained by conjunction of the quantifier restrictions, we obtain following existential closure just the interpretation shown in (26) of the complement clause of (17).

We have noted Giorgi and Pianesi's observation that for matrix V allowing (with some degree of marginality) complementizer deletion, the result of embedding below a matrix past a simple present-tense complement (whether indicative or subjunctive) is ungrammatical; however, the expected meaning is, I am told, intuitively obtained, even if 'forced'. Thus the ungrammatical or at least highly marginal (27) is interpreted as a case of double-access:

(27) ??Gianni credeva (che) Maria sia incinta.
Gianni believed (that) Maria is pregnant.

Conversely, those V that disallow complementizer deletion (with a pre-verbal complement subject; these are, generally speaking, verbs of saying or other forms of communicative behavior) do allow present-tense complements embedded under the past. To account for this correlation, they propose that the complement I is copied into C of the complement clause, the anaphoric copy being the one *in situ*, and the non-anaphoric copy, anchored to the speech time, is in C, indeed in a 'higher' C, which cannot be deleted: hence the first part of their correlation, that verbs not allowing complementizer deletion show typical double-access effects. For the other part, the hypothesis is that V allowing complementizer deletion have only a 'lower', deleteable C, into which I cannot move; hence, on the assumption that the present-tense inflection in the complement clause shown in (27), for example, must move to a higher C but cannot, ungrammaticality results, at least in the Italian case.

There are a number of details of Giorgi and Pianesi's proposal that I will not review here. It is somewhat unclear where the 'forced' interpretation of (27) comes from, since on their view the relevant structure for interpreting it is not available. Zagona (2000) also raises a number of critical points, some with cross-linguistic reference to Spanish. More significantly for the purposes of this chapter, however, we still lack an answer to the question why sequence of tense, or tense anaphora, should be obligatory in complement clauses but optional elsewhere. In the spirit of trying to deduce this phenomenon, rather than positing it as primitive, I explore an alternative below.

Having rejected any metaphysical basis (as in Ogihara's and Abusch's discussions, and in my own earlier work) for the obligatoriness of tense anaphora in complement clauses, we turn first of all (on the assumption that what is in force in that case will apply also to complements, although not conversely) to the simpler case of object relatives. In this respect, two facts stand out: first, −past (an embedded present) can never be anaphoric to a superordinate +past; and second, the +past feature that serves only to trigger anaphora can be anaphoric only to a superordinate +past. Apart from these restrictions, anaphora are entirely optional (recall that we have already rejected, in view of examples such as (16), the suggestion that scopal phenomena are involved). The English paradigm will have superordinate past or present, or future 'will', and subordinate forms including, besides these, the form 'would', which constitutes the anaphoric past of 'will'. To illustrate the first point, observe that (28), unlike (29), requires for its truth that the unicorn Mary found be walking now:

(28)  Mary found a unicorn that is walking.

(29)  Mary found a unicorn that was walking.

Inversely, (29) is triply ambiguous, since the finding could have been simultaneous with the walking (the merely anaphoric past), or following the walking (the true past tense under anaphora), or simply in the speaker's past (no anaphora). To illustrate the second point, note that in (30), if the merely anaphoric past were permitted, we would expect that it could be equivalent to the present-tense (31), which it is not:

(30)  Mary loves a man who was crying.

(31)  Mary loves a man who is crying.

For the merely anaphoric past in the form 'would', we may contrast (32) and (33):

(32)  Mary found a unicorn that would run away.

(33)  Mary found a unicorn that will run away.

The embedded 'will' of (33), being −past, cannot be anaphoric; so if (33) is true then the running away lies in the speaker's future; but the embedded 'would' of (32) is necessarily anaphoric, so that the running away could take place any time after the finding (with perhaps a pragmatic preference for a time between the finding and the time of speech).

I said above that, apart from the restrictions just scouted, tense anaphora in object relative clauses were entirely optional, independently of any issues of scope. Besides the need to make this case by spelling out the examples in detail, the paradigms in question would in a complete story be expanded to include the perfect tenses, and so as to take account of aspectual phenomena. For want of space I omit these details, but invite the reader to verify at leisure the thesis advanced.

Turning now from object relatives to complement clauses, we assume that whatever principles restricted anaphora in the former case restrict them also in the latter, and also that whatever anaphoric relations are allowed from the *in situ* position of the relative clause inflection are allowed in the complement inflection. These assumptions imply that, apart from those restrictions, anaphora are entirely optional, and also that it is the *in situ* position that cannot be anaphoric when it is a present embedded under a past, as in the double-access cases. Hence, they imply that the way in which the double-access interpretation arises is the reverse of that suggested by Giorgi and Pianesi; i.e., that it is the copy of I that moves to C, and not the *in situ* copy that is anaphoric. Suppose so, and suppose further that movement from I to C is obligatory (at least if the +past feature in the embedded clause is not merely triggering anaphora), and that the copy of I there deposited must be anaphoric, independently of the anaphoricity of its source. The properties of the classic double-access cases follow at once. But we obtain also a syntactic/semantic (rather than metaphysical, or stipulative) deduction of the obligatoriness of tense anaphora in complements generally, as follows.

Consider again the English (1), repeated here:

(1)  Gianni said that Maria was ill.

We have the following possibilities:

(a) The embedded past is merely anaphoric. Then the interpretation of the complement is:

$$^\wedge[\exists e' \approx e]\ \text{ill}(\text{Mary}, e')$$

where $e$ is Gianni's (alleged) utterance. Note that, since the embedded past is already anaphoric, any copying into C will not change the interpretation, since it will have the effect merely of adding a redundant conjunct to the quantifier restriction.

(b) The embedded past expresses temporal anteriority $<$. If it is anaphoric, it reduces to:

$$^\wedge[\exists e' < e]\ \text{ill}(\text{Mary}, e')$$

and again any copying is redundant. If not, then after copying and anaphora we have:

$$^\wedge[\exists e': e' < u\ \&\ e' < e]\ \text{ill}(\text{Mary}, e')$$

where the non-anaphoric copy is after all redundant, since $e < u$ (Giorgi and Pianesi note this equivalence as well). So the cases of past embedded below past behave as expected.

I turn now to other embeddings below the past. Evidently, the double-access case (34) will yield the interpretation of the complement (35), as desired:

(34) Gianni said that Maria is ill.

(35) $^\wedge[\exists e': e' \approx u\ \&\ e' \approx e]$ ill(Mary,$e'$)

There is also the embedded future (36):

(36) Gianni said that Maria will be ill.

Here anaphora *in situ* are impossible, because 'will' is −past. After copying and the establishment of anaphora in C we have for the complement clause

$$^\wedge[\exists e': e'>u\ \&\ e'>e]\ \text{ill(Mary},e')$$

where this time it is the anaphoric copy that is redundant, because $e<u$. Finally, there is embedded anaphoric 'would' as in (37):

(37) Gianni said that Maria would be ill.

where, since anaphora are obligatory *in situ*, copying changes nothing, as in (1)(a).

The last paragraph completes the cases I will consider here where the superordinate tense is past. If it is present, as in 'Gianni is saying that Maria was ill', there is of course nothing to discuss, because we are given that $e$ (the saying) and $u$ (the speaker's utterance) are temporally coincident; also, I will pass over the case where 'would' is licensed by a different relation from tense anaphora, as in (38):

(38) Gianni is saying that Maria would be ill (if she were to fail to get a flu shot).

We are left with the cases where the superordinate tense is future, as in (39):

(39) Gianni will say that Maria is ill.

From the case of object relatives we expect anaphora to be optional, and so it is: evidently, both (40) and (41) are fine:

(40) Gianni will say tomorrow that Maria is ill now.

(41) Gianni will say tomorrow that Maria is ill then.

(41) raises no new issues: if the embedded present is anaphoric (as it must be, given the temporal adverb 'then') we obtain:

$$^\wedge[\exists e': e' \approx e]\ \text{ill(Mary},e')$$

If the adverb is omitted from (41), we could have no anaphora *in situ*, but only in the copy in C, obtaining:

$$^\wedge[\exists e': e' \approx u\ \&\ e' \approx e]\ \text{ill(Mary},e')$$

something that can evidently be intended by the speaker. (40), however, is of interest in conspicuously failing to show double access. This case appears, in fact, to be subject to a further curious restriction, upon which I will speculate in closing.

I remarked above that object relative clauses carrying past tense embedded under a non-past could not merely serve to trigger anaphora. The same is true in complement clauses, as in (42):

(42)  Gianni will say that Maria was ill.

That is, we cannot have an interpretation in which Gianni is predicted to say, 'Maria is ill', or the content:

$$^\wedge[\exists e': e' \approx e] \text{ ill}(\text{Mary}, e')$$

With the disappearance of that option, there remains only the case where the embedded past expresses anteriority, and is anaphoric or not. If it is anaphoric, we have:

$$^\wedge[\exists e': e' < e] \text{ ill}(\text{Mary}, e')$$

and if not:

$$^\wedge[\exists e': e' < u \ \& \ e' < e] \text{ ill}(\text{Mary}, e')$$

in which the anaphoric conjunct is redundant, because $u < e$, and which allows, correctly, for both of (43) and (44):

(43)  Gianni will say in two days that Maria was ill the day before.

(44)  Gianni will say tomorrow that Maria was ill yesterday.

To complete the data to be presented here, we may embed the future under a future, as in (45):

(45)  Gianni will say that Maria will be ill.

(the case of embedded 'would' being ruled out as above, where the superordinate tense was present). Here again anaphora are obligatory: I cannot use (45) to predict on Friday that Gianni will say on Sunday that Maria was ill on Saturday. This consequence follows, because where the embedded future is not anaphoric we will obtain:

$$^\wedge[\exists e': e' > u \ \& \ e' > e] \text{ ill}(\text{Mary}, e')$$

where the non-anaphoric conjunct in the quantifier restriction is again redundant. This completes the discussion of the English case, for the core examples given here.

We have shown (*modulo* the example (40), discussed below) that the English data, and the asymmetry between object relative clauses and complement clauses with respect to temporal anaphora, follow from principles (i')–(iii') below, which now replace those given in section 5.2:

(i') −past *in situ* cannot be anaphoric to +past;
(ii') The +past feature can be interpreted either as expressing anteriority <, or as merely triggering anaphora, in the latter case anaphora to a superordinate past;
(iii') In complement clauses, I must move to C, and anaphora from C are obligatory; not so in relatives, where, apart from the restrictions above, they are always *in situ* and optional.

We have now abandoned any orientation-condition on complement clauses, and the observations that led to it fall out purely from the syntactic conditions given, together with the particular principle (iii').

Supposing that the perspective of Giorgi and Pianesi is adopted, but its implementation reversed in the manner suggested, we retain the consequence, and indeed on just their grounds, that there is a correlation in Italian between the possibility of double-access readings and the absence of complementizer deletion. Thus, in cases like (27), repeated here, the embedded tense cannot move to the higher C, and the result is ungrammaticality:

(27)   ??Gianni credeva che Maria sia incinta.
       Gianni believed (that) Maria is pregnant.

(Even the English example in (27) is marginal for some speakers I have consulted; hence the explanation, if correct, may apply cross-linguistically as well.) Further discussion here would take us far afield, both because Italian shows a formal distinction between the imperfect and the past (and distinctions of mood) not found in standard English, and because of other comparative Romance phenomena, as in Zagona's recent work. With respect to the examples we have considered, note that doubling the quantifier restriction wherever the embedded tense is not anaphoric *in situ* is redundant (or, in the case of (41), something that must anyway be allowed), except for the classic double-access case (34) and the entirely non-anaphoric case (40).

I will close with two remarks. The first concerns the difference between tense systems like English and Italian, which show double-access interpretation and have sequence of tense in the classical sense (that is, where an embedded past is not interpreted as a relative past, but as a relative present), and systems like Japanese or Hebrew, which do not. The second considers the example (40).

Again, we owe to Ogihara the careful observation of the Japanese phenomena, where non-past does not show double access, but indeed can be a relative or anaphoric present by itself; and, correlatively, where the past of a complement clause is always a relative past. The resulting system may be taken to obey (iii′) above, but abandons (i′), instead imposing no restriction at all; does not exhibit the ambiguity of interpretation of the +past feature (if, indeed, that is what it is in Japanese; it may be that the formative, or its features, are unlike those of English); and never interprets any but the higher copy of a tense. Evidently, systems that have richer morphology may be the source of interpretations that combine the Japanese with the English features.

Smith (1978) and others have considered the possibility of double-access interpretations with a present tense as complement of a future. Examples include (46):

(46) Gianni will announce next week that Maria is pregnant now.

Such examples are not excluded on the present account; indeed, given I-to-C movement, they are to be expected. But matters are not so clear for (40) and the like. Consider an action-sentence analogue to (40), such as (47):

(47) Gianni will say (next week) that Maria is dancing well (right now).

where the speaker is making a prediction about what Gianni will say later about the quality of Maria's current dancing, then long since over. In my judgement, the speaker (who knows perfectly well, let us say, that Maria is not dancing well) can say (47) if she thinks that Gianni, who is in the studio watching Maria dance, is now of the opinion that Maria is dancing well, even if he has not said so; but she cannot say it if she knows that Gianni is asleep at home, and only later will watch a videotape of Maria's current performance. In the latter case, I believe, the past progressive must be used in the complement clause. The grammaticality of (40) and (47) shows that the complement present tense need not be anaphoric; there is no question here of double access. But it suggests that, while we can sometimes take the complement present just as it is, the circumstances must be exceptional. Thus, it is proper to predict what Gianni will *say* using the present tense if that is what he now *thinks*, even if, when he does say it, it must be with the past tense.

In some other cases, I believe, the result of taking the embedded clause as it stands (without anaphora) is highly questionable. Thus suppose that Maria is known to be touring the United States, one city a day, and that Gianni, who keeps track of her whereabouts, announces each day where she was the day before. Consider the prediction (48):

(48) Gianni will announce tomorrow that Maria ??is/was in New York today.

The example seems highly questionable, as noted. If so, then although the acceptability of (47), under the circumstances described, is problematic for the view presented here (as it is for Giorgi and Pianesi), there may be a dimension of reporting and predicting speech behavior that is not covered by the formal syntactic and semantic conditions under investigation in this chapter.[1]

---

[1] This chapter is an extended and, in section 5.3, somewhat revised version of a paper read at Harvard University, November 1998. That paper was itself a revision of the material in Higginbotham (1993a), which had been presented at the University of Geneva, 1994, and formed part of the basis of a course at the GISSL, Girona, Catalonia, in 1996. I am indebted to the various audiences before whom I have over some years presented the issues of the semantics of sequence of tense, and to individual discussions especially with Dorit Abusch, Alessandra Giorgi, Michela Ippolito, and Terence Parsons. Finally, I should like particularly to note that, although I have come to disagree with the views of Toshi Ogihara (as well as the closely related views of my former self), I am much indebted to his research.

# 6

# Anaphoric Tense

## 6.1 Introduction

In this chapter I extend the discussion of sequence of tense so as to include some properties of the English Perfect, and so as to clarify some pieces of the construction thus far left open. I also call attention to some features of what I call here *indexical mismatch* as between adverbials and tenses, a phenomenon that may well extend in a number of directions, both within individual languages and cross-linguistically. In large part, however, my purpose is critical: I aim to show, despite arguments to the contrary, that anaphoric theories of tense do exactly what needs to be done to explain the dependencies of c-commanded tenses upon c-commanding ones, and that alternatives, notably those of the sort proposed in Ogihara (1995), von Stechow (1995), and Abusch (1994) and (1997), must build back into their respective accounts the anaphoric properties of sequence of tense if those accounts are to be part of an empirically adequate system. The semantics that I deploy here will require abandonment, or at least radical modification, of any framework that takes sentential complements in a 'notation-free' manner, as in possible-worlds semantics; but that framework wants modification anyway, or so (for familiar reasons) I will assume.

Anaphoric theories of tense may be elaborated in several ways. As I am using the term, an anaphoric theory will account for the familiar properties of a sentence such as English (1) by establishing some basis for coreference between the Tense-bearing element of the main clause (in this case futurate *will*), and that of the complement clause (here the present, or −past, inflection on the copula):

(1)  John will say that Mary is happy.

For: (1) can be understood to mean, and be intended to be understood to mean, that John, at some future point or other, will make a statement whose content is that Mary is happy as of the time of that very statement. The complement Present is thus relative to the futurate *will*.

# Anaphoric Tense 103

On the view elaborated in Chapter 5 the anaphoric relation in (1) is established as follows. First, it is assumed that both the main predicate *say* and the complement predicate *happy* (and indeed all heads) have an Event or E-position in the sense of Higginbotham (1985), following the point of view elaborated in several essays in Davidson (1980), and in addition that what it is customary following Reichenbach (1947) to call 'event time' is fixed in each case as the actual time of the events, or alleged events, in question. Second, the tenses are taken, all of them, to express binary relations between times, whether these are given as the times of events or in some other way. Third, a speaker of English who asserts (1) is making a prediction about what will happen in the future of her own speech $u$, an event of utterance; and, fourth, that the complement Present, itself expressing the binary relation $\approx$ of temporal overlap or inclusion, contains an element that is anaphoric to the event time marker of the main clause.

To complete the first steps of the picture, we assume a function, represented here by '$\tau$', that delivers the actual time $\tau(e)$ of events $e$, and (as is customary), existential quantification (default existential closure) at clause boundaries with respect to the E-position, with the temporal relations expressed by Tense figuring in the restriction of such quantification. The main clause, as in (2) below, thus comes out as in (3):

(2)  John will say so-and-so.

(3)  $[\exists e: \tau(e) > \tau(u)]$ Say(John,so-and-so,$e$)

What of the complement clause? In isolation, as the second coordinate of the Present Tense would receive the actual time $\tau(u')$ of its own utterance $u'$ for its value, we would have simply (4):

(4)  $[\exists e': \tau(e') \approx \tau(u')]$ happy(Mary,$e'$)

Embedded as it is in (1), however, this coordinate will receive its value anaphorically, from the first coordinate of the main clause Tense. Its content will therefore be the proposition expressed by (5):

(5)  $[\exists e': \tau(e') \approx \tau(e)]$ happy(Mary,$e'$)

But what is that proposition? Well, for any event $e$ it is the proposition that the actual time of $e$ is included in the actual time of some situation $e'$ of Mary's being happy. Using Montague's notation '$^\wedge$' for λ-abstraction over possible worlds, what I shall call the *modal profile* of this proposition, its intension in the sense of Montague, is that denoted by (6):

(6)  $^\wedge[\exists e': \tau(e') \approx \tau(e)]$ happy(Mary,$e'$)

That modal profile, given the actual world @ so as to fix the function τ, and given a future event *e*, will yield Truth for those possible worlds *w* where the actual time of *e* is included in a time of Mary's being happy in *w*. And it will yield Truth in @, or Truth *simpliciter*, if @ itself is amongst those *w*.

Some further assumptions are certainly required, as for instance the assumption that (1) cannot be made true in virtue of some future utterance of John's in some world other than the actual world; the assumption that temporal intervals and their ordering are fixed across worlds; and the like. Anyway, assembling the pieces, we end up with (7) as giving, up to the limits of the modal profile of the complement clause, the truth conditions of (1):

(7)  $[\exists e\colon \tau(e) > \tau(u)]$ Say(John, $^{\wedge}[\exists e'\colon \tau(e') \approx \tau(e)]$ happy(Mary,$e'$),$e$)

Supposing that any anaphoric theory of sequence of tense must say the functional equivalent of what is proposed above for (1), we may ask what syntactic mechanisms mediate the anaphoric relation as shown in (7), or syntactically through (say) indices as in (8):

(8)  $\ldots [\alpha_i > \beta] \ldots [\gamma \approx \delta_i] \ldots$

where δ, the second coordinate of the complement clause, is anaphoric to α. The syntactic relation depicted in (8) is non-local as stated, in the sense that it proceeds from INFL (or T(ense)) to INFL without mediation. Giorgi and Pianesi (2000) and (2001), however, have shown a strong correlation of this relation with properties of the complementizer position C, and have thus shown that mediation through the clause boundary is wanted; I have adopted a version of their view, involving INFL-to-C movement in complement clauses. This further elaboration, however, does not disrupt the basic contours of the semantics under the anaphoric theory.

## 6.2 General outline

One proposal for English sequence of tense, apart from examples involving the perfect and the progressive, is as follows (repeated from Chapter 5):

(Ø)  The actual time of utterance is default in root clauses.
(i)  Tenses are binary, expressing one of the three relations $\approx$, $<$, or $>$.
(ii) Anaphoric +Past is ambiguous (in English) between (a) facilitating anaphora, but having a −Past interpretation (B-past), and (b) expressing $<$ (A-Past). The antecedent of a B-Past must be +Past, and the clause itself must be stative.

(iii) −Past *in situ* cannot be anaphoric to +Past.
(iv) Tenses in the C position of a complement clause are always anaphoric; movement of one copy of INFL to C is obligatory in these cases.

It follows that sequence of tense is obligatory in complement clauses, but not in relative clauses. The phenomena of English 'double access' likewise fall out. There are a number of languages in which the forced double-access interpretation, as in the well-known example (9), does not occur:

(9) John said that Mary is pregnant.

That is to say, in these languages the analogue of (9) means merely that John said (in the past) that there was such a thing as Mary's being pregnant at the time of his, John's, speaking. English, however, forces an interpretation of (9) according to which the content of John's speech is to the effect that Mary is pregnant both at the time of his own utterance and at the time of the reporter's speech.

In the system assumed here, English double access is a joint consequence of (iii) and (iv) above. For, the complement clause will contain two copies of INFL, one in C and one *in situ*, and these will conjoin in the restriction of the existential quantification over events, as in (10):

(10) $[\exists e' : \tau(e') \approx \alpha \ \& \ \tau(e') \approx \beta]$ pregnant(Mary,$e'$)

The element $\alpha$ will be anaphoric to the first coordinate of the INFL of the main clause (by (iv)), but $\beta$, being −Past, will not (by (iii)). Then $\beta$ will be set at the actual time of the speaker's utterance, thus yielding a content that (whether true or not) locates Mary's alleged pregnancy at both points on the interval between the speaker's utterance and John's, and so by implication throughout that interval.

As for languages that do not show double access, I will assume (until shown otherwise) that condition (iii) above is vacated, and that the B-past doesn't exist (at least with an embedded simple past). There are complications arising from the distinction between perfect and imperfect forms, subjunctive, and the like; but the first parameterization of linguistic differences seems likely to occur at the points mentioned. (From this perspective, English is a poor starting-point for cross-linguistic discussion, as it collapses a number of distinctions that are morphologically expressed in other systems; but my intention here is to explore, in English, the proposition (i), the strictly anaphoric approach to sequence of tense, and the extension of (ii)–(iv) to the English Perfect.)

In my examples, the propositions (∅)–(iv) and their consequences apply between immediately c-commanding and immediately c-commanded clauses.

But such a restriction appears to be sufficient, since, as observed for instance in Ogihara's work (Ogihara (1995)), the operation of sequence of tense is strictly clause-by-clause. As an example, take Hans Kamp's case (11):

(11) John said that in two days he would say to his mother that they were having their last meal together.

The relevant organization of temporal coordinates, according to the anaphoric theory, is as in (12):

(12) $\tau(e) < \tau(u) \ldots \tau(e') > \tau(e) \ldots \tau(e'') \approx \tau(e') \ldots$

Note in particular that the intermediate *would* counts as +Past for the purposes of the anaphoric account. The Past form *were* is also a B-Past, in the terminology adopted here.

## 6.3 Some general questions

On the view that I have summarized above, or on any comparable view, simple examples such as (13) come out as in (14):

(13) Mary thinks that John is asleep.
(14) $[\exists e: \tau(e) \approx \tau(u)]$ thinks(Mary,$^\wedge[\exists e': \tau(e') \approx \tau(e)]$ asleep(John,$e'$),$e$)

where $\tau(e)$ is the time of $e$, and $u$ is the utterance of (13).

Arnim von Stechow, in a couple of places (von Stechow (1995) and (2002)), argues that this sort of view (either in the quantificational terms expressed above, or on more purely referential anaphoric accounts) can't be correct. I quote from one of his arguments (having changed the names in his examples to 'Mary' and 'John', and having adjusted the quotation so as to fit the formulation (14) above):

> We all are wrong about the time most of the time. Mary has her thought at 5 o'clock, but she believes it is 6 o'clock.... We can describe the content of her thought as 'being temporally located at a time which is 6 o'clock and at which John is asleep.' In other words, the time of John's sleeping in the belief worlds is 6 o'clock. Thus [the time of thinking is] 5 o'clock and [the time of sleeping is] 6 o'clock. So, obviously, $[\tau(e')] \neq [\tau(e)]$. Or Mary might not have had any particular time in mind. She just thought: 'John is asleep right now.' The content of the thinking may be described as 'being at a time at which John is asleep.' This formulation makes it obvious once more that the time of sleeping $[\tau(e')]$ has nothing to do with the time of thinking $[\tau(e)]$.
>
> (von Stechow 1995: 4)

# Anaphoric Tense 107

I don't think this argument tells against the anaphoric theory; in fact, as I will elaborate below, it even gets matters backwards, in the sense that the subjective element of time is exactly what *is* revealed in the anaphoric account (14) of (13). First, however, I reconstruct the argument more explicitly.

On the first of the stories just rehearsed, we have the speaker saying (15):

(15)  Mary thinks at 5 o'clock that John is asleep at 6 o'clock.

On the anaphoric theory, we obtain (16):

(16)  [∃e: τ(e)≈τ(u)] {τ(u)=5 o'clock & thinks(Mary,^[∃e′: τ(e′)≈τ(e)] (6 o'clock(τ(e′)) & asleep(John,e′)),e)}

Since τ(u) is by hypothesis 5 o'clock, only that time will truly cash out the existential quantifier in the speaker's statement about what Mary thinks. In the system within which I take von Stechow to be working, and assuming that the temporal designator '5 o'clock' is rigid, there follows (17):

(17)  thinks(Mary,^[∃e′: τ(e′)≈5 o'clock] (6 o'clock(τ(e′)) & asleep(John, e′)),e)

where *e* is the situation of Mary's thinking. But the proposition believed, on this consequence, would appear to be indistinguishable from that believed in thinking that 5 o'clock is 6 o'clock, something of which Mary is certainly not guilty. The conclusion, in what I have offered as a sympathetic reconstruction of von Stechow's line of thought, would be that, since Mary is merely mistaken about the time, and her beliefs are not absurd, there must be something wrong with the anaphoric theory.

But now, why suppose that we can replace the *actual time t* (i.e., the actual time τ(e′) of Mary's thinking) in (18) below with the descriptive designator '5 o'clock'?

(18)  t≈τ(u) & τ(u)=5 o'clock & thinks(Mary,^[∃e′: τ(e′)≈t] 6 o'clock(e′),e)

Mary's thought was about a *thing*, the actual time of her thinking, and that thought is not the same as one involving a descriptive reference (or even a name primitively referring) to that time. So the last step of the argument fails.

It remains correct to remark that Mary's belief about John, under the scenario envisaged, cannot be true (or, that there are no counterfactual situations compatible with her beliefs). The modal profile of her thought, namely that denoted by the expression (19), could yield truth only in a possible world in which 5 o'clock was 6 o'clock; and there are no such worlds.

(19)  ^[∃e′: τ(e′)≈5 o'clock] [6 o'clock(e′) & asleep(John,e′)]

Under the idealization that would view belief and the like as 'personal modalities', in the sense due originally to Jaakko Hintikka, such consequences are a common occurrence; but that just shows the limits of the idealization.

In von Stechow's second example, Mary is simply thinking, 'John is asleep now'. Elsewhere he notes, properly, that the *now* must be 'subjective': it is *her* Present, not *the* Present, that she cares about. I will discuss below the case for taking Mary's thought to have as a constituent the (time of the) event of her thinking it, something that comes out in the speaker's report (13).

Broadly speaking, the distinction between the anaphoric account, as I present it here, and that advocated by von Stechow (1995) is that tense anaphors, for him, are permitted in simple extensional contexts, but not elsewhere; whereas I assume a system in which they are available alike in all contexts, with the difference that they become obligatory in all complements.

Indeed, features of the anaphoric account must eventually be incorporated into von Stechow's own view, because by itself that view does not provide a means for assessing the truth value of what someone is said to have said, believed, realized, etc. Thus take (20) (from von Stechow (2002)):

(20)  Mary thought that it was raining.

On von Stechow's view, the complement clause in (20) gives us only a relation obtained by λ-abstraction over worlds and times: $\lambda w \lambda t(\text{rain}_w(t))$ (or, in the system proposed here, where the times are times of situations: $\lambda w \lambda t[\exists e_w: e_w \text{ at } t]$ $\text{rain}_w(e_w)$). But we now must ask what it is for Mary's thought to be *true*; for I might contradict it, as in (21):

(21)  Mary thought that it was raining, but it wasn't.

(or endorse it, by saying, 'and it was indeed raining', or qualify it, etc.). In the case of (13) the comparable question has an immediate answer: for Mary's belief that John is asleep to be true is for the actual world and time (@,$t_o$) to fall within the relation expressed by the complement. But because sequence of tense is obligatory in complement clauses, in the case of (21) we must allow for a two-way (but not a three-way) ambiguity; that is, we must allow that, on one construal, Mary's thought is true iff rain($t$) at @ at the time of Mary's so thinking, and on another that it is true iff rain($t$) at @ at some time prior to Mary's so thinking; but also we must say somehow that there is no construal such that it is true iff rain($t$) at @ at some time prior to the reporter's speech. Likewise, consider (22):

(22)  Mary said that it will rain.

Supposing that (22) is true, we must bring out the fact that Mary spoke truly if and only if rain($t$) at @ for some time $t$ following the time of the *reporter's* speech (whereas with 'would' for 'will' it would be some time after *Mary's* speech); and so on, through all the cases. In short, the conditions on tense anaphora, whatever they are, must be reproduced *in toto* in a full account of tense in indirect discourse and the like.

The last observation does not imply that the difference between von Stechow's outline and the view advanced here is notational merely; rather, the conclusion should be that there was no compelling reason for von Stechow's detour through properties and relations in the first place; and, as I remarked above, that there are limitations on the view of belief and the like as personal modalities.

Similar remarks apply to accounts of the type advanced by Dorit Abusch, chiefly Abusch (1994). Her work obtains the proper conclusion for (20) and the like through a proposed semantic condition, the 'Upper Limit Constraint', which restricts the times of evaluation of the complement to those less than or equal to the time of the reporter's speech. However, in those languages for which (20) admits only what I called above the A-Past interpretation, the constraint would have to be further modified, or another constraint added, to the effect that the upper limit is not the time of the reporter's speech, but the time of the speech reported. Similarly for languages where, unlike English, the double-access interpretations are not realized, or they are realized only for certain morphological forms, such as the Imperfect. The suggestion in this article, in effect, is that the linguistic parameters governing sequence of tense are all of them syntactic, parts of the binding theory of implicit arguments, and that the semantics is mostly routine once the syntax is solved for.

There are material points as well. The constraint proposed by Abusch would rule out (23), as noted with approval in von Stechow (1995: 19):

(23)   Mary expects to marry a man who loved her.

at least on the interpretation in which Mary's expectation is: she will marry (at some future time), a man (some man or other) who loved her (at some time prior to that). I don't agree with the judgement that this sort of interpretation is not possible. It becomes salient with proper time-delineations, as in (24):

(24)   Mary expects within the next six months to marry a man who fell in love with her only a little while before that.

Of course, the matter is not one of simple counterexample, as the properties of infinitives must be brought into the picture: if the complement is tensed, as in (25) below, we expect, and I believe we get, fully acceptable results, as the anaphoric theory would predict.

(25)   Mary expects that she will marry a man who fell in love with her only a little while before.

In this section I have argued that the anaphoric penetration of complement clause Tense by main clause Tense is not threatened by the kinds of semantic considerations advanced in the literature. I will return only in closing to the question how to make clear the 'subjective' aspect of the time in complement clauses to predicates such as 'say', 'know', or 'think'. Before doing so I sketch, rather briefly, some issues with the English Perfect (taken up more fully in Chapter 9), and with indexicals, which may help to emphasize how the semantics of complements must be sensitive, not only to their modal profiles, but also to the notation in which these are expressed.

## 6.4 Adding the perfect

To this point I have considered only simple verbal forms, abstracting away from the perfect and progressive heads (*pace* Kamp's example (11), which does not raise any of the peculiar issues connected with the progressive). Here I briefly consider the application of the general account to the perfect; see Chapter 9 for further discussion.

Does the English Perfect have temporal properties? Jespersen (1924: 270), urged that it characterizes 'present results of past events', and not the past events themselves. (He further noted that English was what he called a 'conservative' language in this regard, as most Germanic and Romance languages had to a large degree mutated the Perfect somehow so as to become part of a system of tense.) To the extent that Jespersen's view of English holds up, the temporal properties of the Perfect would have to be derived from its aspectual meaning. Parsons (1990) makes Jespersen's account, or part of it anyway, explicit in contemporary logical or truth-conditional terms. I will not summarize these discussions, but turn directly to their implementation in the system proposed here.

I assume that perfect morphology plus tense combine in English in the standard way: there is a head Perf within the scope of +past or −past INFL, and the auxiliary 'have' raises to Tense, whereas the Verb moves to the head position of Perf, marked by '-en'. Perf has two argument positions, and is satisfied by a pair $(e',e)$ of situations just in case $e'$ is a result (in some sense or senses to be determined) of $e$. The Tense, which c-commands Perf, applies therefore to its first argument position, marked by $e'$. In simple sentences existential closure applies to both E-positions.

As Jespersen remarked, his basic view has the consequence that the Present Perfect is just what it seems to be, as in his famous example (26):

(26)  Now I have eaten enough.

where the present predicate *now* must apply to the present result, not the past activity. Taking it step by step, we would have (projections of) the sentential ingredients 'eat enough$(x,e)$' and Perf$(e',e'')$, sisters in the syntactic structure, combining through conjunction (that is, through θ-identification of $e$ with $e''$) to produce (27); and would have these combining again with the raised subject, and with the −past head in Tense as in (28), to produce (29):

(27)  Perf$(e',e)$ & eat enough$(x,e)$
(28)  −past$(\tau(u),\tau(e'''))$
(29)  −past$(\tau(e'),\tau(u))$ & Perf$(e',e)$ & eat enough$(I,e)$

We assume that the sentence is by default existentially closed, as proposed in Davidson (1980). Where the adverb 'now' is predicated of the higher position marked by $e'$, and the feature −past is interpreted as expressing the relation ≈ of temporal inclusion, the result is (30):

(30)  $[\exists e': \tau(e') \approx \tau(u)]$ $(\exists e)$ (Now$(e')$ & Perf$(e',e)$ & eat enough$(I,e)$)

## 6.5 Rigidity and indexical mismatch

Examples like (31) show the semantic effects of Sequence of Tense: as the complement V 'leave' is not stative, the assertion is to the effect that John made a past Past-tense utterance (an A-Past, in the terminology used here).

(31)  John said yesterday that Mary left.

An indexical temporal adverbial construed with the complement clause, however, does not shift its reference because of this. So in (32) 'yesterday', no matter how construed, necessarily refers to the day before the speaker's speech; and in the (for me) somewhat awkward, but as to its meaning perfectly clear, (33), both occurrences of 'yesterday' refer to that day.

(32)  John said [that Mary left yesterday].
(33)  John said yesterday that Mary left yesterday.

The semantic contrast between (33) and, say, (34) could not be greater:

(34)  John said yesterday that Mary left the day before.

It is a widely appreciated thesis, exemplified by the above examples, that indexical expressions in complement clauses behave just as they would in isolation. This is the 'no monsters' thesis discussed in Kaplan (1977), or, equivalently, the 'semantic innocence' thesis of Donald Davidson. Without going too far into details, I may note that for Davidson the thesis is an immediate consequence of his 'paratactic' account of clausal embedding. For Kaplan, however, it takes the form of a general postulate; that is to say, nothing in the formal system prevents the introduction of 'monsters', so that any principle restricting their occurrence, or forbidding them altogether, must come from elsewhere. In Chapter 10, elaborating an early discussion by Tyler Burge, I will offer an account of semantic innocence that differs from Davidson's, but also makes the thesis effectively analytic to the form of the semantic theory. The tenses themselves might be offered as counterexamples to semantic innocence; but it is part of the anaphoric theory of tense that this is only an appearance, induced by tense anaphora.

Indexical temporal expressions are rigid designators; but they also impart what I shall call a *perspective* on their referents. This perspective, following semantic innocence, is always that of the speaker. But those whom the speaker is reporting (including her own past or future self) have their perspectives too. In several recent discussions (Pancheva (2004), Giorgi (2005), Wurmbrand (2001), and Byun (2006)), examples have been offered that appear to show that these perspectives can, as I shall put it, *clash* with the embedded tense, in different ways in English, Korean, Italian, and German. I don't know of any thorough survey of these phenomena even in English, let alone across languages; but I shall remark some of their extent, drawing in part on the work cited.

Consider first of all (35):

(35)  John will say tomorrow that Mary is leaving that day.

with 'that day' anaphoric to 'tomorrow'. What John is predicted to be saying tomorrow is, 'Mary is leaving today', or words to that effect. But (36) is bizarre:

(36)  *John will say tomorrow that Mary is leaving tomorrow.

Of course we can have (37):

(37)  John will say that Mary is leaving tomorrow.

But John is then predicted to be saying the Futurate Progressive, 'Mary is leaving tomorrow', or words to that effect, *today*. Moreover, if we add material so as to restore the relative temporal ordering, as in 'John will say tomorrow that Mary is leaving tomorrow night', then the situation improves somewhat.

There are similar examples with the Past (the judgements are weaker here, however). Thus (33) is for me and some others I have asked relatively unacceptable even if clear, though not so unacceptable as (36). But (38), with 'that day' anaphoric to 'yesterday', is perfectly acceptable, and semantically identical to (33):

(38)  John said yesterday that Mary left that day.

Hyuna Byun (2006) observes that in Korean (where the embedded −past, unlike English, can be anaphoric) one cannot have the analogue of (39):

(39)  *John said that Mary is (=anaphoric 'was') in Seattle yesterday.

The examples suggest that, rigidity of reference apart, certain *clashes of temporal perspective* are not permitted in complement clauses. To put it another way, temporal content must be measured in part through the notation that expresses it. As a perhaps extreme example, consider (40):

(40)  John will say in two days that Mary was happy the previous day/-*tomorrow.

To these facts, let me add that the cases above are in the context of ordinary embedding (they are not cases of free indirect discourse), and that the embedded adverbials are all understood (and can only be understood) as deriving their reference from the speaker's perspective. The examples also go through with a variety of indexicals, as 'last/next year', etc.

The whole arrangement, however, cannot be explained by positing any simple conflict between the tense the subject would use and the indexical employed. Thus (41) is of course fine:

(41)  John said two days ago that Mary would be happy yesterday.

even though the speaker's yesterday was John's tomorrow when he, John, spoke.

The phenomena just illustrated must be seen as syntactic. They do point to the conclusion that the notation of reports of saying and belief is critical for the identity of the contents of those reports, and cannot be abstracted away from. It will not do, therefore, to stick with conceptions of propositional content as stemming just from the modal profile of complement expressions; rather, the notation itself, as in section 6.3 above, must be taken into account.

## 6.6 Subjective time

In this last section I briefly take up the point remarked above, that a number of examples, including von Stechow's illustrations, require a subjective treatment of time.

In Chapters 3 and 4 I discussed some aspects of temporal subjectivity; that is, of judgements that something belongs, not necessarily to *the* Past, Present, or Future, but to the *thinker's* Past, Present, or Future. To deploy once again the famous example of A.N. Prior, suppose I am just leaving the dentist's office after a painful operation. I think to myself, 'I am so glad *that's* over!' Supposing the date to be 30 September 2005, my statement is hardly equivalent to, 'I'm so glad *that's* over as of 30 September 2005'. Not only is the date irrelevant to my feeling of relief, but also mentioning it gives the wrong impression. What I care about is that the operation is over as of the time of my thinking that, that it lies in *my* Past. The point is brought out in the semantics as in (42):

(42) $[\exists e\colon \tau(e) \approx \tau(u)]$ glad(I,^$[\exists e'\colon \tau(e') \approx \tau(e)]$ over(operation,$e'$),$e$)

Here my thinking is itself a constituent of the thought. Insertion of a date for $\tau(e)$ would be misleading.

Similar considerations, I think, apply also to the '*de se*' interpretations of embedded elements, elaborated in Chapter 12. In these, as in (43), the subject is given to herself as the subject of the thought, or desire:

(43)  Mary wants [PRO to visit Paris].

Because she is given to herself in this way, it is not possible for Mary to have misidentified the subject of her thought; not possible, that is, that it should seem to her that she wants to visit Paris, whereas in fact she wants someone else to visit Paris. Such misidentification is possible in (44):

(44)  Mary wants herself to visit Paris (because she wants the top graduate to visit Paris, and doesn't realize that she herself is the top graduate).

The cases of the *de se*, on the one hand, and tense anaphora, on the other, have in common the formal feature that they are paradigmatically realized by empty elements: PRO in the case of the *de se* (as noted some time back by John Perry, Gennaro Chierchia, and others), and implicit arguments in INFL in the case of the tenses. No referential formative can take their place with equivalent (or equivalently restricted) meaning. In the temporal case, even when a time is mentioned, it is merely a modifier of the implicit argument, and does not replace it.

This last point also gives a bit of a handle on von Stechow's case, say as in (45):

(45)  Mary thought at 5 o'clock that it was 6 o'clock.

which of course must be distinguished from (46):

(46)  Mary thought at 5 o'clock that 5 o'clock was 6 o'clock.

The indexicality of tense is not extinguished in (46): on the contrary, it comes out as in (47):

(47)  $[\exists e\colon \tau(e) \approx \tau(u)]\ \tau(u) = 5$ o'clock & thinks(Mary,$^\wedge[\exists e'\colon \tau(e') \approx \tau(e)]$ $(5=6,e'),e)$

That is, she thought that the situation of 5 o'clock's being 6 o'clock held at the time of her thinking that. That thought involves a mathematical falsehood: $5 \neq 6$. But the thought reported in (45), even though necessarily false, does not, and is not self-contradictory.

At this point, one may worry that the conditions that I propose must be satisfied to have the kinds of thoughts that we routinely have about time, or about ourselves, are not too restrictive: for it follows from the above discussion that only creatures with complex propositional attitudes can have first-personal thoughts about themselves, or about their own Past, Present, or Future. They could indeed have thoughts of which they, or the time of their thinking, were constituents; but they could not cross-reference these elements with superordinate presentations of themselves, or the time. Thus (if dogs don't have propositional attitudes of the needed complexity) the dog could want $^\wedge[\exists e]$ Get Bone($\alpha,e$), where $\alpha$ is the dog itself; but it couldn't want $^\wedge[\exists e]$ get bone(subject of $e',e$), where $e'$ is the wanting. It could think $^\wedge$bone($x,t$), that the object $x$ is a bone at $t$, where $t$ is the time of the thinking; but it couldn't think $^\wedge$Bone($x,t$) & $t \approx \tau(e)$, where $e$ is the situation of its thinking that. With human beings, on the other hand, such cross-reference is taken for granted. To paraphrase Immanuel Kant, our epistemic powers reflect the 'I think' that accompanies all our representations.

# 7

# Accomplishments

## 7.1 Introduction

In this chapter I review some arguments (going back to discussions with James Pustejovsky in 1989 and class presentations at MIT in 1990, publicly presented in Higginbotham (1993c) and (1995a)) that accomplishments are syntactically represented by ordered pairs of positions for events, and that the 'accomplishment' interpretation of a predicate may stem from the complex thematic structure $<E,E'>$ of a preposition, a syntactic adjunct, rather than from the head verb. The structures $<E,E'>$ are *telic pairs*; and I hold that the formation of telic pairs is a compositional, rather than a lexical, process. This thesis is applied to a number of constructions, yielding, if I am right, the basis for family of distinctions between English- (or Chinese-) type languages, on the one hand, and Romance (or Korean or Japanese) on the other. The conceptions in this first part of what follows are then applied to the location and locatum Verbs of Ken Hale and Jay Keyser. I suggest an alternative derivation of these Verbs, at least in English. Further, whilst acknowledging the cogency of the comments in Kiparsky (1996) I defend a version of their syntactic theory against his objections. In particular, I argue that certain semantic properties of the location and locatum Verbs are not a matter of primitive stipulation, in the lexicon or elsewhere, but rather follow from the nature of the construction, together with a certain notion of normativity, explained below. The chief novelty, however, in what follows is a systematic response to standard arguments such as those of Fodor and Lepore (1998) against lexical decomposition, arguments that must be answered if contemporary morphosyntax is to correspond in any but an impressionistic way to what might be called morphosemantics. My defense turns partly upon demoting the role of causation; that is, upon seeing causation as a consequence of the semantics of accomplishment predicates, rather than the core conception from which their meaning is to be derived.

## 7.2 Telic pairs

Telic and atelic predicates are distinguished in that telics make some reference to the notion of an end, which may be the end of a process given by the predicate itself (an accomplishment predicate, in the sense of Vendler), or recovered by implication (an achievement predicate). We argue here, based upon a distinction in language design surveyed in some detail in Talmy (1985), that the telic–atelic distinction is syntactically represented, and semantically interpreted through modes of composition for which the notion of what we shall call a *telic pair* of events or situations is crucial. Higginbotham (1995a) gave an illustration of telic pairs (though not by that name), in analyzing Donald Davidson's example (1), which is telic, and whose main predicate is the humble Preposition 'to', bearing an ordered pair of event positions, the first (process) one of which is identified with the event position in the Verb 'fly', as shown schematically in (2):

(1)  I flew my spaceship to the morning star.

(2)  fly(I,my spaceship,$e$) & to(the morning star,($e,e'$))

The point was to explain why deletion of the PP, whose semantic content appears as a simple conjunct in (2), gives rise to atelic (3):

(3)  I flew my spaceship.

with univocal 'fly'. (It would be possible, given this datum alone, to maintain that 'fly' is ambiguous, as between merely applying to motions of the flying sort, and applying only to such motions as constitute progress toward a goal; but we shall see later that this proposal is at best redundant.) Extending this analysis, we propose that telic pairs can also arise from V+PP combinations where the P is purely locative. Talmy (1985) discussed pairs such as English (3) versus Italian (4):

(3)  The boat is floating under the bridge. [ambiguous]

(4)  La barca galleggia sotto il ponte. [unambiguous]

The Italian V, with θ-structure $<1,E>$ (E an activity) combines with the PP 'sotto $x$' with θ-structure $<2,E'>$ (E' a (locative) state) in the obvious way, by identifying 2 with 1, and E' with E (or alternatively by distinguishing E from E', but requiring their spatiotemporal overlap, or inclusion of figure within ground, a nicety that we avoid in what follows). We then have for the combination of Preposition and Verb:

$$galleggia(y,e) \; \& \; sotto(y,x,e)$$

or in English:

$$\text{float}(y,e) \;\&\; \text{under}(y,x,e)$$

The English (3), besides the interpretation of the Italian, has a telic (accomplishment) interpretation, paraphraseable as, 'The boat went to some space under the bridge, floating the while'. For the extra meaning in English, Talmy suggested that English 'float', unlike Italian 'galleggiare', is ambiguous. We propose instead that the English and Italian V and P are effectively synonymous, and both unambiguous. If so, then the 'motion' interpretation of English 'float under the bridge' is the result of a combinatorial operation that is not available in the Italian case, namely that the combination of E and E' should project as a telic pair, yielding an accomplishment predicate. Thus we have, in the relevant reading:

$$\text{float}(y,e) \;\&\; \text{under}(y,x,e') \;\&\; \text{telic-pair}(e,e')$$

Extending these modes to resultative and verb-particle constructions, we offer a semantic parameter that distinguishes languages such as English and Chinese, which abound in telic predicates derived by composition, from the Romance languages or Korean and Japanese, for which this mode of derivation is either entirely absent or severely restricted. In part, the parameter can be expressed lexically: languages disallowing telic-pair combination will not contain P comparable to English 'into', or (one sense of) 'over' or 'across', which imply motion towards an end; and indeed these are absent, for example, in Italian and Spanish. But the lexical parameter is itself to be derived from the combinatorial parameter. It cannot be that the lexical parameter is some sort of accident, or reflects a simple failure to happen to have the P in question. (It is a natural speculation that the parameter is linked to morphological divergences between the language types: that English is, so to speak, a 'give up', 'come in' language, while Italian is a 'resign', 'enter' language; the difference is not merely in the amount of morphology (since German is like English in being a 'give up' language, for example) but in permissible or impermissible word-formation. But we do not take this question further here.)

I assume that resultatives and verb-particle constructions are realized by small clauses, as argued in Kayne (1985) and Hoekstra (1992). Thus we have examples like (5)–(6):

(5) I wept [my handkerchief wet].

(6) They took [the company over].

The semantic nexus, e.g. between 'wept' and 'wet' in (5), is taken up by Hoekstra as simple conjunction. Of course, much more must be said, because of the tight relation that is established between the main clause V and the resultative predicate; moreover, there is the matter of accounting for the selection of resultatives, as in (7):

(7)  I wiped [the table clean/??dirty].

on which children learning English are known to overgeneralize. The view will be that these are complex accomplishment structures, formed by the same process that produces the 'motion' meaning of (3) and the like. Thus in the acceptable example in (7), the complex 'wipe clean' forms an accomplishment predicate. These structures are expected to be present in languages like English or Chinese, absent from languages disallowing the appropriate semantic combination, as indeed they are from Romance.

Our survey has suggested two ways in which telic pairs may be formed by a prepositional adjunct: (i) the P is itself an accomplishment predicate; and (ii) the P is an 'achievement' predicate, whose combination with the verbal head gives a telic pair. Now, Italian for example does have telic pairs of the type (ii), with locative P; but the language contains no accomplishment P such as the 'to' of (1), 'into', etc. But containing, or not containing, accomplishment P is not a plausible parametric difference between languages. We can reduce it to a semantic parameter (which is represented in the syntax, assuming that unification or θ-identification is so represented) if we suppose that the identification process is not available; for that would imply that an accomplishment P could not be semantically merged with V: it would die as soon as it was born.

There is further evidence that the distinction between accomplishment P and merely locative P, which form telic pairs in distinct ways, is exemplified in English, which has both types. Consider derived nominals such as (8):

(8)  John's walk to the store (in ten minutes)

The derived nominal 'John's walk' here purports to refer to an event of John's getting to the store by walking there: (8) is, so to say, an accomplishment nominal. There is a contrast, however, between the sentence (9) and the derived nominal (10), in that the sentence, but not the nominal, has an accomplishment reading:

(9)   John walked under the bridge (to inspect it).
(10)  John's walk under the bridge (to inspect it).

Furthermore, in ordinary N+PP constructions, accomplishment P are disallowed except with ordinal modifiers:

(11)  the *(first) man into the house, the *(next) person through the tunnel

(The situation is analogous to that of subject infinitival relatives, discussed recently in Bhatt (2001: 79 ff.): cf. *'the (first) man to fall down'.) In the same contexts, non-accomplishment (locative) P are of course fine, but never except with ordinal modifiers implicate any motion: thus 'the coin under the carpet' does not refer to the coin that *went* under the carpet, but only to the coin that *is* under the carpet. The distinction between the two classes of Prepositions is therefore supported language-internally.

Tortora (1998) has argued that (12) is in fact a resultative, a conclusion that would be unfortunate if true, since counterparts in Romance and other languages lacking (what are traditionally called) resultatives regularly admit the construction.

(12)   They arrived at the airport.

However, we need not concur with this thesis. Instead, we can regard 'arrive' as a predicate applying to (instantaneous) events of being at a place, which constitute the terminus or telos of events of journeying to that place, formally as:

$\text{arrive}(x,e) \leftrightarrow (\exists p)[\text{at}(x,p,e)\ \&\ (\exists e')\ (e'\ \text{is a journey by}\ x\ \&\ (e',e)\ \text{is a telic pair}]$

If so, then the adjunct does not express a result of the arrival, but simply identifies the place in question. Furthermore, 'arrive' does not admit a resultative, since it classifies events that are themselves already results. I believe that all of the counterexamples given in Tortora (1998) to the thesis that unaccusatives allow resultatives admit the same explanation.

We have taken the notion of a telic pair as primitive. There are some paradigms, such as motion terminating at a place; intentional activity whose agent aims at some specific end, etc., and there are a few, relatively superficial, points that can be made about the relation of process to telos, involving spatiotemporal contiguity and 'directness' of causation. In addition, we will suggest, there is an element of *normativity*; that is, the notion of the *proper end* of an activity. It is this notion that distinguishes acceptable from unacceptable resultatives in many cases, including (7) above: the proper end of wiping is removal of material from a surface.

## 7.3 Applications to causatives and location-locatum constructions

We begin with the familiar causative-inchoative alternation, as in (13)–(14):

(13)   The glass broke.

(14)   John broke the glass.

The forms of 'break' in these examples must be semantically related; but there have been notorious difficulties in saying just what the relation is. Assume (i) that (13) is conceptually prior, and (ii) that causation is a relation between individual events, as in Davidson. It is a piece of common wisdom, at least given these assumptions, that (14) *almost* means that for some event $e$ of which John was the agent, $e$ caused some event $e'$ which was a breaking of the glass; and also that it does *not* quite mean that, because of a further general condition on the construction, traditionally referred to as the requirement of 'directness' of causation. This condition is somewhat obscure; but it seems to amount to the restriction that the causal chain from $e$ to $e'$ may not go through the activities of another agent (the condition is not exceptionless for all causative-inchoative pairs). Although the source of the restriction be obscure, we can, assuming it in the background, give a simple syntax and semantics relating (13) and (14). For (14), following much recent syntactic discussion, we begin with (15):

(15)  [John [cause [the glass [break]]]]

In syntax, the embedded inchoative V moves to the position marked by 'cause'. The semantics is (elementarily) computed from (15).

But now we have a puzzle, emphasized most recently by Jerry Fodor and Ernie Lepore (1998): why, given that the underlying structure of (14), namely (15), contains two distinct predicates, do we not have the possibility of ambiguity with certain adverbial modifiers? Thus, to use an example related to theirs, but free in my view from certain obscurities, why does the adverbial quantifier (which quantifies over events) not show the ambiguity in (16) that it does in (17)?

(16)  John sat his guests down frequently/repeatedly.

(17)  John caused his guests to sit down frequently/repeatedly.

Furthermore, Fodor in particular has expatiated at length about the gap between 'cause to be in state $s$', which is all the semantics we are entitled to on the basis of the representation (15) and the obvious combinatorics, and the particular meanings of actual causative V.

Hale and Keyser (1998) have responded to the first problem, seen also in the notorious suggested derivation of 'kill' from 'cause to die', by suggesting that 'kill', or transitive 'break', really have only one argument position for an event. But this response cannot be correct if, as I have proposed, the deployment of 'in an hour' adverbials requires two event positions.[1] We can have, e.g., all of (18)–(20):

[1] See also Chapter 2 above.

(18) John broke the glass in 5 minutes (by subjecting it to intense pressure).

(19) Totò Riina killed his rival in a short time (by strangling him).

(20) Mary sat her guests on the floor in a few seconds (by giving them various instructions).

Anyway, Hale and Keyser's suggestion really abandons the productive theme of causative derived V, and sacrifices even the insight that the parenthetical 'by'-phrases in (18)–(20) identify in each case what it was the agent did that brought about the final state.[2]

It would appear, then, that the causal relation in the transitive forms should be explicitly represented. But then, in (16) as well as in (17), the event-position for what was caused should be visible for all adverbials, not just the temporal ones as in (18)–(20): for instance, it should be possible, contrary to fact, that (16) should mean that John did something or another frequently or repeatedly, as a consequence of which his guests sat down (once). As for the second problem, how exactly to understand the 'directness' of causation case by case, there is no clear answer. Killing is indeed causing to die +X: but what is X? No definitions, no lexical decomposition, no derivations of causative (14) as in (15).

The answer that I will suggest may be motivated by considering a related question, to which Hale and Keyser have given much attention, the derivation of certain denominal V, the *location* and *locatum* V. For Hale and Keyser, verbs such as 'saddle' and 'stable' are derived from structures as in (21):

(21) [DP [$_V$ Ø [DP [P – N]]]]

where N moves to position P, and P+N moves to the empty V position. Thus, starting from (22) we derive (23):

(22) [John [Ø [the horse [P – saddle/stable]]]]

(23) John saddled/stabled the horse.

The nature of P determines whether the denominal V has a location or a locatum meaning. These constructions are obviously causative, but for Hale and Keyser the V in question has no meaning, the relevant notion of causation arising from the structure.

In critical discussion, Paul Kiparsky (1996) has proposed a non-syntactic treatment of location and locatum V. I do not consider his criticisms of the syntactic account here, but call attention to some points to be made about their characteristic interpretation, modifying Kiparsky's observations somewhat as we proceed.

---

[2] I am indebted here to discussion with Judith Thomson.

First, whereas the subject of an ordinary causative (derived, we are supposing, from an inchoative) need not be an intentional agent (and it can even be an event, as in *the storm/hitting the ground broke the glass*) the subject of a location or locatum V can only be an intentional agent (on pain of a category mistake, however these are ultimately understood). The storm can break the window, but even if it blows a saddle onto the horse's back in just the right way, the storm cannot saddle the horse. Neither Hale and Keyser's derivation, nor endowing what is marked above with 'Ø' with a causal interpretation, has this consequence. Second, causation is again 'direct' (i.e., at least does not go through the activities of another agent, though once more there are cases and cases). Third, and critically, there is a normative, teleological dimension. Kiparsky writes that it must be a 'canonical use' of the reference of N to be related in the appropriate way to the object DP. We might go further, and suggest that, at least in many crucial cases involving human artefacts, the crucial notion is what the object N is *for*, in a strong, teleological sense. Stables are for housing animals; that is why (to use Kiparsky's facetious example) Joseph and Mary, in putting the infant Jesus in a stable, did not stable the infant Jesus.

Taking these restrictions on board, and in view of the fact that location and locatum V are always accomplishment predicates, we might suppose that the unpronounced V; that is, Ø above, has a complicated content, something like *e causes e′ in virtue of the action of an intentional agent, in such a way as to deploy an object (of the kind a word for which is N) so as to fulfil or promote its purpose with respect to a patient*. But in fact, it seems, we can do better.

Notice first that besides the denominal V as in 'saddle (the horse)', 'slipper (one's feet)', 'shelve (the book)', 'shelve (the kitchen)', there are participial adjectives derived from the N as well, as in 'the horse is saddled', 'the saddled horse', etc. So we might take 'saddle the horse' as, roughly, 'cause the horse to be saddled'.[3] In support of this suggestion, notice that the participial constructions already show the third point above, taken with modifications from Kiparsky; that is, they obey the same teleological restrictions as the V. But here there is no question of causation, let alone agency. For example, a horse could be born stabled (so nothing ever stabled it); and somewhat more outlandish examples, but in our opinion reasonable in this context, can be constructed. Then we might propose a structure as in (24) as underlying denominals:

(24)  [DP [$_V$ Ø [DP [N+en]]]]

---

[3] I am indebted here to Terence Parsons.

('-en' being realized a zero morpheme, chosen to suggest the semantic effect already observed). Then N+-en moves into the empty V slot.

But now we may go further. Suppose that the position marked by Ø above ranges over events (whose nature is, however, unspecified), and that in the semantics this element, together with the state (e.g., being saddled) over which the participle ranges, form up a telic pair. We then have the interpretation of (23) indicated in (25):

(25)    ($\exists e$) ($\exists e'$) [agent(John,$e$) & saddled(the horse,$e'$) & ($e,e'$) is a telic pair]

It then follows: (i) that the derived V involves causation, because all telic pairs do; (ii) that the causal route must be 'direct', because all telic pairs have that property; and, plausibly, (iii) that the subject must be an intentional agent, because it is a presupposition of the second conjunct of the matrix of (25) that the state $e'$ fulfilled the purposes of whatever served as the saddle with respect to the object saddled; and only intentional agents can fulfil the purposes of things (or, to advert to Kiparsky's formulation, only intentional agents can *use* things). We therefore derive the properties of the location and locatum V from two premises, one that posits a denominal predicate classifying the telos (a substantive, primitive operation), and the other the formation, at the projection of V, of a telic pair. The notion of causation turned out to be a distraction, being derived from the accomplishment nature of the predicate, rather than a source of it.

Returning now to the problems for syntactic causative formation posed by Fodor and Lepore, suppose that what is called the 'causative' form of the V comes about through the process just described for the denominals; i.e., by the formation of a telic pair. Then the causal nature of the causative is again derived, together with its 'directness'. But also we may immediately conclude that frequency adverbs and the like cannot quantify only over the telos or final state; rather, just as with ordinary accomplishment predicates, they must quantify over whole ordered pairs (e.g., we don't have 'John crossed the street frequently', meaning that as a result of some single street-crossing he was frequently on the other side). On the other hand, the final state, identified as it is with the state classified by the inchoative root, is visible in the usual way for other purposes, such as becoming the second argument of time adverbials like 'in an hour'.

What now of definitions? As an example, a V like 'kill', with arguments such as:

$$\text{kill}(x,y,(e,e'))$$

will be defined by:

$P(x,(e,e'))$ & $e'$ is a death of $y$.

The conditions on *P* are whatever they are (naturally, we investigate *P* by scrutinizing our exact usage of 'kill'). Directness of causation is already involved here (as Chomsky remarked long ago, I don't kill Bill in virtue of inducing him to drive across the country with a homicidal maniac). More must be said, because killing is a moral and legal concept, not merely a causal one. But a definition is a definition for all that, and our procedure deprives Fodor of at least one reason for advancing the thesis that the lexicon of a human language is in his terms 'atomistic'.

I conclude that lexical decomposition, at least of the sort given here in syntactic or morphosyntactic terms, is viable, and that we were always wrong to pay such close attention to causation, a notion that, where applicable, is derivative upon the formation of primitive accomplishment predicates.

# 8

# The English Progressive

## 8.1 Preliminary remarks

I examine here the English Progressive, concentrating upon the issues surrounding what David Dowty (1977) dubbed the 'imperfective paradox'. My discussion concerns a single part of the general problem of tense and aspect, both within languages and cross-linguistically. That general problem has three pieces, namely: (i) what is the interpretation of tense and aspect? (ii) what is the nature of the syntactic structures to be interpreted? and (iii) what are the principles through which the mapping from these structures to the meaning is effected? None of these pieces can be assumed in advance: all must be solved simultaneously. A remarkable point about tense and aspect is that, although they belong to what we may regard as some of the most basic parts of language, their interpretation (unlike that of quantification, say) is not obvious, even to a first approximation. Native speakers, unreflectively, get things right; but what they are getting right is a matter for research. I shall begin this discussion by remarking some assumptions about the nature of tense and aspect, including assumptions about question (iii), the nature of the mapping from structure to meaning. I shall assume here without argument that the mapping is effectively trivial; that is, that it consists in putting together by locally compositional means the open or closed elements in simple ways, such as 'for example' those outlined in Higginbotham (1985).

The English progressive is 'be'+'-ing', or as we shall see simply '-ing' in certain of the environments that allow omission of the copula. Its elementary syntax is, I will assume, as given in Chomsky (1957), augmented by contemporary research suggesting that the linear order of 'auxiliary' elements is also their hierarchical order:

$$\text{Tense} - (\text{modal}) - (\text{have}+\text{-en}) - (\text{be}+\text{-ing})$$

with stems raising to affixes, e.g. 'cross' to '-ing' and 'be' to Tense, giving for example the structure of sentences like (1):

(1) John is crossing the street.

*The English Progressive*    127

We expect (in the unmarked case) the hierarchical order of the auxiliary elements to correspond to the order of their semantic composition; and therefore we expect that in (2) we have, as a matter of semantic fact, the Present of the Perfect of the Progressive, and not any other order:

(2)    John has been crossing the street.

Before launching into the Progressive, we require a few preliminary words about Tense, about the English Perfect, and about the telic/atelic distinction, all of which will have subsequent roles to play. My own view of these matters will occupy section 8.2. Section 8.3 rehearses traditional material on the Progressive, and in section 8.4 I consider, and suggest a revision of, David Dowty's important early work on the subject. In section 8.5 I turn to Terence Parsons's view (Parsons (1989) and (1990)), and to some very serious problems for it, several of them due to Zucchi (1997). Section 8.6 gives the bare bones of the view in Landman (1992), and sketches some issues raised by that view. Sections 8.7–8.9 attempt a synthesis. A major theme of my discussion will be the *contextuality* of the Progressive; but this theme has many threads, which are collected only in section 8.10. I conclude in section 8.11 with some cross-linguistic speculations.

## 8.2 Semantic elements

I will assume that the tenses are binary predicates expressing temporal relations, and so depart from the 'Reichenbachian' view that we have all of 'event-time', 'speech-time', and 'reference-time', regarding the second as merely a special case of 'reference-time'. Assuming as we will throughout that stems contain a position E for events, we take up a simple sentence such as (3) as true if and only if there is a state of happiness accruing to John that surrounds the time of the context, here the time of utterance by default:

(3)    John is happy.

The syntax from which this meaning is computed is effectively as in (4):

(4)    [$_T$ –past <1,2> [$_{VP}$ John happy<3>]]

where the numerals in angled brackets stand for the open positions or implicit arguments in the head T and the VP.[1] In the semantic computation, the implicit argument 3 of the VP, which ranges over events, is identified with argument 1 of

---

[1] What we hear in hearing (3) is the result of raising the subject out of the VP; but this movement, I shall assume, is semantically vacuous, and so I shall simplify the syntactic exposition here and in what follows.

T, and argument 2 of T set to the speech-time or utterance $u$. The feature −past is interpreted as meaning that 1 surrounds 2 This notion is expressed below by '≈', said of times (and of events through their times). Finally there is default existential closure of argument 1, with the result for (1) that we may write as (5):

(5) [∃e≈u] happy(John,e)

i.e., there is a state of John's being happy whose time surrounds that of the utterance $u$. Where the non-past is interpreted by ≈, the past and future tenses, periphrastic or otherwise, are taken up as expressing the obvious relations of anteriority < and posteriority >.

With each event $e$ there is associated its *time* $\tau(e)$. In the cases considered here, $\tau(e)$ will always be an interval (possibly half-closed or closed), or else a point; and, for simplicity, that $\tau(e)$ for each $e$ is constant across counterfactual situations.

For the (English) Perfect, we assume with Parsons (1990) and others that it expresses a relation between events and their *result* or *resultant* states (these are distinguished as needed below). Thus in (6) we have the interpretation shown in (7):

(6) John has been happy.

(7) [∃e′≈u: e′ a result(ant) of e] happy(John,e)

Note in particular that since result and resultant states must follow the states of which they are the results or resultants, John was happy in the past if (6) is true, even though any result or resultant state $e′$ that makes (7) true is non-past. The Perfect will be of significance for certain interpretations of Progressive sentences.

As in Chapter 2, I suppose that the predicates that Zeno Vendler called 'accomplishments' contain an ordered pair of implicit arguments for events, and that those he called 'achievements' may be taken up with that status through syntactic combinatorics of various kinds. Thus in an accomplishment predication as in (8) we will have the interpretation shown in (9):

(8) John crossed the street.

(9) [∃(e,e′)<u] cross(John,the street,(e,e′))

Here (assuming (8) is true) we have an event $e$ consisting of John's progress toward the other side of the street, and an event $e′$ consisting of (the onset of) his being on the other side, the ensemble, taken in that order, constituting the crossing of the street.

Particular notice should be taken of the case where an accomplishment predicate is formed by syntactic means, as in a verb-particle or resultative construction, as in Chapter 7; see also Folli (2002). Thus examples like (10) are ambiguous, with the syntactic adjunct 'upstairs' indicating either (a) merely the direction of motion, or (b) the telos of the activity (Mary got upstairs by running there). In the latter case, the adjunct is as much a part of the predicate as the Verb.

(10)   Mary ran upstairs.

## 8.3 Background to the English progressive

In early discussion of the Progressive in generative grammar it was recognized (as in traditional grammar) that:

(A) Progressive predicates constitute 'activities' in the sense of Vendler, even when the verbal constructions to which they applied were accomplishments or achievements, and that in these cases there was no implication that the ends of the activity were reached, or the achievement attained, as in (11) or (12):

(11)   John is dying.
(12)   Mary is going to work.

(11) may be true now although John does not die in the end; and (12) may be true although Mary never makes it to work. (A version of this point goes back to Aristotle.) On the other hand, the Progressive of an activity predicate has no such effect: thus from 'John was running' there follows 'John ran'.

(B) Stative predicates do not allow the Progressive. Thus (13) allows only the (rather strange) 'agentive' reading, and (14) is simply impossible (it attributes agency, which never holds for knowledge):

(13)   John is being happy.
(14)   Mary is knowing the answer.

(C) There exists a possibly distinct 'futurate' Progressive, signifying that something is 'scheduled' or 'on the agenda', as in (15) or (16):

(15)   But I am singing in New York tomorrow!
(16)   They said the world was ending tonight (but here it is midnight and we are still around).

(D) It appears that existential generalization is not always valid for the Progressive of a sentence (or VP) for which it is valid, a point that seems especially clear for V of creation, as in (17):

(17)   John is building a house.

For: the skeletal form 'John build a house' (with any tense) implies that for some house x, John build(s) x; but (17) may be true although there is no house anywhere, so it appears.

Any thorough account of the Progressive should incorporate material from which the above and other generalizations noted below will follow.

## 8.4 Counterfactuals: Dowty (1977)

The phenomenon (A) above received special attention in Dowty (1977) and (1979), who suggested that Progressives were to be assimilated to a variety of conditional, such conditionals to be clarified in turn through modality, understood as in possible-worlds semantics. The central idea (the revision in Dowty (1979) of the original proposal of Dowty (1977)) is that a Progressive is true if, in all (possibly counterfactual) relevant situations (of which there must be at least one) in which things go on 'as they might be expected to' (the 'inertia worlds', in Dowty's terminology), the end of the accomplishment (or the existence of the activity) is to be found (Dowty (1979: 149)).

I take the liberty of transposing Dowty's account into a scheme with event-positions, and with temporal reference interpreted as in section 8.2 above. (Dowty's original exposition, self-consciously, did not take events as primitive.) Where truth is relative to pairs $(w,i)$ of possible worlds and intervals of time, Dowty's intensional Progressive operator *Prog* is definable by (18):

(18) $Prog(p)$ is true at $(w,i) \leftrightarrow [\forall w': w'$ is inertial with respect to $(w,i)]$
$[\exists i': i' \supset i]$ ($p$ is true at $(w',i')$).

(The containment '$i' \supset i$' is proper.) If we 'extensionalize' this operator, the Progressive of a proposition $p$ amounts to (19):

(19) $[\forall w': w'$ is inertial with respect to $(w,i)] [\exists i': i \subset i'] \ p_{(w',i')}$

With the possible-worlds reference explicit, we should take up 'John was running' as in (20), where '$\tau(e)$' denotes the actual time of $e$, and '@' the actual world:

(20) $[\exists e < u] [\forall w: w$ is inertial with respect to $(@,\tau(e))] [\exists e': \tau(e) \subset \tau(e')]$
$\text{run}_{(w,\tau(e'))}(\text{John}, e')$

(I assume for simplicity that the name 'John' is rigid.) Now, $w'$ is inertial with respect to $(w,i)$ only if (intuitively speaking) the histories of $w$ and $w'$ are the same through the interval $i$. From the fact that an event of the type of running (as with other activities) is made up of subevents of the same type, we are guaranteed as of the last moment of $\tau(e') \geq \tau(u)$ that $[\exists e] \ \text{run}_{(w,\tau(e))}(\text{John}, e)$ in any *w* inertial with respect to (@,τ(*e*)); hence that it would be true at τ(*u*) to say 'John ran'. The result, then, is to make the Progressive of an activity trivially true if its interior is true; to make (11) true if John dies in each of the relevant situations (even if not in the actual world); and to make (12) true if Mary gets to work in all such situations, even if something detains her as things are.

A difficulty for Dowty's original account, elaborated especially in Vlach (1981), is that the interval semantics did not capture the fact that for a Progressive as in (11) or (12) to be true at a time, there must at that time be a relevant ongoing *process*: we cannot say that John is dying simply because his death is inevitable, or that Mary is going to work at the very moment when she retires for the night, even if, provided that things go on as expected, she will go to work in some hours.[2] This difficulty is not immediately overcome by requiring that the speech-time of, say, 'Mary is going to work' be an element of each interval *i'* such that 'Mary go to work' is true at (*w',i'*). For, where *i''* is an interval such that 'Mary go to work' is true at (*w',i''*), and the speech-time τ happens to precede every moment in *i''*, let *i'* be the whole interval that includes both τ and *i''*. We would have to declare that in some cases, but not all, 'Mary go to work' is not after all true at (*w',i'*); but which cases are these? Intuitively, they are those in which no process has begun as of τ that will, if successful, get Mary to work sometime later. There is, to be sure, some vagueness about exactly when Mary's going to work commences; but that is not the issue. Rather, the difficulty is that the formulation (18) gives no way even to mark the distinctions that are wanted. However, the difficulty can be set aside, I believe, if we modify Dowty's view in accordance with the picture of accomplishment predicates given in section 8.2 above, where the reference to events is explicit. For (12), repeated here, we would have (21):

(12)  Mary is going to work.

(21)  [∃*e*≈*u*] [∀*w*: *w* is inertial with respect to (@,τ(*e*))] (∃*e'*) go to work$_{(w,\tau(e+e'))}$(Mary,(*e,e'*)).

where *e+e'* is the sum of *e* and *e'* (i.e., the least event of which both are parts). Recalling that we postulate the existence of at least one *w* inertial with respect to (@,τ(*e*)), and that the history of any such *w* will be that of (@,τ(*e*)) through τ(*e*), (21) implies the existence in *w* of a process *e* that, in *w*, terminates with an event *e'* of Mary's being at work (it being understood that, in a telic predication φ(*e, e'*), τ(*e*)⊂τ(*e+e'*)). Where the actual world is not inertial with respect to itself and τ(*e*), we may have Mary going to work without actually getting there. In a

---

[2] Dowty was well aware of this problem, as well as of issues concerning the status of events: see Dowty (1977: 58).

further refinement, we may take it that *e* itself is only an initial stage of a process *e''*, possibly different in different inertia worlds *w*, such that (*e''*,*e'*) is the entire process plus termination of Mary's going to work. (The refinement does not affect the case of activity predicates, because an initial stage of an activity of type *T* is already an activity of type *T*.) The final formulation is therefore (22):

(22) [∃*e*≈*u*] [∀*w*: *w* is inertial with respect to (@,τ(*e*))] [∃(*e''*,*e'*): τ(*e*) ⊂ τ(*e''*)] go to work$_{(w,τ(e''+e'))}$(Mary,(*e''*,*e'*))

We agree to this extent with Dowty's interval semantics, but only where the intervals are conceived as the intervals *of* underlying events, a more fundamental structure.

A virtue of Dowty's account, retained under the revision just suggested, is that the Progressive of an impossibility must be false, as in the examples (23)–(24):

(23) John is squaring the circle.

(24) Cyrano is rising to the moon in a balloon.

(there being no relevant counterfactual situations, whereas there must be at least one inertia world). However, problems remain.

For one thing, the construction given does not allow the conjunction of incompatibles, as in (25), an example that, I take it, may be truly uttered:

(25) John is dying of cancer and heart disease, although only one of these will kill him (and it is a random matter which one it is).

For if John is dying of cancer, so that the ensemble of inertia worlds makes 'John is dying of cancer' true, then he must in all of these die of cancer, rather than heart disease; but that falsifies the conjunction. Nor, evidently, can Dowty's condition be weakened so as to be said to hold at interval *i* provided its interior comes to be true merely at some interval *i'* properly containing *i*. That is too weak, since it would make it true, for example, to say both 'Mary is going to work' and 'Mary is going to the baseball game' when Mary is debating which to do, and hasn't yet decided. In Dowty (1977: 59), where the truth conditions for the Progressive were existential rather than universal, it was noted that conjunctions of incompatibles were allowed to come out true, contrary to intuition at least in many cases. The scheme with universal quantification, as in (18) above, or the extensionalized (19), disallows all such, on the assumption (independently necessary) that for every (*w*,*i*) there is a world *w'* inertial to it. But if (25) is acceptable, then further distinctions are required: I return to this matter below.

Several authors, especially Fred Landman (1992) and Andrea Bonomi in (1997) and elsewhere, have emphasized the contextuality of the Progressive, which goes largely untreated in Dowty. Standard example: Mary takes an airplane in New York, bound for London; the plane is hijacked en route and flown to Havana. Early on in the flight, would it be true to say that Mary is flying to London? That she is flying to Havana? Both? Neither?

It is noteworthy that in this case, unlike (25), the possibility of saying, 'Both' is precluded: under the scenario envisaged, it is not true that Mary is flying to London and flying to Cuba. It seems equally clear that she is either flying to London or flying to Cuba, so that 'Neither' is ruled out as well. However, incompatibles are sometimes possible, as in (25), so there is a serious question why (26) is false (no matter when asserted):

(26)  Mary is flying to London and to Cuba.

In sum, Dowty's counterfactual theory can be recast with events as primitives, in such a way that Vlach's objection can be turned aside. As for the traditional matters, outlined in section 8.3: that stative predicates do not admit the Progressive will have to be stipulated (on the grounds, perhaps, that nothing is 'going on' when a stative is true), and the futurate Progressive simply set aside as a different construction, perhaps (as suggested in Ippolito (1999)) as analogous to the Italian Imperfect, which has no distinctive morphological realization in English. Existential generalization is in general invalid, and the valid cases will have to be treated independently. But there remain problems with the contextuality of the Progressive, and, of course, with the determination of inertia worlds.

## 8.5 An extensional view: Parsons (1990)

Terence Parsons, in articles reprinted with emendations in Parsons (1990), formulated a simple and purely extensional view of the English Progressive, whose central tenets are: (i) that all (verbal, non-stative) predicates range over events; (ii) that a present or past progressive has it that some event of the sort classified by the predicate is or was going on; and (iii) that the simple past (future) of a predicate adds, besides a temporal relation of anteriority (posteriority), the notion that whatever event it was 'culminated' (will 'culminate'), where what it is for $e$ to culminate is given by the nature of $e$.

Thus our example (8) above, repeated here, comes out for Parsons as in (27), whereas the Progressive (28) simply lacks the final clause of (27), expressing culmination:

(8)   John crossed the street.

(27)   [∃e<u] [cross(John,the street,e) & culminate(e)]

(28)   John was crossing the street.

(I have suppressed some redundancies in Parsons's formulation.) The suggestion of this chapter, and of Higginbotham (1995a), may be seen as providing a further and more explicit elucidation of Parsons's notion of culmination, one that puts the situation constituting the telos of the accomplishment directly into the representation.

There are several phenomena that Parsons's account does not address. It is not easy, for example, to apply it to achievement predicates such as 'die' which appear to contain within themselves no hint of a process that could be said to culminate. But attention has focused on other issues, to which we now turn.

Parsons's account allows, indeed demands, that predications such as that of 'John cross the street' can hold of events even if they do not culminate; their accomplishment character in the past tense, as in (29), is said to arise from the tense itself:

(29)   John crossed the street.

However, a quick survey of gerundive vs root-verb contexts appears to show that, in English at least, the predicate is itself an accomplishment:

(30)   (a) I saw John cross the street.

(30)   (b) I saw John crossing the street.

(31)   (a) For Mary to cross the street would be a mistake.

(31)   (b) For Mary to be crossing the street would be a mistake.

(32)   I didn't let John cross the street (although I let him start to cross, I didn't let him get to the other side).

(33)   [John quickly crossing the street] is a welcome sight.

(34)   (a) At this point in the story, John crosses/will cross Broadway.

(34)   (b) At this point in the story, John is crossing/will be crossing Broadway.

(I discussed these examples with Parsons as early as the lecture Higginbotham (1993c); no doubt they were known to others as well. Zucchi (1997) notes the point, and attempts a repair, which I will not discuss here.) If (30)(a) is true, John must have reached the other side of the street; not so with (30)(b). Likewise, we can imagine situations where a terrible danger awaits Mary if she reaches the other side of the street, so justifying the assertion of (31)(a); but there is no danger in her crossing itself, and indeed one could say that for

Mary to be crossing the street wouldn't be a mistake, so long as she doesn't actually cross it. Further, (32) is a fine defense of one's conduct when charged with not letting John cross the street. In (33), the use of the verbal gerundive subject clearly refers to what is seen when one spots John in mid-crossing, independently of whether he gets to the other side. Finally, (34)(a) but not (34)(b) implies that, in the story, John gets to the other side of Broadway.

The contexts in (30)–(34) are all non-finite, and in the case of (30) and (32)–(33) in particular show every evidence of lacking inflection altogether. Yet the examples with the bare V, where available, signal telicity, whereas those with '-ing' do not. Furthermore, the examples in (34) underscore the independence of the distinction between Progressive and non-Progressive forms from the specific matter of Tense.

The cross-linguistic evidence that the root construction is telic for predications such as 'cross the street' is complicated by the fact that the English simple present, unlike that of Romance and most of Germanic, cannot be used as a report of contemporaneous goings-on, and, moreover, that in those languages where the simple present can be so used it carries no implication of telicity. The English (35) (by itself, and not as an understood 'habitual' assertion), cannot be a report of what John is now doing; and when it can be used as a non-habitual, as in the recounting of what happens in a story or play, it is, like (34)(a), clearly telic:

(35)  John eats an apple.

Whereas, to use Italian for contrast, (36) can be a report of what is presently going on, and in any use can be atelic:

(36)  Gianni mangia una mela.

Moreover, the tests that we have used in (30)–(33) to distinguish the bare V from the progressive are not in general available in Romance or Germanic, the reason being that V cannot occur without inflection. It is, therefore, not so straightforward to conclude that the bare English construction, consisting of the V and its arguments, is intrinsically telic, rather than atelic; or in some way underspecified; or ambiguous.

However, for instance in Italian, one finds that what has been traditionally considered the Progressive is anyway distinguished from the simple present. As reported in Giorgi and Pianesi (1997), the simple present of an achievement, corresponding to English 'reach the top', is anomalous, at least in the situation where Mary is merely approaching the top:

(37)  *Maria   raggiunge   la    vetta.
       Mary    reaches     the   top.

Now, achievements can be progressivized, as in 'John is dying', (11) above, or (38):

(38)  Mary is reaching the top of the Himalayas.

and what is generally taken to be the Italian progressive, namely the gerund form with auxiliary 'stare', is likewise acceptable with achievements:

(39)  Maria sta raggiungendo la vetta dell'Himalaya.

(37) therefore contrasts with (39), something that would be unexpected if the Italian Progressive added nothing to the simple present.

I will not discuss further here the various possibilities for the source of the semantic distinction for instance between English and Italian simple present; suffice to say that the ambiguity of the Italian (36) as between telic and atelic interpretations cannot be used straightforwardly in support of Parsons's suggestion. For further cross-linguistic discussion, see Giorgi and Pianesi (1997), and section 8.11 below.

Parsons speaks as though, given an event *e*, we could say at once what it is for *e* to culminate. But consider again the early part of Mary's flight, on a plane bound for London that is hijacked to Cuba: is that an event which did not culminate (because she never reached London), or did culminate (because we can say that, unbeknownst to her, she was flying to Cuba, and she really did get there)?

Or, as remarked in Zucchi (1997: 185–186): suppose that Gianni catches the train in Milan, intending to go to Florence. Unfortunately for him, there is a strike just as he reaches Piacenza, a town on the way. Now we have an event *e* that makes (28) true. But this same event is among those that make (41) true:

(40)  Gianni went to Piacenza.
(41)  Gianni was going to Florence.

Then *e* is an event that both culminates and does not culminate, a contradiction.

Notice that Zucchi's example is different from the hijacking case. There, we could not say that the agent was going to both places, Havana and London; but in Zucchi's example, Piacenza being on the way to Florence, it is true at the beginning of the journey, and all the way until arrival in Piacenza, that the agent was going to both. Hence, at least from the start through the time the train stops in Piacenza, it is true to say that Gianni is going to Florence.

Now, there is an evident form of answer available to Parsons for these last issues. The notion of culmination may be interpreted, not just as a property that an event has or does not have, but rather as a relation between an individual event and a classification of events *as* of one sort or another. Zucchi, taking Landman's discussion as a point of departure, relativizes in this way Parsons's predicates *Hold* and *Cul* ('culminate'), which were advanced as a simple predicates of events. Suppose, for instance, that $P$ is the property of an event's being a street-crossing (by something or other), and that we take up reference to properties as suggested in Montague (1960). Then

$$P = {}^{\wedge}\lambda e\,(\exists x)(\exists y)\,[\text{street}(y)\ \&\ \text{cross}(x,y,e)]$$

We could propose that culmination is a relation $C$ between events and properties. Then Mary's flight $e$ culminates *qua* flight of someone to Havana, but not *qua* flight of someone to London. On the other hand, if our earlier objection is correct, then $C$ must be independent of the Tense.

In Parsons's account existential generalization applies, even in the case of V of creation: it actually does follow that if John was building a house, then there is a house $x$ such that he was building $x$. To the challenge to provide the alleged house (say, in the case where the builder had done no more than lay a brick or two before abandoning the project), he responds that the house that was being built is 'incomplete'. As we can say that John is building a house even when he has done no more than get the wherewithal together to commence the project, this response must be available even where there are no physical traces of house-building to be found.

There is no doubt that Parsons's account is correct for many contexts, for we do have examples, such as Schubert's 'Unfinished' symphony, Dickens's incomplete novel *The Mystery of Edwin Drood*, and so forth. However, Zucchi (1997), citing an example due to Landman (1992), presents cases where (perhaps) a progressive construction with a verb of creation fails to imply the existence of anything at all of the kind indicated by the direct object.[3] He further notes that we should be able to go from the likes of (42) to (43):

(42)   John was making an apple pie.

(43)   John made an apple pie.

But this is precisely the contrast, it would seem, that wants explanation. For, (42) can be truly said when John had done no more than get out the apples,

---

[3] The example is (i)

(i)   God was creating the unicorn when He changed His mind.

The thought is that (i) may be true even though no unicorn was created. If (i) is not contradictory, *and* it is contradictory to speak of uncreated unicorns, then existential generalization must fail. My doubts about this example stem from doubts about the second thesis. However, as noted below, existential generalization seems anyway to fail on other grounds.

flour, and so forth, and so, it would seem, can be true even if there is no pie at all later on; and if the assembled ingredients can count as an 'incomplete' pie *a*, then in making *a* John made an apple pie.

I conclude this section with two further difficulties: in Parsons's account, there is no explanation of why the progressive of impossible accomplishments or achievements is false. (Of course, they can't 'culminate', but nothing follows from that.) Furthermore, that account fails to apply to the case of what I called in Chapter 7 'accomplishment prepositions', yielding telic predicates as in (27):

(44)  The train was rattling into the station (when it broke down and stopped).

I return to both points below.

## 8.6 Counterfactuals again: Landman (1992)

In an important discussion, Landman (1992) suggested that the Progressive expresses a relation between an event and a property (in Montague's sense, that is, a function from objects and possible worlds into truth values), cashed out as a relation between an event and a possible event. Intuitively, the possible event (which must exist in some possible world) is the completion of the event in question. Naturally, much is going to depend upon how remote the possibility of the completion is. But we should note right away some problems for this view.

Although verbal heads are construed as having positions for events, in the way familiar from Davidson (and adopted here, with some modifications), no principled distinction is made in the logical forms of predicates. The consequence (a point made by Mittwoch (1988) in discussion of Dowty's original proposal, but applying equally to Landman) is that examples like (45), which are evidently anomalous, should be fine:

(45)  #Just as I arrived, the lake was rising ten feet.

(Suppose I arrive at 3:30, when the lake has risen five feet, and it will go on to rise by five more over the next hour; still I cannot say (45).) Another consequence is that there is no way immediately to apply the theory to achievements.

Given an event $e^*$ in the actual world @, and the question whether $e^*$ there satisfies the Progressive of the condition $P$ on events, we are, on Landman's view, to consider close possible worlds $w$, and those events $f$ in $w$ such that $e^*$ is an initial stage of $f$. If $P(f)$ holds in $w$, and $w$ is a possible world that is close, or sufficiently close, to @, then $e^*$ satisfies the progressive of $P$ in @ (and if there is no such $f$, then further considerations, which we pass over here, come into play). The difficulty here is that by an 'initial stage' of $f$ cannot be meant simply an initial temporal part of $f$: my smoking one cigarette is an initial temporal part of my smoking twenty cigarettes, but when I am smoking one cigarette I am not smoking twenty cigarettes. Conversely, suppose that John's crossing the street halfway is the event $e^*$. To determine whether, given $e^*$, we are justified in saying that John is crossing the street, we need, in Landman's terminology, to know whether there are any 'close' possible worlds in which some 'continuation' of $e$ constitutes a street-crossing by John. Well, which events, if any, *are* continuations of $e$ (suppose John's intention was to walk to the middle of the street and stop there)? This last problem is quite general, and it is a counterpart of the critical point for Parsons's notion of 'culmination': there is simply not enough information given in $e$ itself to determine what it is for $f$ to be a 'continuation' of $e$, or what it is for $e$ to 'culminate'.

Toward resolving these questions, I turn now to a modification of Landman (1992) (parts of which overlap with Landman, but were suggested independently in my unpublished (1990); I am grateful to Landman for suggesting some years back that I need not scrap my ms.).

## 8.7 Revision I: Making telicity explicit

Our problem is twofold: (a) to solve for the logical syntax of the Progressive head (assumed now to be just '-ing' in view of examples above), and (b) to interpret the non-logical predicates that appear given (a). As in Landman (1992), I take the Progressive head to express a relation between events $e$ and *properties* of events. We denote this relation by '*Prog*'. For property abstraction it will be convenient for this exposition to follow Montague's formulation, so that for instance the property (task, activity) of (John's) eating chow mein is as in (46):

(46) $^\wedge \lambda e'$ eat(John,chow mein,$e'$)

and 'John is eating chow mein' is therefore as in (47):

(47) $[\exists e {\approx} u]$ $Prog(e,^\wedge \lambda e'$ eat(John,chow mein,$e'$))

Extending Landman's proposal, we suggest that for accomplishment predicates (and achievement predicates for which a preliminary process may be contextually supplied) the abstraction is over the ordered pair of process and telos. Thus for 'John is crossing the street' we have (48):

(48) [∃e≈u] $Prog(e,^\wedge\lambda(e',e'')$ cross(John,the street,$(e',e'')$))

(Here and below I allow λ-abstraction over ordered pairs as a derived notation.)

The computation of the interpretation of 'John is crossing the street' proceeds from the syntactic structure (49):

(49) [$_T$ –Past <1,2>) [$_{Prog}$ –ing <3,4>) [$_{VP}$ John cross the street <5>]]]

where the Progressive head '-ing' θ-marks the VP through position 4, with the interpretation shown in (50):

(50) $^\wedge\lambda(e',e'')$ cross(John,the street,$(e',e'')$))

and position 3, which ranges over events, is identified with the first position of the Tense.

We must now focus upon the nature of the abstraction, and upon the relation *Prog*. Notice, however, that the logical syntax, together with other assumptions mentioned in the preliminaries and elsewhere, already disposes of several of the more problematic issues discussed above.

First, we recognize that the bare predicate can be an accomplishment (involve a 'culmination' in Parsons's sense), although the culmination is not attained.

Second, the problem of what constitutes a 'continuation' of an event disappears. A continuation of an event *e* such that $Prog(e,^\wedge\lambda(e',e'')$ cross (John,the street,$(e',e'')$)) is an event $e'''$ such that *e* is an initial segment of $e'''$, $e'''$ is small as possible spacewise, and $e+e'''$ is closer than *e* to the state $e''$ of being on the other side of the street; and similarly in other cases. Thus the notion of a continuation is not only relative to the event-type of the complement VP, but is also cashed out in terms of what state would constitute the explicitly represented telos.

Third, by breaking accomplishments down into process and telos, the account provides the equipment needed to secure the Progressive of achievements, and it does this by means independently wanted. Suppose we have (51):

(51) John died in ten minutes.

Examples of this sort can constitute accomplishments, because we can quantify over the process leading to death as well as the death itself (and in this case, in the absence of any other time determination, the difference between the onset of the process and the death is what the adverbial 'in ten minutes' measures; see Higginbotham (1995a) and Chapter 2 above). With this understanding, we can interpret 'John is dying', although the lexical item 'die' itself is true only of achievements. (For detailed discussion of a number of cases of this phenomenon, see Rothstein (2000).)

As a corollary, the theory applies in the case of accomplishment prepositions, as in (44) above, repeated here:

(44) The train was rattling into the station (when it broke down and stopped).

In the root form (52), the main predicate is 'into', which carries two event positions:

(52) The train rattle into the station.

The main V serves merely to describe the process of getting into the station as accompanied by rattling. (For the explicit semantics, see Chapter 7 and Folli (2002), and for a treatment in Montague Grammar, Dowty (1979: 207 ff.).)

Fourth, the account answers the puzzles about what constitutes a 'culmination' of an event. Events do not inherently have or lack culminations; rather, when we speak of these, as in telic predication, we conceive of a pair of events taken together, and in atelic predicates we speak of them singly. As for Zucchi's problem: it will be the ordered pair (travel to Piacenza, the onset of being in Piacenza) that makes it true that John went to Piacenza, but the *sum* (travel to Piacenza+being in Piacenza) that makes it true that John was going to Florence.

Fifth, the account can distinguish between those predications licensing temporal adverbials such as 'in ten minutes' that are truly telic, and those which are licensed by measure phrases, as in (53):

(53) The lake rose ten feet in two hours.

We have noted Mittwoch's example (45), repeated here:

(45) #Just as I arrived, the lake was rising ten feet.

The predicate 'rise' in this case is not telic, so that the VP in 'the lake rose ten feet' is just (54):

(54) rise(the lake,$e$) & $\mu_{feet}(e)=10$

That is, $e$ is a rising of the lake whose measure in feet is ten. The temporal adverbial then measures the temporal distance between the onset of $e$ and the point at which $\mu_{feet}(e)=10$; but this is not telic predication.

Lakes are not in the habit of getting themselves to rise, by ten feet or anything else. Predicates with measure phrases that accept the temporal adverbials characteristic of telic predication may, however, themselves be telic. Consider (55):

(55) Just as I arrived, John was running a mile.

The example is acceptable if, just as I arrived, John was engaged in the intentional project of running a mile, his having run a mile thus constituting the telos of his activity (see the related discussion in Zucchi (1997: 204)). The VP in 'John run a mile', in this sense, is as in (56):

(56)   run(John,$(e,e')$) & $\mu_{mile}(e)=1$

and in this case the adjunct 'in ten minutes' measures the temporal distance between the onset of $e$ and the attainment of the telos $e'$ of having run a mile. The importance of the telos, in the original Aristotelian sense of 'that for the sake of which the thing is done', can be seen from the fact that (57) is acceptable only with the intentional telic interpretation, whereas (58) (because of what we know about lakes) is ridiculous:

(57)   Just as I arrived, John was running a mile in ten minutes.
(58)   Just as I arrived, the lake was rising ten feet in two hours.

The aim of the agent in (57) is not just to run a mile, but rather to run a mile in ten minutes, or perhaps to run a mile as fast as possible. Thus an example like 'Just as I arrived, John was proving the deduction theorem in ten minutes' is acceptable only in contexts in which John has a stake in how fast he can prove the theorem: it is not enough for him merely to have intended to prove the theorem, and to have happened to take ten minutes to do so.[4]

Still, what is wrong with (45), going over as it will into (59)?

(59)   [$\exists e < u$: $e \approx$my arrival] $Prog(e, \char`\^ \lambda e'$ (rise(the lake,$e'$) & $\mu_{feet}(e')=10$)

It would appear (as Zucchi, if I understand him correctly, suggests) that the trouble stems from the condition that $e \approx$my arrival, for there is no evidence in the local scene as of the time of $e$ that would warrant the belief that there would be a continuation $e'$ of $e$ such that $\mu_{feet}(e')=10$. Note that this evidential condition must be peculiar to the Progressive, inasmuch as (60) is fine:

(60)   Just as I arrived, the lake was in the course of (what would prove to be) a ten-foot rise.

[4] I am indebted here to questions raised by Andrea Bonomi.

## 8.8 Revision II: Telics and stages

In the last section I scouted the prospects for a logical form for the progressive, with telicity of predication made explicit, and using the primitive relation *Prog*, informally explained. It is only through a close examination of property abstraction and that relation that the progressive can be further elucidated. But we may set down a few points at once.

First of all, we can understand the relation $Prog(e, ^\wedge\lambda e'\ \varphi(e'))$ in such a way that if $e$ really *has* the property in question; i.e., if $\varphi(e)$, then $Prog(e, ^\wedge\lambda(e')\ \varphi(e'))$. Such an axiom accounts for the triviality of the progressive of an activity. (Note that this axiom does not allow Mittwoch's (45), as the scene $e$ as of my arrival doesn't have the property that $\mu_{\text{feet}}(e)=10$.)

Second, it is part of the game that the complement of the progressive head be of the form '$^\wedge\lambda e\ \varphi(e)$' or '$^\wedge\lambda(e,e')\ \varphi(e,e')$'. But this can be only if in the logical form the nothing else takes scope between head and complement. Thus if we start from the underlying VP (61):

(61)  Jim smoke 20 cigarettes.

and we give the object wide scope, as in (62):

(62)  [20 cigarettes $x$] smoke(Jim,$x$,$e$)

then we are stuck. It therefore follows that in the progressive (63) the object must take scope outside the progressive head, or else scope internal to the abstraction:

(63)  Jim is smoking 20 cigarettes.

We may take 'smoke' as atelic.[5] Assuming with Schein (1993) that there is no prospect of taking the scope of '20 cigarettes' immediately within the tacit existential quantification over events, there are two scopal possibilities for this expression, as shown in (64) and (65):

(64)  [20 cigarettes $x$] [$\exists e{\approx}u$] $Prog(e, ^\wedge\lambda e'$ smoke(Jim,$x$!,$e'$))

(65)  [$\exists e{\approx}u$] $Prog(e, ^\wedge\lambda e'$ [$\exists X$] [$X$ comprises 20 cigarettes & smoke(Jim,$X$!, $e'$)][6]

---

[5] Naturally, a predicate such as 'smoke a cigarette' may also be taken as telic. That is because a cigarette is consumed by smoking it, so we can say 'smoke a cigarette in five minutes', as well as 'smoke a cigarette for five minutes'. The atelic construction is chosen here for simplicity.

[6] Both (64) and (65) should be understood as imposing a *uniqueness* requirement on the object, indicated by the exclamation mark '!'. Thus, (64) implies that $x$ was the one and only cigarette involved (in the appropriate θ-role) in $e'$. The notation

For (64), there must be 20 events $e$, one for each cigarette $x$, each of which is appropriately related to the property of being an event $e'$ such that smoke $(Jim,x,e')$. This condition might conceivably be realized if Jim has lit each of 20 cigarettes and is taking puffs from each in turn. In (65), there must be a single big event, appropriately related to the smoking of each cigarette, simultaneously or sequentially (or in some combination of the two). Suppose the smoking is sequential, and recall now the problem of stages $e$ of an event $f$: at the time when Jim is smoking the first of the 20 cigarettes he will eventually smoke, (64) is false, and (63) is not in general true, even though smoking the first cigarette is an event $e$ that is in fact an initial segment of an event $f$ of smoking 20 cigarettes. If, on the other hand, Jim is embarking upon the project of smoking 20 cigarettes, then one who is aware of this can volunteer (66), and with that intention (63) as well:

(66) Now Jim is smoking his usual 20 cigarettes, one right after the other.

But this suggests that, as in the case of (55) above, it is the implication of an intentional project that accounts for the acceptability of the example. On the other hand, intentional agency is too strong a requirement in general, it would appear. Suppose that the morning fog is coming, and has covered half the sky. Knowing as we do that the fog will infallibly obscure the sky altogether in a few minutes, we can volunteer (67):

(67) Look! The fog is covering the sky!

It seems, then, that the presumption of causal inevitability justifies assertions like (67), and would justify Mittwoch's (45) if it obtained.

Third, it is an old observation that quantifiers are generally confined within the progressive. Thus there is a contrast between (68) and (69):

(68) I saw Nolan Ryan pitch two no-hitters.
(69) I saw Nolan Ryan pitching two no-hitters.

In particular, (69) is strange, because Nolan Ryan never pitched two games simultaneously. We saw above that, despite the absence of the copula, the perception verb complement in (69) is a Progressive. Assuming that the complement is a quantifier over events, rather than a clausal complement, it

$$\lambda e'\ \text{smoke}(Jim,x!,e')$$

is short for

$$\lambda e'\ \{\text{smoke}(Jim,x,e')\ \&\ [\forall y\text{: cigarette}(y)]\ y=x\}$$

and similarly for (66). See Schein (1993) for a full unpacking of the issues here.

would appear to be a syntactic condition that favours the reading in (70) rather than that in (71):

(70) [∃e<u] Prog(e,^λe′ (∃X) (X comprises 2 no-hitters & pitch(Nolan Ryan,X,e′)))

(71) [2 no-hitters x] [∃e<u] Prog(e,^λe′ pitch(Nolan Ryan,x,e′))

Again, since pitching a no-hitter is not something even Nolan Ryan can intend to do (though he can of course try), still less do at will, (69) resists the kind of telicity that can be associated with (63). Hence for (69) we obtain as the only interpretation that in which he is pitching two games at once.

The above examples serve to reinforce the thesis that the temporal stages of an event can be initial segments that fail to involve every object implicated in the abstract given by the root VP only when the construction is truly telic; i.e., only when the abstract is '^λ(e,e′) φ((e,e′))', the events in the ordered pair standing in the special relation that they have when e′ is the telos or *terminus ad quem* of e in the sense of Chapter 2.

A last point for this part of the discussion. It will have been noted that in Landman's formulation, adopted here, the norm will be a failure of existential generalization. Above, I expressed some doubts about whether this failure could be pinned on verbs of creation; but in any case the need for an opaque construal of the arguments is not best revealed by verbs of creation, but rather (as one might say) by verbs of *selection*. The following is cited in von Stechow (2001: 281), and is due to Angelika Kratzer:

(72) They were picking out a pumpkin.

Evidently, 'they' may be in the course of picking out (or selecting, or choosing, or deciding upon, etc.) a pumpkin, without there being any pumpkin that they were in the course of picking out. Yet the past-tense variant of (72) surely has existential implication:

(73) They picked out a pumpkin.

(contrary to doubts expressed by von Stechow, *ibid.*); for if anybody asserts to me (73) I can surely ask, 'Which pumpkin?' The same question is absurd in the ordinary context of (72).[7] Whatever in the end may be the truth about Parsons's view that in the case of verbs of creation there is existential

---

[7] As Jacqueline Guéron pointed out to me, there are even examples where the implication that something is eventually picked out or selected is vacated: so a panel, engaged in selecting a prize-winner, may conclude that none is worthy of the prize.

generalization, albeit over 'incomplete' objects, Kratzer's example shows that to require existential generalization is too strong.

## 8.9 Revision III: Defining '*Prog*' with counterfactuals

Our previous discussion has removed some major difficulties for Landman's account noted in section 8.6, and suggests a synthesis with the modification of Dowty's proposal given in section 8.4 above. On the modified proposal, the progressive of an accomplishment predicate $\varphi(e,e')$, under a tense expressing the temporal relation $R$, is schematically as in (74):

(74)  $[\exists eRu] \ [\forall w\colon w \text{ is inertial with respect to } (@,\tau(e))] \ [\exists (e'',e')\colon \tau(e) \subset \tau(e'')]$
$\varphi_{(w,\tau(e''+e'))}((e'',e'))$.

whereas on Landman's proposal, modified as suggested above, it is (75):

(75)  $[\exists e''Ru] \ Prog(e'',^{\wedge}\lambda(e,e') \ \varphi(e,e'))$.

However, there are a number of assumptions built into Landman's account, and the further additions of the last section, that would require to be treated in a demonstration of equivalence. But also, the notion of a world inertial to $(@,\tau(e''))$ is sufficiently loose that the equivalence may be all too easy to obtain! Landman's definition of his progressive relation PROG is (76):

(76)  $PROG_w(e,P) \leftrightarrow [\exists e'][\exists w'] \ [(e',w') \in CON(e,w) \ \& \ P_{w'}(e')$

where $CON(e,w)$ is a family of ordered pairs of events and worlds determined by $e$ and $w$ (the 'continuation branch' of $e$ and $w$). Under the modification suggested here, where accomplishments involve ordered pairs of events, a natural modification of (76) is first of all (77):

(77)  $PROG_w(e,P) \leftrightarrow [\exists (e',e'')][\exists w'] \ [((e',e''),w') \in CON(e,w) \ \& \ P_{w'}(e',e'')]$

Recalling now that what it is for one event to 'continue' another is obscure, to the extent that we can replace Landman's condition

$$((e',e''),w') \in CON(e,w)$$

with the simple statement that $e$ is an initial segment$_{(w,e)}$ of $e'$, and $w'$ is inertial with respect to $(w,e)$; and, finally, that we can assume that for each $(w,e)$ there is a unique inertial world $w'$, the definition reduces to (78):

(78)  $PROG_w(e,P) \leftrightarrow$ the world $w'$ that is inertial with respect to $(w,e)$ is such that
$(\exists (e',e'')) \ [e \text{ is an initial segment}_{(w,e)} \text{ of } e' \ \& \ P_{w'}((e',e''))]$

so that, if the position marked by '$P$' is filled with a property abstract '$^\wedge\lambda(e',e'')\varphi(e',e'')$', we have almost the proposal offered above as a modification of Dowty (the only difference is that we have replaced inclusions of times with segments of events).[8] Indeed, we could look upon Landman's notion of a continuation branch as a way of delivering the relevant inertial world: it will be the closest world, if there is one, where the telos $e''$ is to be found at the end of a process $e'$ of which $e$ is an initial segment, and therefore the actual world if the accomplishment comes off.[9]

## 8.10 Revision IV: Some influences of context

The discussion to this point has left us with several open questions concerning the effects of context. These questions divide into two parts. First of all, there is the issue of spelling out what it is for $w'$ to be the inertial world for $(w,e)$, as measured by some conception of 'closeness' to the actual world. Second, there are the contextual issues that remain even when this notion is taken for granted. These are distinct: for any actual event $e$, nothing is closer to $(@,e)$ than the actual world $@$ itself; but that can hardly always be the inertial world, or else we should make every progressive true just in case the progressivized clause will come to be true, whereas what we want is that if the progressivized clause comes to be true, then the progressive was true, but not conversely. It must be the case that if John dies of cancer, then he was dying of cancer: and this can be so only if, John having died of cancer, we consider at an earlier point the inertial world or worlds to be just those in which he does die of cancer; or, in Landman's formulation, we consider only those continuation branches from $(e,@)$, where $e$ is some (perhaps slender) initial segment of the process of his dying, that eventuate in his death from cancer. Now, at that initial segment, it might have been highly unlikely that John would in fact die of cancer (e.g., it was highly improbable bad luck that the appropriate therapy didn't reach him in time); but this improbability is now irrelevant, given that he did in fact die of cancer.

All of which follows from the fact that the actual world is closer than any other to itself, for any actual event $e$. But now certain other issues arise.

---

[8] The distinction could become important, inasmuch as events may have their temporal locations, if not their participants, only contingently.

[9] I am aware that the assumption that there is at most one inertial world will be controversial; just as, in accounts of indicative conditionals, the assumption is controversial that there is at most one closest possible world in which the antecedent is true. If this assumption is vacated, then, as urged in Bonomi (1998), we could have a true disjunction of incompatible progressives, such that neither disjunct is true. The account given here admits adjustment if this is the case, however: replace 'the inertial world' by 'every closest inertia world'. The general method is given in Lewis (1973: 77 ff.).

Consider first the 'imperfective paradox' in its simplest form. Mary is taking her flight to London, the one that will end up in Havana. At some point early on, I say (79):

(79)  Mary is flying to London.

I speak truly, although, as luck will have it, the hijackers have boarded, and will commandeer the aircraft. Accounts of the Progressive, including those surveyed and suggested here, are all intended to allow for the truth of (79) under such circumstances. But suppose I know that the aircraft will be flown to Havana. I can then, at an early point in Mary's flight, speak truly by saying either (80) or (81):

(80)  Mary is flying to London, but she will never make it.

(81)  Mary thinks she is flying to London, but in fact she is flying to Havana.

Similarly, once the hijackers have flown the aircraft to Havana, I can say truly either (82) or (83):

(82)  Mary was flying to London, but she never made it.

(83)  Mary thought she was flying to London, but in fact she was flying to Havana.

At *no* point is a true utterance of (84) possible:

(84)  Mary is/was flying to London and (she is/was flying) to Havana.

(since, by hypothesis, neither destination is *en route* to the other). The conjuncts in (84) are incompatible, even though each individually may be asserted; and, as we have seen, once we are given what happened in the actual world, then the Past Progressive (84) is licensed, however improbable the attainment of the telos may have been.

Parsons's account of the Progressive, at least in its unadulterated form, fails to account for the possibility that both of (80)–(81), or (82)–(83), can be true assertions. On that account, (79) is fine, since we merely have a flying to London that does not culminate; and so is 'Mary is flying to Havana' on the hijacker scenario. But then the conjunction (84) should be true, contrary to fact; and it could not be as in (83) that Mary only thinks she is flying to London.

Landman's ingenious construction (Landman (1992: 26–28)) tells us, in constructing the continuation branch of an event *e* in a world *w*, to stick to *w* as long as *e* can be continued there, and to hop to another world (if possible), only if *e* 'stops'. As Landman recognizes, this condition on continuation branches will have the desired consequence that it must be true that Mary was flying to Havana if that is where she ended up, that John was dying of cancer if that is what he eventually died of, etc. So (83) will be true. But then how can (80) be true? For any initial segment $e$ of Mary's flight, there is a segment $e'$ with $e \subset e'$ such that, in the actual world, $e'$ stops only when Mary reaches Havana. If, therefore, we are not permitted in constructing the continuation branch to leave @ until $e$ stops, we shall never leave it, and (80) is therefore false.

Landman discusses the issues here in terms of what he calls the *perspective* that one brings to the evaluation of the Progressive. However, now that we have at our disposal the breakdown of events into process and telos, we may suggest simply that, in imaginatively or counterfactually continuing an event $e$, we follow $e$, not 'until it stops' (or 'until it stops being a flight to London'; for our question must be, given that it *was* a flight to Havana, whether it *ever* was a flight to London), but rather *until it ceases to bring us closer to the telos*.

Notice that universal quantification over inertia worlds as in Dowty's original proposal does make (84) false (at the cost, noted above, of making absolutely all conjunctions of incompatibles false, a point to which I return below). But that happens just because the inertia worlds are independent of all but the world and the temporal interval under consideration, and that in turn makes it impossible to have both (82) and (83) true. The same defect obviously attends the revised condition (78) above. This circumstance, together with our suggestion above, suggests that we relativize the inertia world, not merely to $w$ and $e$, but also to the predicate in question. Then (78) would give way to (85):

(85) $\text{PROG}_w(e,P) \leftrightarrow$ the world $w'$ that is inertial with respect to $(w,e,P)$ is such that
$(\exists (e',e''))\, [e \text{ is an initial segment}_{(w',e)} \text{ of } e'\ \&\ P_{w'}((e',e''))]$

Under the revision suggested, (79) is true because the inertial world for

$(w,e,\char`\^\lambda(e',e'')\ \text{fly to London}(\text{Mary},(e',e'')))$

is the (closest) one in which there was no hijacking. And 'Mary was flying to Havana' is true, as before, because she actually did fly there. But then (relativizing the inertia worlds to the two different properties of accomplishment predicates), (84) is true as well.

For this last, it may be suggested that, perhaps as a pragmatic matter, a single perspective or inertial world must be chosen for a single assertion. Then (84) will not be true, and the correction (81) is appropriate as well. As we shall see, however, matters are not so simple.

Suppose that Mary makes it to London as scheduled, even though it was nearly certain early on that the hijackers would act (one of them had an allergic reaction to a rotten airline peanut, so they decided at the last moment to call it off). Then (86) is true, and (87) is false:

(86)  Mary was (then) flying to London.

(87)  Mary was (then) flying to Havana.

This is the case even though it was then almost certain that she would never make it to London. To round out the story, we may assume that the early part of Mary's flight, even beyond the point where the hijackers take control, would be exactly the same whether the hijackers acted or not.

The case just considered points to a general asymmetry in Progressives, in that the circumstances invoked to account for the truth of the Progressive of an accomplishment in the absence of the attainment of the telos do not by their absence imply the truth of the Progressive of an alternative accomplishment. Thus under the circumstances of our last example, it is simply not true that Mary was *ever* flying to Havana. But why not? Had it not been for the, antecedently highly unlikely, allergic reaction, Mary would have flown to Havana. Note that the following response is not available: 'Well, when the aircraft, however improbably, escapes hijacking, then the early part of Mary's flight is not a flight *e* that formed, as an event in @, something whose continuation in any world *w* was a flight to Havana.' The response is not available, because it begs the question: in a world *w* in which the debilitating peanut is not consumed, isn't *e* the first part of a flight to Havana by Mary? If not, why not?

Any individual example of the asymmetry in question will carry with it some substantial contextual baggage, and so might be disarmed in various ways. Thus it might be suggested that Mary's flight was given in advance as a flight to London, not Havana, and that this colours our evaluation of the case. Anyway, let us note the asymmetry by noting the truth of (88) (where the aircraft was hijacked; call this scenario (1), and the falsehood of (89) (where the hijacking was called off; call this scenario (2):

(88)  Mary was flying to London, but she flew to Havana [scenario 1].

(89)  Mary was flying to Havana, but she flew to London [scenario 2].

Consider now the following case (Dowty (1977), credited to Richmond Thomason): a certain coin is tossed; while it is in the air it is true to say, 'The coin is landing heads or tails'; and which of 'the coin is landing heads' and 'the coin is landing tails' is true depends only upon what actually happens. (In Dowty's original terms, this could only be because just the actual world counts as an inertia world—but then why should this not be so in every case?) Note that the Progressive here is not futurate: neither the coin's landing heads nor its landing tails is determined or on the agenda. Nor is it a matter of probabilities. Let $c$ be a coin that is biased 99.99% in favor of tails, and let $c$ be tossed in the air. Suppose that $c$ lands heads on that toss. Then (as Landman's account would predict), 'the coin was landing heads' is true. But 'the coin was landing tails' is false, and this fact is unexplained. In short, (90) is false when the coin lands heads, just as (91) is false when it lands tails:

(90)  The coin was landing tails, but it landed heads.

(91)  The coin was landing heads, but it landed tails.

Finally, there are symmetric cases; i.e., cases where both Progressives are assertible. Above I gave the example (23), repeated here:

(23)  John is dying of cancer and of heart disease, although only one of these will kill him (and it is a random matter which it is).

I believe that, where John dies in the end of cancer, (92) is assertible, and where he dies of heart disease, (93) is assertible:

(92)  John was dying of heart disease, but he died in the end of cancer.

(93)  John was dying of cancer, but he died in the end of heart disease.

I sketch two other, perhaps more convincing, examples of the same phenomenon.

$B$ is a book in the Bodleian Library in Oxford that is growing yellow with age. If nothing is done, it will be destroyed, having been printed on paper with acid in it. Thus (94) is true:

(94)  The oxidation of its pages is destroying $B$.

$V$ is a vandal who wishes to destroy $B$. Having little time to act in the vicinity of $B$, he is ripping out pages surreptitiously, one page a day. So far he has destroyed two. Hence (95):

(95)  $V$ is destroying $B$.

Scenario 1: the oxidation of $B$'s pages is proceeding so rapidly (owing to new ventilation in the library) that $B$ crumbles to dust long before $V$ has a chance to remove any but a few pages. On this scenario, we have (96):

(96)  $V$ was destroying $B$, but the oxidation of its pages destroyed it.

152  *Tense, Aspect, and Indexicality*

Scenario 2: *V* is able to accelerate the pace of destruction (owing to lax security in the library), so that the pages are all ripped out in a few days. Then we have (97):

(97)   The oxidation of its pages was destroying *B*, but *V* destroyed it.

Similarly: suppose that Dorothy Gale is crossing a street whose surface is something like the Deadly Desert of the *Oz* books. The street, being filled with sand from the Deadly Desert, will slowly turn to sand anything in contact with it. But if one crosses fast enough, one suffers only the most superficial and harmless transformations of bits of one's body into sand. Scenario 1: Dorothy crosses quickly, so that (98) is true:

(98)   Dorothy was turning into sand when she crossed the street (but she didn't turn into sand).

Scenario 2: Dorothy trips and falls on the way, and turns into sand before she can recover. Then (99) is true:

(99)   Dorothy was crossing the street when she turned into sand (so she never crossed the street).

In place of (98)–(99) we may, in analogy with (88)–(89), put (100)–(101):

(100)  Dorothy was turning into sand, but she didn't, since she crossed the street quickly. [scenario 1]

(101)  Dorothy was crossing the street, but she didn't cross it, because she turned into sand. [scenario 2]

Our question, now, is what may account for the symmetry in (100)–(101) and the asymmetry in (88)–(89).

Dowty (1977: 58) more than hints at the asymmetry remarked upon here when he asks why, in the familiar scenario, 'John is crossing the street' is true at some intervals when 'John is being knocked down by a truck' is not. He resolves the question by noting that 'John is being knocked down' can't be true until John's body has commenced to be displaced by the truck (thus conceding, or perhaps anticipating, that a process must have begun for the Progressive to be true). As we have seen, however, there are examples that cannot be resolved in this way, as well as examples, like those above, where symmetry is maintained.

The symmetric examples, such as (96)–(97) or (100)–(101), allow conjunctions of Progressives, as in (102)–(103):

(102)   The oxidation of its pages was destroying *B*, and vandal *V* was destroying *B*.

(103)   Dorothy was turning into sand while crossing the street.

and these conjunctions hold no matter what happens, so that whether *V* or the oxidation of its pages destroys *B*, (102) is true; and whether Dorothy turns into sand before getting across the street or not, (103) is true. We therefore conclude that the contradictoriness of the conjunction (84) is not pragmatic; likewise the falsehood, say, of 'the coin is landing heads and is landing tails'. It is time to think about taking further semantic steps.

First of all, note that, in the first two of the symmetric cases discussed above, there are two distinct ongoing processes, each tending to the same end (John's death, the destruction of book *B*), which are causally independent. In the last case, there are again two independent processes, tending toward different ends, and it is just a question who gets there first. In all symmetric cases, I suggest, such causal independence is observed, and the Progressive, applied to either process, is assertible, as is the conjunction (because the conjuncts select their inertia worlds with respect to different properties *P*).

There remain the cases where there is only one causal process (say, the toss of the coin in the air), and the cases where there are two, one of which (as in the hijackers commandeering Mary's aircraft) *interferes* with the operation of the other (Mary's flight proceeding smoothly to London). In the first case, the truth or falsehood of the Progressive depends exactly and only upon what actually happens. In particular, as we have seen, probability of the outcomes is irrelevant. In the second case, where interference plays a role, we typically have asymmetry: whereas the hijackers' act does interfere with the flight to London, their calling the whole thing off does not interfere with the (proposed) flight to Havana.

The contextually given notions of *interference*, or the *interruption* of one event by another, thus appear to play a critical role in the evaluation of Progressives. But they are not reducible to simple preclusion of one event by another. *V*'s rapidly ripping the pages out of the library book did not interrupt the oxidation of those pages, and thus did not interfere with that event's destroying the book, even though the book was not in the end thus destroyed. Dorothy's getting across the street did not interrupt her turning into sand, although it prevented that from happening; and so on in like cases. To put it another way: when we choose the inertial world for a Progressive, that world cannot be described as one in which 'things go as expected', for if something as simple as that were the case, then the coin (biased 99.99% in favor of tails) would be landing tails even on tosses in which it landed heads, and Mary would be flying to Havana when, surprisingly, one of the would-be hijackers had an allergic reaction to a peanut. Rather, when the inertial world is not the actual world, and the Progressive is true although the simple past will never be true, it is one in which the process tending toward the telos was, however probably or improbably, interrupted by an event that deflected it from the attainment of the telos.

The formula (85) above cannot, of itself, distinguish amongst the cases discussed above. Rather, the distinctions among them belong to the interpretation of the notion of an inertial world $w'$ for $(w,e,P)$. There being no evident context-neutral way to distinguish *interference* of one event by another from mere *preclusion*, it appears that there is an ineradicably contextual element in our evaluations of the Progressive.

## 8.11 Cross-linguistic questions

Historically, the origin of the English Progressive is a nominal construction with a gerundive object, as in (104):

(104)   John is at [PRO crossing the street]

(the relic of the preposition is still heard, of course, in those English speakers who say 'John is a'crossing (of) the street'). The prepositional head 'at' will have its own position for events $e$, and will take the complement as an argument. We might conjecture, therefore, that the interpretation of the complement was just as in Landman's proposal, namely

$$^\wedge\lambda(e,e')\text{ PRO cross the street}(e,e')$$

with the role of the subject of the complement, and the subject 'John', to be determined. If, in view of the fact that expletive 'it' can be the subject of a Progressive, we can take the further step of abstracting away from any semantic difference between the ordered pair of arguments ('John', 'PRO crossing the street') and 'John crossing the street', we arrive at just the logical syntax that the analysis of (104) above would suggest: the preposition 'at' expresses a relation between events $e$ and properties of events $P$. The further development of the English Progressive, if this is correct, would consist in a grammatical reduction of the structure, leaving the interpretation unchanged.

In section 8.2 above I sketched Parsons's view of the English Perfect, which would give for (105) the logical form (106):

(105)   John has crossed the street.

(106)   $[\exists e'' \approx u\!\!: e''$ is a resultant state of $(e,e')]$ cross(John,the street,$(e,e'))$

When we turn to the Perfect Progressive, as in (107), we have two interpretations:

(107)  John has been crossing the street (for the last five minutes).

The first has John still in the midst of crossing, and not having made it yet to the other side of the street; this one is obtained by applying the Perfect directly to the Progressive head. The second is the 'over and over' reading: John has crossed the street several times over the last five minutes. This latter reading I take to be a consequence of what amounts to a pluralization of the event position in the Progressive head (see similar examples in Chapter 2). There are, then, multiple events $e$ over the last five minutes, each of which is the resultant state of an initial segment of a crossing of the street. Formally, we have (108):

(108)  $[\exists E \approx u]$ $[\forall e \in E]$ $[\exists e': e$ is a resultant of $e']$ $Prog(e',{}^\wedge\lambda(e'',e'''))$ cross (John,the street,$(e'',e''')))$.

Since one crossing of the street cannot commence until its predecessor is concluded, the 'over and over' interpretation follows. In other cases, free from such a restriction, the various initial segments of what may or may not turn out to be multiple accomplishments can be interleaved, as in (109):

(109)  Mary has been writing several papers for the last hour.

I conclude that, as would be expected from both the phrasal hierarchy and the historical development of English, the Perfect of a Progressive takes the heads in that sequential order, and no other.

Historical inquiry about the English Progressive is but one dimension of a variety of cross-linguistic work that would be required to see whether what is called 'the Progressive' in human languages is a unified phenomenon. The account suggested here would be supported if it were. It is striking, for instance, that the Chinese Progressive (discussed for instance in Carlota Smith's work, Smith (1991)) appears to reveal the same structure as the historical English. We have examples such as (110):

(110)  Jangsan tsai chih fan.
       Jangsan at eat (rice)
       'Jangsan is eating'

(where *tsai* is the ordinary locative). It would be worthwhile to know whether the semantic properties scouted above carry over here—only if very different languages are thus united can we speak of *the* Progressive. One point is clear: Chinese does not permit the Progressive of an accomplishment. One cannot have (111):

(111)  *Jangsan tsai sz
       Jangsan at die
       'Jangsan is dying'

What accounts for this gap remains, so far as I am aware, to be explained.

Finally, there are cross-linguistic issues in the representation and source of telicity. Throughout this discussion, I have assumed that root predicates may be telic, so that (for instance) the distinction between atelic 'eat apples' and telic 'eat an apple' reflects a lexical ambiguity. But the Italian examples discussed in section 8.5, where it was observed that the simple present 'mangia una mela' ('eat (of) an apple') was not necessarily telic, are problematic for this view, as are other cases where various contrasts between English Progressive and non-Progressive forms do not carry over into Italian. I do think that, contrary to Parsons's suggestion, it won't do to lay the emergence of telicity, or his notion of culmination, down to the influence of Tense; but it is not out of the question that telicity stems from compositional, rather than lexical, semantics. In any case, it appears that the Romance Progressive (say Italian '-ndo' with 'stare') is comparable to the English, and is to be sharply distinguished from the simple present (Giorgi and Pianesi (1997)). The study of the questions here requires native judgements, and subtle ones at that. But, the problems of comparative semantics will necessarily involve both syntactic and semantic unknowns.[10]

---

[10] The material presented here was a long time percolating. The central hypothesis, that the Progressive '-ing' expresses a relation between events and properties of events, formed the core of a critical paper presented at the University of Maryland, College Park, and subsequently at the Scuola Normale Superiore, Pisa, Italy, in the spring of 1990 (these presentations, and the accompanying manuscript, account for the occasional references to the paper in the literature). Besides the audiences at those presentations, I am indebted to Terence Parsons for comments upon and discussion of that paper. Seeing that my hypothesis as to logical form was, some notation and other issues aside, independently advanced by Fred Landman in his article then to appear in *Natural Language Semantics*, which I reviewed for that journal's first issue, I elected not to submit my own piece for publication anywhere. (Fred's later kind encouragement did not change my mind.) Discussion of the Progressive from the point of view developed here did, however, figure in my lectures in Oxford over the years, as well as constituting part of a course I gave as Visiting Professor at Rutgers in 1998, and of a lecture at MIT that same year. In preparing for the Paris meetings, I was struck anew by the critical analysis in Zucchi (1997). The present chapter is prompted in part my reaction to this work; and observations by Andrea Bonomi also led me to rethink several issues.

I sent a full draft of the July 2002 version to several people. I am particularly indebted to David Dowty, Andrea Bonomi, and Alessandro Zucchi for comments on that version, and indebted also for comments and suggestions from my editors, the Jacquelines.

# 9

# The English Perfect and the Metaphysics of Events

## 9.1 Introduction

The general thesis that I explore here is that the English Perfect is purely aspectual, serving to shift from a predicate of events *e* to a predicate of events that are results of *e*, as explained more fully below. To the extent that this thesis is defensible, the Perfect is not involved in the Tense system at all, except derivatively (because Tense applies to the Perfect itself). The investigation of the Perfect interlocks with a number of metaphysical questions concerning the nature of events and situations, and further issues in the syntax and semantics of sequence of tense in English. In exploring these I shall draw upon earlier chapters in this volume, and Higginbotham (2005).

The general thesis, that the Perfect concerns aspect rather than Tense, is an old one. Jespersen (1924: 269) proposed that the English Present Perfect characterizes 'present results of past events', and not the past events themselves. Parsons (1990) makes at least one part of this account explicit. Consider a simple assertion such as (1):

(1)   Mary has solved the problem.

We assume that the heads line up as in (2):

(2)   [Tense [Perf [VP]]

with V moving to the head Perf, and auxiliary 'have' to Tense. The V 'solved' expresses a 3-place relation $S(x,y,e)$ that is satisfied by a triple $(\alpha,\beta,\gamma)$ just in case $\gamma$ is an event of $\alpha$'s solving $\beta$. The head Perf has two argument positions and expresses a relation $R(e',e)$, satisfied by an ordered pair of events such that $e'$ is a 'result' of $e$, in a sense or senses to be determined. The interpretation of the Perfect Phrase in construction with VP is then as in (3):

(3)   $Result(e',e)$ & $solve(Mary, the\ problem, e)$

I shall assume that the Present expresses the relation ≈ of temporal overlap or inclusion as between (the actual time of) an event and (the actual time of) the speaker's utterance *u*. Following existential closure (as originally suggested in Donald Davidson's work), we obtain (4):

(4)  [∃e'≈u] [∃e] [R(e',e) & solve(Mary,the problem,e)]

In Present Perfect assertions, and in tensed Perfects generally, it is the result that carries the tense, and is said to surround the time of the clause (the utterance time, in the case of root sentences). But because, by assumption, results temporally follow, and do not overlap, the states or events of which they are the results, it follows that the situations characterized by a predicate F (e) are past with respect to a present result e' of e.

Present Perfects are distinct from Pasts (Preterits). Jespersen (1924: 270), himself following earlier observations, notes that:

Sentences containing words like *yesterday* or *in 1879* require the simple preterit, so also sentences about people who are dead, except when something is stated about the present effect of their doings, e.g. in *Newton has explained the movements of the moon* (the movements of the moon have been explained—namely by Newton).

Jespersen further characterized English as relatively 'conservative' in these respects; conservative, that is, with respect to his proposed evolution of the Germanic and Romance language families. If this is right, then the Present Perfect is just what it seems to be, namely the present of a Perfect, as in Jespersen's famous example (5):

(5)  Now I have eaten enough.

where the present predicate 'now' must apply to the present result, not the past activity. Where the adverbial 'now' is predicated of the higher position, marked by e', and the inflectional feature—past is interpreted as expressing the relation ≈, the interpretation is as in (6):

(6)  [∃e'≈u][∃e] [Now(e') & R(e',e) & eat enough(I,e)]

We next distinguish *Results* from *Resultants* (the latter in the sense of Parsons (1990)). Resultant states are states that commence when an event *e* is over, and continue forever. The meaning of the sentences in which they constitute the interpretation of the Perfect is, as it were, 'been there, done that', salient for instance in (7):

(7)  I have been to Japan/driven a truck/been shot at.

For a Perfect of Result (not Resultant) consider (8):

(8)  I have spilled my coffee!

The announcement (8) is only in order as long as there is spilled coffee around. Likewise, (5) is fine when just setting down one's knife and fork after dinner, and for some time afterwards, but not upon waking up the next morning (unless one has just resolved to go on hunger strike). And so on in like cases, as both result and resultant states commence immediately after the events of which they are the results or resultants.[1] For notation in what follows we use '*R*' for result states, and '*RR*' for resultant states.

Some further preliminary remarks. First, it is evident that Perfect morpheme '-en' of English can all by itself contribute a result state. The point is seen in examples like those in (9):

(9)  saddled (the saddled horse); botoxed (the botoxed face); treed (the treed cat)

derived from Nouns (I assume that the corresponding Verb is causative on the participle, as in Chapter 7), and those in (10), derived from Verbs:

(10)  burned (the burned tree); spilled (the spilled coffee); demolished (the demolished house)

Second, the same point is underscored by the existence of adverbials that cannot be Verbal modifiers, but may modify perfective adjectives, as in (11) versus (12), or (13) versus (14):

(11)  the freshly caught fish, the newly appointed assistant professor
(12)  *We freshly caught the fish, *They newly appointed an assistant professor.
(13)  John is newly divorced.
(14)  *John newly divorced.

Third and last, the presence of the result is seen in the favored interpretation of expressions like 'John's broken arm' (not the arm that he broke, but the one that is now broken; i.e., in the result state of a breaking), or 'the stolen painting' (the painting that is now stolen, and so not recovered). Comparable evidence is of course found in the Romance and Germanic languages.[2]

---

[1] It is perhaps worth noting that the Perfect head, even when happening to favor in context a Result interpretation, can always be understood as expressing a Resultant, as in (i) for instance:

(i)  I have done many foolish things in my life—I have spilled my coffee, I have lost my wallet, etc.

[2] Boogaart (1999) and references cited therein provides a contemporary survey, with special reference to English and Dutch.

The Perfect of Result is thus widely attested, and the question is whether all Perfects in English fit the mould.

The above syntactic and semantic points leave questions about the nature of the elements—events, situations, results, and resultants—that have been invoked in their characterization. In section 9.2 below these, with consequences for the Perfect, will come to the fore. In section 9.3 I take up the matter of the integration of the Perfect into the English system of sequence of tense, and in 9.4 I offer a generalization of the puzzles of the Present Perfect, as noted for instance in the quotation above from Jespersen. A number of further issues remain, and I will note some of these in passing.

## 9.2 Metaphysical issues

We are recognizing, in ordinary heads, positions for arguments, plus the event-position (hereafter: E-position), as in (1) above. In heads giving rise to Accomplishment interpretations in the sense of Vendler the E-position is complex, consisting of an ordered pair of positions, one for process and one for telos or end, as in 'cross the street', where the positions are $(x,(e,e'))$, with the first reserved for the agent, $e$ for the process of crossing, and $e'$ for the end, the onset of the agent's being on the other side of the street.

Events or situations in this sense are to have to following properties and relations to the syntax:

(A) They are the relata of causal relations. To say that striking the match caused it to light is to say that one event $e$, the striking, caused another $e'$, the lighting. (The relation between process and end as in 'cross the street' is causal as well, but of a rather special kind, namely one where the process—proceeding from the curb more or less toward the other side of the street—continues until the end—being on the other side—comes about.)

(B) In gerundive and mixed nominals, and in many derived nominals as well, it is just the E-position in the head that is bound by the Determiner; thus 'the striking of the match' is a definite description as in (15):

(15)   (the $e$) strike(the match,$e$)

Moreover, sentences in general allow gerundive nominals, and many allow nominals of the other kinds as well.

(C) Such nominals, and complete sentences in some contexts, may refer to or quantify over events and states. An example of the first kind is (16), of the second (17):

(16)   Mary enjoys/remembers [walking to work]

(17) [John fell down] after [Bill hit him]

The expressions in square brackets involve events, not propositions.

(D) Events and other situations may be described in any number of ways (they are objects). The event descriptions given by nominalization or in full sentences admit without exception the substitutivity of identity for singular terms. So, to deploy a well-worn example, the nominals (18) and (19), if they refer at all, refer to the same thing, even though at one point Oedipus didn't know that:

(18)  Oedipus's marriage to Jocasta

(19)  Oedipus's marriage to his mother

(E) Adverbial modifiers of the simplest sort, the manner adverbials, characteristically modify, by conjoining with, the E-position of the head; adverbial quantifiers may also bind this position. So, in standard manner-adverbial cases like (20) the interpretation is as in (21) (with perhaps the qualification that the crossing was only relatively quick); and in standard quantificational cases like (22) one of the salient interpretations, indicated in (23), is that amongst Mary's journeys to work some reasonable proportion are walks:

(20)  John crossed the street quickly.

(21)  [∃e] [Cross(John,the street,e) & quick(e)]

(22)  Mary occasionally walks to work.

(23)  [Occasional e: travel to work(Mary,e)] walk to work(Mary,e)

Assembling the above pieces, however, generates a number of problems, of which I concentrate on two, one involving causation and the other involving complex nominalizations. I will argue that these problems have the same solution, a solution that, while it may appear extravagant, is nevertheless practically a deductive consequence of the basic assumptions above.

The problem with causation (noted by many, and folkloric so far as I know) is that, according to the hypothesis that takes (20) up as (21), the nominalizations in (24), one gerundive and one mixed, come out as in (25):

(24)  John's crossing the street quickly/John's quick crossing of the street

(25)  (the e) (cross the street(John,e) & quick(e))

These nominalizations occur as the subjects and objects of causation, say as in (26):

(26)  The traffic light's changing to amber caused John's quick crossing of the street.

(or, for the object of (26), the infinitival, 'John to cross the street quickly'). But now it may well be that John's quick crossing of the street was his one and only crossing of the street. In that case we have the identity (27):

(27) (the *e*) (cross the street(John,*e*) & quick(*e*))=(the *e*) cross the street (John,*e*)

But then we may put equals for equals in (26), deriving (28):

(28) The traffic light's changing to amber caused John's crossing of the street.

But we can readily conceive that (28) is false whilst (26) is true, a contradiction.

There are many variations on the above theme.[3] One can imagine responses that would deny one of (A) or (B), that causal relations are relations between events, or that nominalizations purport to refer to them, or (D), that events are objects. Note that the very success of hypothesis (E), that modifiers such as 'quickly' may be understood as simply conjoining with what they modify, is what brings down the conjunction of the others; and conversely, that abandoning (E) would call (A)–(D) into serious question. Davidson himself suggested that examples such as (26) equivocated between statements about causation pure and simple and statements of putative causal explanation, between *causes* and *becauses*, as he put it. Certainly, statements *A because/ causally explains B* display properties very different from singular causal statements: they relate sentences (or propositions), and they do not admit the substitutivity of identity for singular terms. But the move deprives the major thesis (A) of much of its credibility.

There is, however, another, very different, solution to the puzzle, one that suggests itself as soon as notice is taken of the generality of the process of forming event nominals. Consider again assumption (B), and note that nominals with adverbial heads come in as a special case, as in (29):

(29) the quickness of John's crossing of the street

These nominals themselves refer to situations: just as 'John's happiness' refers to the situation *e* such that happy(John,*e*), so should (29) be construed as in (30):

(30) (the *e*) [∃*e′*] [quick(*e*,*e′*) & cross(John,the street,*e′*)]

---

[3] The example chosen is one where the alternative descriptions are of the caused, rather than the causing, event. But examples of the latter kind are easily constructed as well, e.g. (i):

(i) John's quick crossing of the street caused him to be early.

for the nominal refers, not to the crossing, but to the quickness of the crossing. But now we may conclude that there is an E-position *also* in the Adverb, in addition to the position that is identified with that of the Verb.[4]

In place of (21) for (20), then, we have (31), revealing the extra E-position:

(31)　[∃e][∃e′] [cross(John,the street,e) & quick(e,e′)]

and when we nominalize (20), or take the infinitival complement as referring to an event, we may nominalize either with respect to the E-position in the head, or with respect to that in the adverbial. If we nominalize with respect to the syntactic head 'cross', then for 'John's quick crossing of the street' we have the innocent identity corresponding to (27), namely (32):

(32)　(the e) [∃e′] [cross the street(John,e) & quick(e,e′)]= (the e) cross the street(John,e)

but if we nominalize with respect to the Adverb (as we must do in (29)), we have (30), referring not to the crossing, but to its quickness. With the object nominal so understood, there is no question of identity, and the implication from (27) to (28) fails, even on the assumption that John crossed the street just once, in a quick crossing.

But must the object nominal be understood as a nominalization of the adverbial position? I am inclined to think not, at least for the case of mixed nominals; that is, there may be a way of understanding (28) that makes it true after all (though perhaps misleading as an assertion). For infinitival objects as in (33) below, however, my judgement is that only the interpretation that describes the quickness of the crossing is possible:

(33)　The traffic light's changing to amber caused John to cross the street quickly.

The problem just addressed, and the suggested solution, extend through countless similar examples. Of these I mention one, which I heard delivered by Robert Hambourger in discussion with Davidson at a colloquium at Columbia University in 1971. Suppose I am going home late at night, and I fear that I am being followed by a mugger. I quickly fumble for my keys. I have two keys for my door, one green and one red. As it happens, the one I grab is the green key. Then: my fear caused me to open the door; and it caused me to open the door with a key; but it did not cause me to open the door with the green key. That is to say: it was not the state *e* of the key's being green that caused me to open the door with that key. In the 1971 discussion, Davidson

---

[4] This point is briefly noted in Higginbotham (2005).

responded to the example with the distinction between 'causes' and 'becauses', noted above. In a way the response was correct; what was not noticed was that the 'becauses' could be located in the events themselves, through the E-positions in non-heads such as 'quickly' above, or 'green' in Hambourger's example.

Assuming now that at least causal contexts bring out E-positions in non-heads, I turn to a second case where the proposals (A)–(E) come into apparent conflict both with the data and with each other. Consider contexts where complement clauses evidently involve reference to events, as in (34) and the like:

(34) Mary enjoyed/remembered walking to work this morning.

The complement purports to be a definite or indefinite description of an event, namely that of walking to work. The E-position in the complement is accessible to adverbial quantification, as in (35):

(35) Mary occasionally walks to work.

An assertion of (35) will be made against a background according to which Mary's walks to work are occasional—her travels to work, for instance. Then the truth conditions of (35) will be as in (36):

(36) [Occasional $e$: travel to work(Mary,$e$)] walk to work(Mary,$e$)

But now we may embed such clauses as gerundive complements, as in (37):

(37) Mary enjoyed/remembered occasionally walking to work.

where the quantificational adverb is interpreted with respect to the clause in which it appears. What Mary is said to enjoy or remember is *occasionally walking to work*—the occasionality of it, as one might say. But the theory allows no such interpretation. The complement is supposed to describe something, but, unlike the complement in (35), it is not a predicate but a closed expression (the adverbial has bound the E-position).

In light of our discussion above of causal contexts, a solution to this conundrum suggests itself: why not allow an E-position *also* in the adverbial? It then can become a definite or indefinite description of an event, and we shall obtain truth conditions as in (38):

(38) [$\exists e$] [Occasional($e,e'$): travel to work(Mary,$e'$)] walk to work(Mary,$e'$) & enjoy/remember(Mary,$e$)][5]

---

[5] I recall this suggestion as having been made in passing by Paul Portner.

Indeed, quite apart from contexts such as (37) we must recognize an E-position, or the potential for such a position, in (35), because of the possibility of nominalization:

(39)  the occasionality of Mary's walking to work

The general solution, then, to the issues that arise when we put proposals (A)–(E) together is a flourishing of E-positions, and therefore of reference to events, particularly with respect to modifiers, quantifiers, and other non-heads. Viewed in this light, the invocation of such elements as Result and Resultant states (particularly the latter, as they are defined only by what they are the Resultants of) is the least of it.

Turning back to the Perfect, it is a consequence of the discussion to this point that Results and Resultants may be given in terms, not only of the events described in the verbal heads, but also of those that come in through modification or quantification. Some causal contexts will exemplify the situation. In (40), for example, it is not the fire's having burned out, but its having burned out slowly that causes the bricks to become warm:

(40)  The fire's having burned out slowly warmed the bricks.

and indeed the result of the fire's burning out—namely, no more fire—and the result of its burning out slowly—ambient heat—are intuitively different. If this is right, then we have further evidence that it is Perfect Aspect, and not the E-position in the head 'burn', upon which Tense operates.

## 9.3 Interactions with sequence of tense

I understand the phenomenon of sequence of tense in English to comprise anaphoric relations, optional or obligatory, between inflectional heads. The Tenses themselves express binary relations between events (more precisely, their actual times; but we abstract away from this detail for ease of exposition); and we assume the obvious relations of temporal priority and temporal inclusion for Past and Non-past. The periphrastic future 'will' is −Past, and 'would' is the +Past inflection of *will*. The +Past feature, I shall suppose, need not actually express the past, but may function so as to facilitate, in some way, the anaphoric connection. The ambiguity of (41) is a case in point:

(41)  John said that Mary was late.

(41) may be taken as a report of a past past-tense utterance, 'Mary was late' say, made by John; or a report of a past present-tense utterance, 'Mary is late'. In the former case, the speaker of (41) is attributing a content to John's speech

that places Mary as late prior to the time of that speech. The truth conditions of an utterance $u$ of (41) are then as in (42):

(42) [∃e<u] Say(John,^[∃e'<e] late(Mary,e'),e)

The anaphoric relation consists in the matching of the second coordinate of the embedded Tense with the first coordinate of the superordinate Tense. In the latter case, the speaker is attributing a content that places Mary's lateness at the time of that speech itself. The +Past feature is not interpreted as expressing priority <, but rather temporal inclusion ≈. The result is (43):

(43) [∃e<u] Say(John,^[∃e'≈e] late(Mary,e'),e)

In Chapter 5 I outlined a system for English sequence of tense that included only basic forms, in complement clauses and in relative clauses. The premises of the system, repeated here, are as follows:

- (Ø) The time of utterance is default in root clauses.
- (ii) Tenses are binary, expressing one of the three relations ≈, <, or >.
- (II) Anaphoric +Past is ambiguous (in English) between (a) facilitating anaphora, but carrying a −Past interpretation (B-past), and (b) expressing < (A-Past). The antecedent of a B-Past must be +Past, and the clause itself must be Stative.
- (III) −Past *in situ* cannot be anaphoric to +Past.
- (IV) Tenses in the C position of a complement clause are always anaphoric; movement of one copy of I to C is obligatory in these cases. The Tense in I and the Tense in C are both interpreted.

Details of the system as applied to the basic (non-aspectual) cases are given in Chapter 5. Here I enumerate some points that must be satisfied if the account of the Perfect as purely aspectual is to be retained, and offer some examples in support.

By (III) above, if the Present Perfect and the Future Perfect are as hypothesized −Past, then they must display the behavior characteristic of the simple Present and Future. The complement Present gives rise to the notorious double-access phenomenon, canonically illustrated by (44):

(44) John said that Mary is pregnant.

The complement Future places the temporal location of the subject's content in the future of the *speaker's* (not the subject's) speech, as in (45):

(45) John said that Mary will be pregnant.

Thus (45) has truth conditions as in (46) (note that as required by (IV) the Tense is interpreted twice over, once as anaphoric, and once as non-anaphoric):

(46)  [∃e<u] Say(John,^[∃e′>e] [Pregnant(Mary,e′) & e′>u],e)

The restriction on the quantifier in the content (complement) clause is of course redundant, as we have (if John speaks truly) the ordering e′>u>e, and so in particular e′>e. But for (44) it is not redundant, as we obtain (47):

(47)  [∃e<u] Say(John,^[∃e′≈e] [Pregnant(Mary,e′) & e′≈u],e)

so that the temporal content of the complement includes both the time of the subject's alleged speech and that of the speaker.

Transposing the scheme to Perfect complements, we examine (48) and (49):

(48)  John said that Mary has been pregnant.
(49)  John said that Mary will have been pregnant.

(48) should show double access, with the result or resultant state given in the complement as including the time of the subject's alleged utterance and the time of the speaker's. But 'pregnant' is a stative, hence implicates no result state; and the peculiar property of resultant states, that they are temporally unbounded, implies that, in contrast to (44), the non-anaphoric copy of the complement –Past has no work to do: if the alleged resultant state e′ temporally surrounds e, then it also surrounds u. With Result contexts things are different. Consider (50), for instance:

(50)  The mayor announced that he has signed the legislation.

Assertions such as (50) are proper on the day that the mayor did the signing, but (so I believe) not the next week, let alone after a longer lapse. But (51) will always be assertible:

(51)  The mayor announced that he signed the legislation.

Examples such as (50), then, do provide evidence that the complement Present Perfect is aspectual merely. As for the Future Perfect (49), we shall want to ensure that the context is purely temporal, and not the 'will' of 'assurance', whatever that may come to exactly.[6] Bearing that point in mind, and so rendering the truth conditions of (49) straightforwardly as in (52), we

---

[6] I have in mind cases such as, 'The sum of those digits will be a prime number', where there is no question of temporality.

have John reported as predicting a Resultant of Mary's being pregnant whose onset lies in the future of the speaker's report:

(52) $[\exists e<u]$ Say(John,$^\wedge[\exists RR(e')>e]$ [Pregnant(Mary,$e'$) & $RR(e')>u$],$e$)

Similarly for Result states. We may contrast Future Perfect complements above all with the 'future in the past' 'would', as in (53)–(54):

(53) John said that Bill would spill his coffee.

(54) John said that Bill will have spilled his coffee.

Turning now to complements in the Past Perfect, we have the possibility of an A-Past (where the Past retains its temporal interpretation) and a B-Past (where the complement is not interpreted as Past), together with the resultant or result interpretations of the Perfect. The A-Past together with a resultant interpretation is seen in (55):

(55) John said that Mary had once been happy.

The temporal relations as shown in (56) are appropriate, implying that the content of John's alleged speech placed the onset of the resultant state prior to that speech:

(56) $e<u\ldots[\ldots RR(e')<e$ & $RR(e')<u\ldots]$

But again we have redundancy, as the first embedded temporal location of $RR(e')$ implies the second. But result interpretations of the construction are in order as well, where there is no implication that the result state survives to the present. B-Past interpretations are then easily obtained, as for instance when one is telling a story in the middle of which one goes on as in (57):

(57) ... then John noticed that I had spilled my coffee...,

the reference time having been reset from the time of speech to some past time determined by the narrative. In this case too, I think, we can observe that the Perfect retains its interpretation: the story line (57) is appropriate only if, at the reference time, the coffee is in a spilled (not mopped-up) state.

We have seen that, where the effects can be semantically visible, the complement Perfects behave as expected on the general account summarized in (Ø)–(IV). However, as noted in Ogihara (1995) (also in Iatridou *et al.* (2005)), the Present Perfect does indeed often behave like a Past when it is superordinate. Consider (58):

(58) John has said that Mary was ill.

If (58) were a true Present, like (59) below, we would expect it to have a unique interpretation, that in which John is reported as having made a past-tense utterance, 'Mary was ill', or words to that effect.

(59)  John is saying that Mary was ill.

But (58) is in fact ambiguous as between reports of past-tense and present-tense utterances (between A-past and B-past, in terms of the classification (II) above). We must, then, have communication between the complement Past and the superordinate E-position in 'say', as in (60):

(60)  $[\exists e' \approx u]$ $[\exists e\colon R(e',e)]$ Say(John,$^\wedge[\exists e'' </\approx e]$ ill(Mary,$e''$),$e$)

with the choice between $<$ (A-Past) and $\approx$ (B-Past). Of course, a complement Present Perfect may be superordinate with respect to its own complement, as in (61):

(61)  John said that the mayor has made it widely known that he was ill.

The mayor's announcement could have been either present tense or past tense; but the content attributed to John may involve a present result.[7]

## 9.4 Shifted perfects

As Jespersen remarked in the passage I quoted above, the Present Perfect is incompatible with temporal adverbials such as 'yesterday' and 'in 1879'. In this section I offer a partial account of this fact in terms that are, if I read him correctly, rather close to those offered in Portner (2003); I also observe that the phenomenon persists under certain cases of sequence of tense, suggesting, again, that the aspectual properties of the Perfect are always visible.

---

[7] In an article that became known to me only after this paper was first in press, Kiparsky (2002: 8), citing earlier work by Declerk, observes that the B-Past disappears in what he calls 'resultative perfects'. Certainly, it disappears if the superordinate predicate is a straightforward activity or achievement predicate, as in (i) or (ii) say:

(i)  The president has realized that the economy was in bad shape.
(ii)  Mary has announced that John was leaving.

From the point of view taken here, these cases would be as expected, and the anomalous case would be the relative acceptability of the B-Past in (59) or (61). Kiparsky himself closely follows Reichenbach's system, and divides the English Perfect into various readings. If, however, it is right to suggest as above that the B-Past is only available because the lower Tense can 'see' the E-position in the superordinate 'say' (but not in 'realize' or 'announce'), then such division may not be necessary, even for these cases.

The question concerns first of all the generalization that governs the ungrammaticality in examples such as (62):

(62) *I have visited the museum yesterday/last year.

Pancheva and von Stechow (2004) suggest that the generalization is that, in English, the temporal adverbial must apply only to intervals that include the speech time. Thus in 'Alicia has danced this year', in their view, we intend the whole interval constituting this year up to and including the time of speech, and say that some dancing by Alicia lies temporally within this interval. As 'last year' or 'yesterday' exclude the time of speech, they are unsuitable. However, this cannot be entirely right, because of examples (of a sort that have not much been considered in the literature) such as (63) and (64):

(63) I have visited that museum in the past/before (now).

(64) I have been to Copenhagen twice, a long time ago.

An interval described as 'in the past' or 'before (now)' presumably cannot include the present; and the parenthetical 'a long time ago' is acceptable in (64). The first remark is no mere quibble, as Pancheva and von Stechow take the necessity of the English Present's overlapping the speech time as crucial in their account of the difference between English and, for example, German, which freely allows the Present Perfect with adverbials that exclude the time of speech. The second observation raises problems of its own, as the parenthetical in (64) must somehow be combined properly, without producing ungrammaticality. I shall not be considering these cases further here (but see footnote 10 below).

To fix matters more precisely, consider adverbials that, unlike 'yesterday', 'today', and 'in 1879', do not refer to precise periods of time, but describe matters more loosely. We obtain the partial classification shown in (65)–(66):

(65) Possible with the present perfect: 'recently', 'in the past', 'within/during the last week', 'lately', 'yesterday and today', 'from childhood'.

(66) Not possible with the Present Perfect: 'none too recently', 'in the distant past', 'long ago', 'then', 'during last week', 'awhile/a little while back'.

It appears that the predicates $P$ possible with the Present Perfect have the property that the past times (hence, times of past situations) of which they are true are *closed under temporal succession*; i.e., if $\tau < \tau'$ and $P(\tau)$, then $P(\tau')$, for all times $\tau$ before the speech time. Thus if Thursday is within the last week, then the Friday following it is as well; if $\tau$ is a past interval, and $\tau'$ is a past interval following it, $\tau'$ remains a past interval; and so on. But intervals more recent than intervals that are none too recent are some of them recent; so 'none too recent' is not closed under temporal succession. For the moment, then, we may put the condition down as (**P**):

(**P**)  *[e′≈u) & Perf(e′,e) & VP(e) & A(e)] if A is not closed under temporal succession.

I have been supposing that temporal predicates such as 'recently' are true of various sets of points (which may be intervals, or scattered, or even singletons). An alternative, the one I take to have been adopted by Pancheva and von Stechow, is to suppose that they pick out a more or less large period of past time—for 'recently', the recent past, as one says—so that my predicate 'recent (e)', which holds if the time τ(e) of e is recent, would be understood as τ(e)⊆ Recent Past. Evidently, so long as the temporal modifiers can be construed as referring to single intervals, the methods are equivalent.

To account for the properties of the English Perfect, Pancheva and von Stechow propose a 'competition model', which selects the Past over the Present Perfect in contexts where there is (in terms of the generalization (**P**)) a temporal gap between the times falling within the extension of the adverbial and the Present. They suggest that the distinction between English and other Germanic languages for which the puzzle arises, and those for which it does not arise, is correlated with the distinction between those that allow the equivalent of, e.g., 'John is here since noon' and those that do not; but the data here are somewhat obscure, as noted in Giorgi and Pianesi (1998a: 140). In what follows, I will offer a conjecture that is independent of questions of correlation, and says nothing of competition.

Consider first of all obviously unacceptable examples that constitute clashes of some sort between tense and modifying adverbial, such as (67):

(67)  John is here yesterday.

It will not suffice to observe that they are contradictory: lots of things are contradictory without being intuitively weird in the way that (67) is. Nor will it do to suggest that (67) is simply ungrammatical. Indeed, as we know that 'John is here' allows stretches of the present of arbitrary length, the contradictoriness of (67) is by no means obvious. Why, for instance, can I not make the inference in (68)?

(68)  Today there have been no more dinosaurs for a long time; therefore, yesterday there are no more dinosaurs.

An obvious in-between suggestion for (67) is that it has something of the status of a category mistake, an expression like 'blue concept', 'sleep furiously', or 'Wednesday is in bed'. But even this proposal fails to account for (68). The word 'yesterday', like 'today', admits extensions: in saying (69) I am not speaking just of the day preceding my speech, and it will be obvious to my hearers that this is so.

(69) Yesterday children obeyed their parents.

The above phenomena may, however, have an explanation of the sort associated above all with McTaggart (1908). In speech and thought, we set up present, past, and future. We may set them up in different ways, depending upon our interest; but however we do this they exclude one another. To quote from McTaggart:

> Past, present, and future are incompatible determinations. Every event must be one or the other, but no event can be more than one. This is essential to the meaning of the terms. (McTaggart (1908: 467))

In (67), by virtue of using the word 'yesterday', the situation of John's being here is said to be past; but then it is not *also* present. In this sense, (67) is a category mistake. Similarly in the conclusion of (68). It does no good that I have asserted in the premiss that there have not been any dinosaurs for a very long time; for *my very use* of 'yesterday' in the conclusion forces the situation of there not being any dinosaurs to be past, and that conflicts with my statement that it is present.

Supposing that the above conjecture concerning (67) and the like is on track, we may go further. In a routine Present Perfect such as (70), in virtue of the fact that 'recently' is closed under temporal succession, we note that both the situation $e$ of my visiting the museum and the onset of the resultant state $e'$ are recent:

(70) I have visited the museum recently.

But in the paradigm case (62), repeated here, supposing as we do that the visit $e$ is confined to the past, the onset of its resultant state $e'$ must also be so confined:

(62) *I have visited the museum yesterday.

(The first moment of the onset is the accumulation point of the time $\tau(e)$ of the visit $e$: on the assumption that 'yesterday' selects a closed interval, this point must belong to yesterday if $\tau(e)$ does.) Suppose that for a resultant (or result) state to be present requires that its onset be present. We then have a contradiction (in McTaggart's terms), or a category mistake induced by the triadic division of indexically given time: every situation is past, present, or future, and none is any two of these.

I hasten to note that the contradiction in question is not some formal contradiction: the negation of (62), 'I have not visited the museum yesterday', is just as weird a sentence as (62) itself. Perhaps in part for this reason, Portner (2003) (to whose view the suggestion in the text is perhaps closest) holds that his rather similar condition (which does not, however, involve resultant states) is 'pragmatic', as he puts it. On the view advanced here it is not at all pragmatic (it attaches to the expressions in question in virtue of their linguistic form). Rather, the conflict arises because, in English, the trichotomy of past, present, and future applies so as to disallow the expression of quantification over or reference to a resultant state that is both present (because of the Tense) and, in virtue of the explicit use of the adverbial 'yesterday', or another that is not closed under temporal precedence, also past. The restriction thus comes in addition to the fundamental, and presumably universal, restriction that rules out 'John is here yesterday' and the like.

Of course, none of the above, even if correct, shows that competition models of the sort suggested by Pancheva and von Stechow are wrong. It is worth noting, however, that the puzzle does not persist under sequence of tense applied to Past Perfects, either with relative clause objects or with complement clauses. Thus consider (71):

(71) John met a man today who had spilled his coffee yesterday/two days ago.

The Past Perfect (like English 'would') requires a licenser (which need not be tense anaphora, as shown by counterfactual contexts). In (71) the only licenser around is the superordinate Past, and the complement adverbial yesterday compels a B-Past ('shifted') interpretation, applying to the Result state. So the second temporal coordinate of the complement INFL is anaphoric to the first coordinate of the superordinate INFL, giving (in relevant detail) (72):

(72) $[\exists e < u] \ldots [\exists e' \approx e][\exists e''] \ [R(e',e'') \ \& \ \text{spill}(e'') \ \& \ \text{yesterday/two days ago}(e'')]$

But now, one can have also (73):

(73) John met a man today who spilled his coffee yesterday/two days ago.

so that (71) and (73) are in free variation. It's not clear, however, why, on a competition model, the competition between the Present Perfect and the Past does not extend to this case.[8]

---

[8] As noted above, Pancheva and von Stechow intend their account to mark the distinction between languages for which (i) and (ii) differ:

(i) I live in London since 1995. (*English, OK German etc.)
(ii) I have lived in London since 1995. (OK English)

We may propose that the account sketched above is compatible with the fact that (71) is acceptable. It is true that, just as the onset of the resultant state in (62) is said to lie in the past of the time of visiting the museum, so the onset of the result state in the relative clause in (71) is said to lie in the past of $\tau(e)$, the time of meeting: the cases are formally identical, except that $\tau(e)$ has replaced $\tau(u)$. But $\tau(e)$ is itself past from the point of view of the whole assertion, to which the division past, present, future applies. Hence the adverbials in the relative clause are not restricted to those that, within the temporal perspective provided by that clause, are closed under temporal succession.

Similar remarks would apply to cases with complement clauses, as in (74):

(74)  Mary said yesterday that John had visited the museum two days ago.

Mary, being a competent speaker of English, could not have said, 'John has visited the museum yesterday'. But if she said, 'John visited the museum yesterday', then I can report her as in (74) nonetheless.

Despite the absence of a shifted puzzle with the Past Perfect, there is further evidence that distinguishes it from the embedded Past. The B-Past or interpretation of an embedded Past is (as noted above) generally only possible with statives. Thus Giorgi and Pianesi (1998a) remark that interpretations of the like of (75), where the complement is a relative Present rather than a relative Past, are not in general possible even for languages where the bare Verb in the Present (unlike English) can be used to report current goings-on:

(75)  John said that Mary left.

That is, (75) cannot be made true in virtue of John's past utterance of 'Mary leaves', or (in English) 'Mary is leaving'. But the Past Perfect under sequence of tense does indeed admit B-past interpretations, as in (76):

(76)  John said that Mary had left.

---

But *this* difference persists in the Past Perfect:

(iii)   I met a man yesterday who lived in London (ever) since 1995.

(iv)   I met a man yesterday who had lived in London (ever) since 1995.

at least in the sense that (iv) is completely natural English, and (iii) is not. But then the absence of any, or any obvious, contrast between (71) and (73) cannot simply consist in a neutralization of the competition between Perfect and Past. Of course, the above observation itself doesn't provide an alternative account of the cross-linguistic distinction that Pancheva and von Stechow are rightly after; but it does suggest that their competition parameter alone is not adequate to capture it.

(John made a past Present Perfect utterance); which is natural enough if, as I am suggesting here, the Perfect, in virtue of moving the application of INFL from the underlying situation, expressed by the main predicate, to the result or resultant state, produces a stative. A true preterit would not be expected to do that.

I conclude this discussion by presenting, first, a diagrammatic representation of cases such as (62) on the view taken here, and then observing a case that exemplifies the persistence of the properties of the Present Perfect under sequence of tense. The truth conditions of (62) are as in (77):

(77)  $[\exists e' \approx u][\exists e]$ [RR($e'$,$e$) & I visit the museum($e$) & Yesterday($e$)]

As the visit $e$ was Yesterday, $\tau(e)$ is confined to that day, and the onset of the resultant $e'$ of $e$ is also there. By using *yesterday*, one puts all of yesterday as PAST. As the tense is −Past, $\tau(e')$ is PRESENT; but its onset is PAST, and this is a category mistake, as seen in (78):

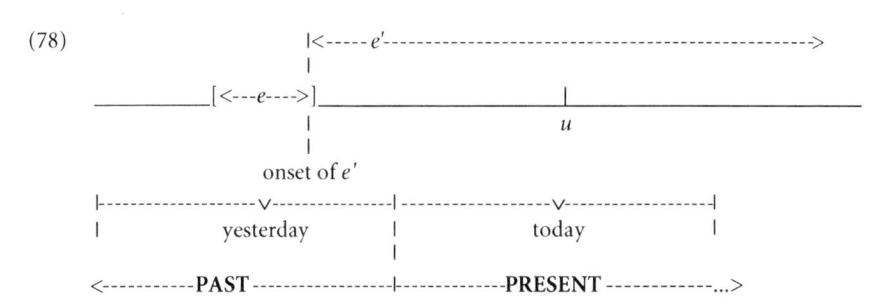

(78)
```
                    |<----- e'---------------------------------->
                    |
        [<---e--->] |
_____|_____|_____
                    |                u
                    |
               onset of e'
|-------------------v----------------|-------------------v----------------|
|              yesterday             |                today              |
                                     |
<----------PAST-------------------+-------------PRESENT-----------...>
```

Replacement of 'yesterday' with 'recently', however, gives (79):

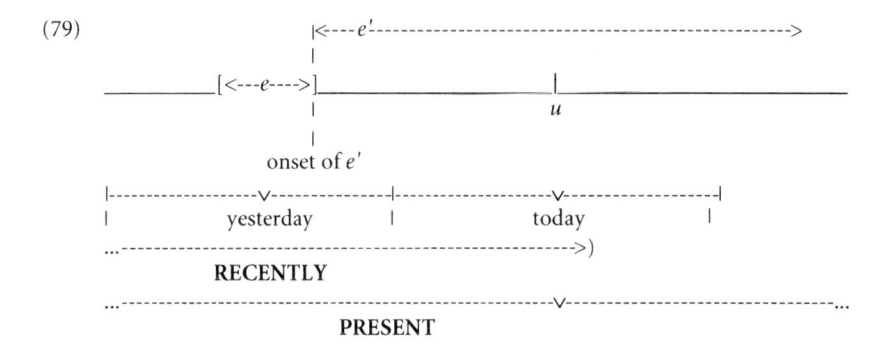

(79)
```
                    |<---e'----------------------------------->
                    |
        [<---e--->] |
_____|_____|_____
                    |                u
                    |
               onset of e'
|-------------------v----------------|-------------------v----------------|
|              yesterday             |                today              |
...----------------------------------------------------->)
              RECENTLY
...----------------------------------------v-----------------------------...
                              PRESENT
```

The visit $e$ is concluded before the utterance $u$, and so the onset $e'$ of $e$ is before $u$ as well. The adverbial predicate is closed under temporal succession, so that the RECENT period can be as in (79). Nothing prevents the PRESENT from subsuming a period that includes the onset of $e'$.

The general conditions on English sequence of tense allow a −Past as well as a +Past complement to be anaphoric to a −Past superordinate INFL, as in (80):

(80)  John will say that Mary is happy.

In (80) the speaker may predict a future, present-tense, utterance by John. Similarly for (81):

(81)  In his speech next year, the president will say that the legislation he will sign next week is working well.

As for +Past complements, we have examples like those in (82)–(84):

(82)  John will say two days hence that Mary was happy that day.

(83)  John will say two days hence that Mary was happy today.

(84)  John will say two days hence that Mary was happy the day before.

Replacing the complement Past with the Present Perfect, we have first of all (85)–(86):

(85)  John will say two days hence that Mary has been happy that day.

(86)  John will say two days hence that Mary has been happy today.[9]

But also (87):

(87)  *John will say two days hence that Mary has been happy the day before.

I believe that (87) represents an anaphoric or shifted violation of the conditions on the Present Perfect. Under sequence of tense it will have the truth conditions shown in (88):

(88)  $[\exists e > u]$ {Say (John,$^\wedge[\exists e' \approx e]$ $[\exists e'']$ {$RR(e',e'')$ & Happy(Mary,$e''$) & $e'$ on the day before the day of $e$],$e$) & $e$ is two days after the day of $u$}

---

[9] This example is, I think, comparable to cases such as (i), discussed in Higginbotham (2002a) (Chapter 5 above):

(i)  John will say that Mary is dancing well.

in that they become the more natural the more one considers that John already believes the complement, at the time of saying (i).

The speaker's present is unaffected; but we may suppose that the tense anaphora sets up a relative past and present as shown in (89):

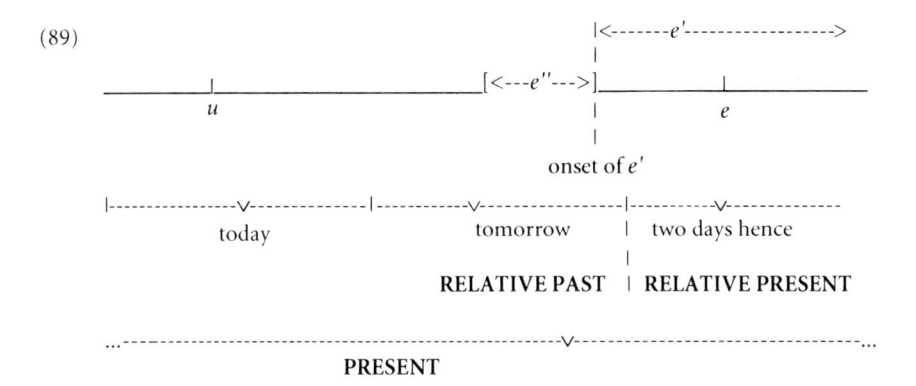

(89)
```
                                    |<-------e'------------------>
                                    |
_____|_____[<---e"--->]_____|_____
         u                          |                e
                                    |
                                onset of e'

|----------------v---------------|-------------v-----------------|----------v--------------
               today                       tomorrow              |   two days hence
                                                                 |
                                                       RELATIVE PAST | RELATIVE PRESENT

...--------------------------------------------------v-----------------------------------...
                                PRESENT
```

Briefly: because 'the day before' stands to 'two days hence' just as 'yesterday' stands to 'today', the condition (P) on the Present Perfect is violated: 'the day before' is not closed under temporal succession.

Very well, assuming the datum (87). However, at least one speaker of British English with whom I have discussed these matters does not particularly object to (87). I noted above, as many have observed, that the 'Perfect Puzzle' disappears with the Past Perfect in (74) and the like. It may be that for some speakers the puzzle disappears altogether under tense anaphora; in other words, that even though the reported utterance in (87) could not have been a Present Perfect (John is not predicted to say, 'Mary has been happy yesterday'), its content can be reported indirectly with that form. A further, possibly interfering, factor is that the Perfect Puzzle itself can be attenuated, as illustrated above in (64). Other illustrations may include (90) and the like:

(90)   John is not happy now, but he HAS been happy, long ago.[10]

---

[10] Thus compare (i) to (ii) (my judgements):

(i)    *John will say in three years that Mary has been happy the year before.
(ii)   (?)John will say in three years that Mary HAS been happy, the year before.

or with the stress pattern and contraction as in (iii):

(iii)  *John will say in three years that Mary's been HAPPY the year before.

I find (iii) out of the question, (ii) somewhat marginal.

Finally, I note that the context (87) does limit the ways in which the day in the complement clause can be designated; in particular, it cannot be designated with a speaker's Future indexical, as in (91):

(91) \*\*John will say two days hence that Mary has been happy tomorrow.

For some further discussion and references, see Chapter 6.

## 9.5 Conclusion

In this chapter I have examined the scope of the Result Perfect in English, observing *en route* that, quite apart from bringing in such objects as result and resultant states, any account that takes positions for events and situations as implicated in the semantics of human first languages must find them in a variety of causal and other contexts, and even in adverbial and quantificational expressions. It is well of course to look at individual and detailed examples; but the overall picture is that of a very general hypothesis, the evidence for which must rest on a manifold of consequences.[11]

---

[11] Versions of this chapter, or of parts or longer discussions related to it, were presented at the Paris conference on Tense and Modality, December 2005, and later at Kyoto University and Sendai University Japan; MIT; the University of London; University College Dublin; and the Scuola Normale Superiore, Pisa, Italy. I am grateful to the audiences at these events, and further to Jacqueline Guéron and Jacqueline Lecarme for a number of comments.

# 10

# Competence with Demonstratives

## 10.1 Introduction

Some of the simplest uses of language involve two distinct phases. We set things up, by actions or by words, or simply take advantage of the local scene and the hearer's expectations of us; and having set them up we make, in Wittgenstein's words, our 'moves in the language game'. What we *say*, in the most intuitive sense of that term, is constituted by the move we make, the setup being given; but what we let on that we believe, and intend others to believe that we believe, encompasses much more. (For this reason, it is easy to be misleading without lying.) Because the setting-up phase generally involves a perspective, individual or shared, of one or another party upon an object, or upon the interpretation of a predicate or other referential device, and because the same linguistic or other devices set up the reference or extension in ways that exploit the particular features of that setting, we cannot in general, having moved to a different setting, preserve reference and perspective simultaneously. There is a tension, then, when we attempt to express, from where we are, what a person says or thinks or wonders about from where she is, or was, or will be. Her statements or thoughts are structured in terms of her perspective, which yielded a reference according to linguistic and perhaps other communicative principles open and common to all. In our different setting, all crucial features of reference must be preserved: for the way we put her statements or thoughts must at least admit the same evaluation for truth. But then something of her perspective will be lost.

Suppose that Joan thinks, 'Should I go home for Thanksgiving?' Then she wonders whether she should go home for Thanksgiving. The transition I just made, from quotation to indirect reporting, loses the perspective that Joan had on herself when she wondered about herself in the first person. Not all of her perspective is lost, however. The word 'home', when used as a bare noun and with specific reference, always refers to the home of a particular object of the discourse. Mary's thought showed cross-reference, for she was wondering whether to go to *her* home. This cross-reference is preserved in my indirect report. But that does not help with expression of the first-person perspective.

That the first-person perspective on herself was the perspective that Joan actually had might be indicated parenthetically. I could say that Joan wonders whether she (thinking of herself in the first person) should go home for Thanksgiving. The parenthetical, however, is not a constituent part of what Joan wonders; the information it contains belongs to the setting-up phase, and not to her thought.

The above remarks are impressionistic, and are meant to be. I will argue, nevertheless, that the impression of conflict between the aim of preserving perspective and the aim of preserving reference, induced by the distinction between those aspects of language use that belong to the setting-up phase and those that belong to the phase of saying things, survives under scrutiny, and is even inevitable given the principles that govern our languages.

What I am calling loss of perspective is seen not only in respect of context-dependent expressions, but also in respect of all elements that are contextually anchored, though not expressed overtly. For the special case of ellipsis, we can supply the words that might have been added but were not, as when 'It's raining' is evaluated with respect to the local scene, or as a response to the question, 'What's the weather in Milan?' In the latter case the speaker surely thought, and intended to be understood as asserting, that it was raining in Milan, so that the missing element can be supplied as a constituent of what was said; and in the former the speaker surely thought that it was raining (as she would put it) *here*, so that the intended location that needs to be supplied for evaluation is recovered through an indexical, reducing the case to the previous problem of context-dependent expressions. However, many cases where missing elements are contextually supplied cannot be construed as elliptical, if only because there need be no particular form of words that what is missing is elliptical *for*. A simple example is that of the incomplete definite description or quantificational noun phrase, where the range of the nominal is restricted, say, to objects on the local scene, as in (1):

(1) Each table is covered with books.

The speaker may have intended no particular restriction, but the range of the quantifier may be confined to the local tables just the same. When those same tables are not part of the local scene, something more than the statement itself must be supplied to indicate which were the tables said to be covered with books. Whatever that is, it is foreign to the speaker's original content.

Ellipsis aside, then, the blank spaces whose completion is essential to providing truth conditions, hence content, are as problematic as indexical expressions themselves: one cannot in general preserve both their reference and the salient contextual features upon which it originally depended.

Of the circumstances in which reference and perspective come apart, I spoke above in terms of tension and conflict. I believe that these terms are justified, and not only from a theoretical point of view. A very substantial amount of philosophical thought and ingenuity have gone into relieving the conflict, for instance by packing into indirect discourse, and reports of propositional attitudes and epistemic states, parameters that, taken together, will allow the simultaneous linguistic expression of the now-remote perspective and the reference it there, or then, or under such and such circumstances secured; or alternatively into the construction of a means outside common speech for getting at what we say, or anyway let on, that people say and think.

I will argue here that the conflict is unavoidable, and that nothing even in principle can resolve it. But ordinary linguistic practice, and therefore our linguistic competence in virtue of which we are able to participate in the practice, takes the conflict into account, and gives us the means to live with it. We do convey perspective through the use of language; but we do not, and cannot, do it by saying what it is. Thus we have no difficulty in grasping what Joan wondered when she wondered whether she should go home for Thanksgiving; and we do this because we know, and it is common knowledge that, there is a first-person perspective that one has on oneself when using the word 'I' in accordance with the rules of the language, and we take it that Joan has such a means to refer to herself, and did so in wondering whether she should go home for Thanksgiving.

We may think of the field of reference as the points in a space, and the perspectives as demonstratively established, and often egocentric, coordinate systems for the points. Reference to the same point from different perspectives is not a one-shot affair, but involves a general transformation of coordinate systems, mapping one entire set of perspectives into another. Moreover, the family of all sets of perspectives may be so organized that any one can be transformed into any other by a general routine, known to the speakers of a language, and known by them to be known to other speakers. Such mutual knowledge is part of linguistic competence, or so I will maintain.

In the remainder of this chapter I will endeavor to substantiate the views just advanced, through a consideration of linguistic competence with demonstrative and indexical constructions, and the semantics of complement clauses, and besides analyzing a well-known typical case I will try to support the metaphor of transformations of coordinate systems. If these views are on the right track, then the notion of semantic competence—knowledge of meaning—should be seen as including the principles governing demonstrative and indexical expressions.

## 10.2 Normal forms for demonstrative reference and truth

In 1974, Tyler Burge gave a powerful and persuasive account of the place of demonstrative constructions in theories of truth for historically given natural languages.[1] I begin with two essential features of this account.

Consider a simple demonstrative utterance, say (2), uttered while conspicuously pointing to a dog:

(2)  This is a dog.

A theory of truth for our language should establish about (2) the truth conditions common to all utterances of its type, independently of how the reference of 'this' is secured. The type of the utterance is a syntactic structure $\Sigma$, and so it should establish (3):

(3)  If $u$ is an utterance of $\Sigma$, then $u$ is true iff $\alpha$ is a dog.

where '$\alpha$' holds a place for the reference of the demonstrative. Furthermore, the account should say what is common to all the demonstrative uses of 'this'. The latter is accomplished by relativizing the truth condition to the speaker's act of reference (accomplished by pointing in the example given, but of course not confined to that). The result is the universal closure with respect to $u$, $x$, and $s$ of (4):

(4)  If $u$ is an utterance of $\Sigma$, and the speaker $s$ of $u$ refers with $s$'s utterance of 'this' therein to $x$ and nothing else, then $u$ is true iff $x$ is a dog.

The first feature of the account just sketched, and adapted from Burge's original article, is that truth conditions as in the biconditional consequent of (4) show places on the right, marked there by '$\alpha$', that do not appear on the left. The format is therefore radically different not only from that for languages without indexical expressions, where the right side of the biconditional is always a closed sentence, but also from that advanced in the truth-at-an-index accounts of truth conditions for sentences with demonstratives, which if put in terms of utterances would have been approximately as in (5):

(5)  If $u$ is an utterance of $\Sigma$, then $u$ is true at the index $\alpha$ iff $\alpha$ is a dog.

Truth-at-an-index accounts generally stem from Montague (1968), and were pursued by a number of authors, including especially Lewis (1970). In these

---

[1] An important part of this account is due independently to Scott Weinstein (Weinstein (1974)); but Weinstein's note was not, and was not intended to be, more than a demonstration that demonstrative reference could be accommodated within a standard view of a theory of truth.

accounts the truth predicate is exactly as relative as there are places to be filled by demonstrative referents in the statement of truth conditions. The development in Kaplan (1977), an advance in several respects, is not essentially different in this one: truth is relativized to possible worlds *w* and contexts *c*, and in the case of (2) we will have (6):

(6)  Σ is true in the context *c* in *w* iff the reference of 'this' in *c* is a dog in *w*.[2]

The second feature of Burge's account, exemplified in the passage from (3) to (4), is the construal of the position marked by 'α' as occupied by a bound variable in the full statement of truth conditions. The strategy generalizes across demonstratives and indexical expressions, and what is more across the non-elliptical elements that serve to restrict the range of a predicate. In respect of (1), for example, we will have (7):

(7)  If *u* is an utterance of the syntactic structure for (1) by *s*, and *s* confines the range of the utterance of 'table' therein to tables *x* such that $X(x)$, and refers with the present tense as used therein to the time $\tau(u)$ of *u* itself, then *u* is true iff for each *x* such that $X(x)$, *x* is covered with books at $\tau(u)$.

I will call a statement like (7) a *normal form* for semantic theory.[3] The general structure is as in (8):

(8)  If *u* is an utterance of Σ by *s*, and $\varphi(s,\Sigma,s,x,X)$, then *u* is true iff $\psi(u,\Sigma,s,x,X)$.

where *x* and *X* are objectual and predicate parameters, respectively.

The construction of normal forms for any substantial piece of an actual human language is a theoretical matter. More than this, however, even the successful presentation of normal forms for individual sentences, presupposing the lexicon of non-indexical words, does not of itself answer the obvious question how the semantics of indexical elements is to be stated. Borrowing a terminology from David Kaplan (from his unpublished Gareth Evans Memorial Lecture, Oxford, 1995), let us broadly divide the linguistic pieces of an utterance into those with *meanings*, and those with *rules of use*. Ordinary nouns and verbs have meanings (which may nevertheless be contextually variable, for example along dimensions of strictness—recall J.L. Austin's question whether France is hexagonal). Words like 'this' do not have meanings, but have rules of use that are as much common coin as meanings are,

---

[2] Kaplan's formulation speaks of sentences in contexts rather than utterances, but contexts will be discriminated sufficiently finely that the utterance (if there is one) will be determined from the sentence and the context.

[3] In this I continue the terminology in Higginbotham (1988).

which specify how they are to be employed in setting up an utterance to be evaluated for truth or otherwise appraised.

I shall suppose that rules of use for words, like rules of use for tools and home appliances, are stated in imperatival form, as for example in (9)–(10):

(9) 'this N' is to be used to refer to proximate, salient objects satisfying N.

(10) The periphrastic future 'will' is to be used to restrict times to those (of some interval) following the time of *u*.

There is of course a distinction between expressions that are truly demonstrative as in (9) and those that are merely indexical, as in (10): the speaker has some latitude about what to refer to with 'this N', but none whatever about the periphrastic future, apart from limiting its extent. But the distinction follows from the form of the rule of use itself, together with the fact that it is common knowledge that it is the rule of use; for insofar as the rule fixes the contribution of the expression in all contexts, it will be taken in any given context as making as determinate a contribution as the rule prescribes. We know that there may be many proximate, salient objects satisfying N, even in a given context, and equally that there is just one stretch of time following any *u*. Hence 'this N' is demonstrative, but the future tense more nearly indexical.

The first person is purely indexical, at least on the assumption that an utterance has just one speaker. So the rule of use for it is elementary:

(11) 'I' is to be used to refer to the speaker of *u* (and only in nominative case positions).

The use of a word under a rule of use is grasped as signifying that a certain act is taking place, because referring to a thing with a word is an act. But of course the utterance of the word cannot signify that the act *is* taking place. There cannot be a word signifying that the object referred to is in fact proximate and salient, or that the speaker believes it to be, or believes himself to have referred to something proximate and salient. Donald Davidson pointed out in Davidson (1979) that a hypothetical assertion-sign, signifying that the speaker actually is, or believes himself to be, making an assertion, would once admitted immediately be used on stage, where it signifies no such thing. Similarly, a sign that one was actually or anyway believed oneself to be referring to a proximate and salient object would leave no room for the actor to say, 'Is that my old friend Mary?' while gazing offstage left at nothing in particular.[4]

---

[4] Kaplan's distinction suggests that the imperative mood, like an indexical, is associated with a rule of use, rather than a meaning. If so, then imperative sentences would not have truth conditions,

## 10.3 Complement clauses

Having assembled the elements of Burge's account of demonstrative reference, and having somewhat generalized it, we may take the consequences that substantiate the impressionistic distinction between the setting-up phase and the performance phase of a typical utterance. According to the account, all demonstrative and indexical reference, including the unstated restrictions on a predicate, flows from rules of use and belongs entirely to the setting-up phase, so that the content of the rules does not enter the truth conditions of what is said. This consequence agrees with Kaplan's (1977) discussion of demonstratives and indexicals as referring rigidly across counterfactual situations. That demonstrative reference belongs to the setting-up phase is not a reflection of rigidity, or an equivalent formulation of it, but explains it.

It follows also, given the split of the lexicon into items with meanings and items with rules of use, that we are generally bound to lose the perspectives of those whose sayings or thoughts we report indirectly. Once (2) is embedded, as in (12), and we put its truth conditions into normal form, nothing is left of the demonstrative but its reference:

(12) Mary wonders whether this is a dog.

If circumstances are favorable, I may conspicuously indicate to my hearer that the perspective on the basis of which I call her attention to the object of which I am saying that Mary wonders whether it is a dog is the very perspective that (I believe) Mary had on it when she thought to herself, 'Is that a dog, I wonder?' ('Look at it from over here, and you'll see why Mary wonders whether this is a dog'). In these cases, we may think of the act of reference as carried out in the setting-up phase, not of the whole of (12), but rather within the complement clause. But to examine the possibilities more closely, it will be necessary to formulate the truth conditions for such clauses.

I will assume here without argument an account of the reference of complement clauses that I have defended elsewhere (Higginbotham (1986), (1991a), and (2006b)): they refer to their own syntactic structures, understood as if the speaker uttered them.[5] Let $\Sigma$ be the syntactic structure for 'snow is white'. Then 'Bill Clinton believes that snow is white' is true just in case Bill Clinton believes $\Sigma$, understood as it would be were it an utterance of mine, where what it is for it to be so understood is for the conditions for its truth to

---

although they may have (much more complicated) compliance conditions, depending upon what the form was being used to do.

[5] This way of putting the proviso about how they are to be understood is due to Burge (1978).

be known as I know them.[6] Syntactic structures can be understood as having objects other than words as constituents, so that quantification into the standard contexts is not problematic. What we say are words, but we admit syntactic structures with objects in some positions, as in (13):

(13)   [[Bill Clinton] ['is $F$']]

containing the person Bill Clinton in the subject position, and we stipulate that the truth conditions as apprehended by the competent speaker are that Bill Clinton be among the objects of which 'is $F$' is true; and similarly for other categories of expressions.

Suppose that we conceive the act of reference to the dog (call him 'Rex') by 'this' in (12) to be part of the setting-up of the whole of (12). Then the wonderment attributed to Mary concerns (14):

(14)   [[Rex] ['is a dog']]

understood as if the speaker had said it. So to understand (14) is to know of the dog Rex that (14) is true if and only if he is a dog. Thus the target statements for utterances of syntactic structures with demonstratives will contain objects, and elements in the range of second-order variables, in positions where names and predicates would go in structures made up only of words, and understanding these statements will be knowing about those objects and the second-order referents that the structures are true just in case they satisfy some target condition. But now it follows that whether the act of reference were part of the setting-up of the whole of (12) or only of its complement clause, no difference would ensue; the perspective that the speaker uses and the hearer grasps will not except by accident be any part of what Mary is said to be wondering about.

The liberty granted by the account of demonstrative reference in terms of normal forms as discussed above, to construe the act of reference as taking place with respect to a whole utterance or merely with respect to its complement clause, therefore makes no difference in respect of the content contributed by that clause. This consequence may underscore the point that Kaplan's generalizations follow from the theory of the truth conditions of utterances of sentences with demonstrative elements, as given by the rules of use for

---

[6] More strictly, I assume that the speaker knows, and expects the hearer to know, a target statement of truth conditions reflecting semantic competence. (Such statements are not in general trivial or 'disquotational'.) In general, the hearer understands $\Sigma$ if he knows that it is true if and only if $p$, where that statement is the target. To understand this attribution of knowledge one must understand the target for '$\Sigma$ is true if and only if $p$', say that it is true if and only if $q$, but having the knowledge and understanding the attribution of it are different things.

those elements and the normal forms for the theory of truth and linguistic competence.

## 10.4 Coordinate transformations

Consider the egocentric coordinate system for days:

> ... 2 days ago, yesterday, today, tomorrow, 2 days hence, ...

It is the whole-number sequence whose zero point, today, changes with the day. We regularly use elements from one point in the sequence to refer to days that those whom we report would refer to with another point, as in (15), as said by me on Sunday:

(15) Mary said on Friday that she would leave yesterday, but she didn't leave then.

As I have noted elsewhere (Higginbotham (1994a)), Gareth Evans, in response to John Perry's thesis that indexicals supply only a reference and no Fregean sense, suggested that words like 'yesterday' are understood with what Evans called a 'completing sense'; and Perry in turn has responded to Evans that the completing sense of 'yesterday' in (15) diverges from that of the corresponding word, 'tomorrow', that was no doubt used by Mary, so that the account is false to the Fregean semantics of indirect discourse and attitude reports (Evans (1981); Perry (1993)). But I argued also that neither a completing sense in Evans's sense, nor a view of indexicals as lacking sense, was warranted by the facts; rather, we count the embedded clause in (15) as faithful to Mary's speech when she said on Friday, 'I will leave tomorrow', because we presuppose that all parties to the discourse know and use the egocentric coordinate system. Evans and Perry are both right in a way; but neither has distinguished between senses and rules of use known to the speaker. Given the distinction, we have that what is required to understand 'yesterday' is not a completing Fregean sense as in Evans, but rather a rule of use that not only locates that day as prior to the day of thinking or speaking, but also embeds it as part of the above coordinate system to which it belongs. Conversely, Perry's response to Evans fails to note that my perspective on Saturday when I said (15), although not the same as Mary's when she spoke, is transformable into that perspective by sliding 'today' back two notches, thus superimposing her 'today' onto my 'two days ago', and her 'tomorrow' onto my 'yesterday'.

The example (15) carries another moral, I believe: it is by no means necessary to suppose that my 'yesterday' goes proxy for, or carries in addition to its reference, any imagined replacement such as in (16):

(16) Mary said on Friday that she would leave the day after that, but she didn't leave then.

For one thing, the content of my 'then', which is anaphoric to the embedded 'yesterday', is just what it would be if I had said 'yesterday' itself. For another, we should miss the point that when Mary said 'tomorrow' it is not as if she said 'the day after this one' (indicating a day), but rather as if she said 'the day after today', using a purely indexical expression; so the replacement gets us no closer to Mary's own perspective.

I conclude that the transformation of coordinates exemplified by this simple example is the crucial element involved in the conveyance of perspective. But other cases are not so simple, and may have to be configured as they arise.

## 10.5 Puzzles of perspective

We have been considering complement clauses as they are used to classify acts of speech and states of mind, broadly speaking, thus including speech acts and epistemic states where the truth or falsehood of the complement is presupposed. The states and acts themselves are assumed to have whatever content they have, and our questions have concerned the extent to which our classifications can be faithful to that content, given that the perspective on the reference in the state or original speech may under the situation in which the classification is to be made yield a different reference, or none, and that the reference figuring in the content may allow indication only by means foreign to the original.

I will concentrate on just one of the many puzzles and conundrums that have figured in discussion, due to Mark Richard (Richard (1983)). *A* is talking on the telephone to *B*, whom *A* knows well. *A* is in a telephone booth on one side of Elm Street, and sees on the other side a woman in another telephone booth. *A* sees also that a steamroller is bearing down on her, and is of course horror-stricken to see that she is in such danger. *A* does not know it, but the person in the booth is *B*. Describing the situation over the telephone, *A* may well say (17):

(17) I believe she is in danger.

*B*, who can see the other side of Elm Street and the man in the telephone booth there, observes his panicky behavior and guesses, correctly, that he thinks she is in danger. If *B* were to say (18):

(18) The man watching me thinks I'm in danger.

she would speak truly. Therefore, if *A* were to say, addressing *B*, (19):

(19)  The man watching you believes you are in danger.

*A* would also speak truly. But as a matter of fact if *A* were to say

(20)  I am the man watching you.

he would also speak truly. Putting equals for equals in (19), we have that (21) is true as said by *A*:

(21)  I believe you are in danger.

But if *B* were to ask *A*, 'Do you think I'm in danger?' then *A* would respond, correctly, 'No, I don't think you're in danger.' Contradiction.

The response to the puzzle suggested by Richard (1990: 190 ff.) and by Mark Crimmins in Crimmins (1992: 29–32 and 164) is that more should be put into the content of what is said and would be understood than is given by the words. (Views of this type can be traced at least to Schiffer (1977); see also Schiffer (1987).) There are a number of technical points connected with Crimmins's and Richard's views, and somewhat different treatments are suggested in Salmon (1986), Higginbotham (1991a), and others. But all of these have in common the idea that we should understand (17) and (21) relative to different perspectives (or 'modes of presentation'), taking them up in the semantics as if the perspectives occurred where the indexicals sit.[7]

Abstracting from the details of the various presentations, observe that *A* would speak falsely were he to say (22):

(22)  I believe that [the woman I am talking to] is in danger.

where what appears in the square brackets—the parenthetical of my discussion above—has replaced the simple 'you'. But *A* would speak truly were he to say either (23) or (24):

(23)  I believe that [the woman across the street from me] is in danger.

(24)  The man watching you believes that [the woman across the street from him] is in danger.

If we understand the passage from (19) to (21) as shifting the context so that the second-person pronoun is a proxy for, or invokes in addition to its

---

[7] Similarly, for many discussions including Richard and Crimmins, for comparable issues involving proper names.

reference, the square-bracketed constituents, then we can see why the substitution licensed by (20) should alter our judgement.

However exactly the technical details go, all is well under the rewriting envisaged: no contradiction with intuition ensues. There is a further point to be noted in connection with Richard's ingenious example, which will be taken up further below. Every instance of (25) must be true in $A$'s speech:

(25)   The man watching you believes that $p \leftrightarrow$ I believe that $p$.

Suppose that $B$ actually says (18) to $A$, and $A$ suspends judgement about whether $B$ really is in danger, or the man across the street from her is panicking unnecessarily. Then (24) is as true as before, but (26) is false, or perhaps anomalous:

(26)   I believe that [the woman across the street from him] is in danger.

The reason is that the pronoun 'him' is functioning as a bound variable in (24), but not in (26). There is no contradiction with (25), since the principle holds only for closed sentences, not open sentences. Preserving cross-reference gives the true (23). Obliterating it by a further substitution taken from the perspective $A$ has from $B$ gives (27):

(27)   I believe that [the woman across the street from the man watching you] is in danger.

which is false. Preservation of cross-reference is therefore essential, and we must distinguish

$$\text{For } x=a, a \text{ believes that} \ldots x \ldots$$

from

$$a \text{ believes that} \ldots a \ldots$$

even where '$a$' is the indexical 'I'.[8]

Returning to the main theme, we have observed that transforming the clauses by substituting perspective for indexical removes the counterintuitive or paradoxical appearances. I refer to this as the *substitution* strategy for

---

[8] I believe that this distinction is at work in the intuitions underlying what David Lewis has called *de se* interpretations of the first person (Lewis (1979)). At the time of writing, the point of view defended here seemed to me incompatible with there being such an interpretation, since it was incompatible with there being any more to the first person than the elementary rule of use. I now think my earlier view was incorrect; see Chapter 12 below.

removing the puzzles.[9] The strategy, if correct, must reflect what we do and intend with language, clarifying the rational basis for our intuitive judgements. An alternative strategy, due to Stalnaker (1981), is to evaluate *A*'s and *B*'s actual or potential utterances as they would be evaluated if their beliefs were true. It is part of the story above that *A* believes he is not the man watching *B*, and that *B* is not the woman in the telephone booth across the street from him. In a possible world in which these beliefs are true there are four persons, and two sets of street-opposite telephone booths (and two steamrollers). Let *B*′ different from *B* be the woman across the street from *A*, let *A*′ different from *A* be the man across the street from *B*, and let us preserve the steamroller scenario as before. Then *A*'s 'she' refers to *B*′, who is in danger, his 'you' refers to *B*, 'the man watching you' to *A*′, and 'I' to himself. Then (17) and (19) are true as said by *A*; (18) is true as said by *B*; and (20) and (21) are false as said by *A*. I repeat the examples here:

(17)   I believe she is in danger.

(18)   The man watching me thinks I'm in danger.

(19)   The man watching you believes you are in danger.

(20)   I am the man watching you.

(21)   I believe you are in danger.

The semantics takes 'believes' (or more strictly '*a* believes', for *a* an individual) as a modal operator, so that for a proposition to be believed is for it to be true in every possible world doxastically accessible to *a*; but now Stalnaker proposes the twist, that the English indexical expressions in the complement clauses are to be evaluated in a possible world, not with the reference that they have as we use them, but with the reference that they would have as used *there*. These 'diagonal propositions', as he calls them, are what is expressed (or up for evaluation) in the complements of (17)–(19) and (21).

There are important differences between the substitution strategy and the 'diagonal' strategy just illustrated. But it is clear that the reconstruction of the perspective taken by the person whose words or thoughts are reported is the common aim of both. For many purposes, the results of the two strategies

---

[9] It is not as if the person reported upon might as well have used what the substitution strategy delivers. The substituend is longer than the original, so in the interest of saving breath one would not expect it to be used unless necessary. There is also the fact that, the system of indexical reference being in place, the substitutions if actually carried out would give the wrong impression. If I were to substitute 'the person I am talking to' for 'you', as though being coy about the identity of my addressee, then I would, to put it mildly, be the regular recipient of funny looks. In Richard's example, *A* *ought* to say 'you', even where the intended understanding is 'the woman across the street from him', with 'him' functioning as a bound variable, as we have seen.

will coincide. Given the diagonal strategy, we can generally construct the proper substitution by considering what the reference of the demonstrative would have been, and what perspective would have been taken upon it, in an appropriate counterfactual environment; and conversely, given a substitution that we can recognize as correct, we reach the crucial possible world on the diagonal by endowing the counterfactual environment with properties that make the demonstrative take on the appropriate reference.[10]

## 10.6 Perspective and truth

Does the Richard puzzle call for a revision of the basic conception underlying semantic theory? Some devices that have been suggested in the literature (including attempts by the present author) would effectively answer this question affirmatively. There is no space to outline these devices here, which in any case are rather different from one proposal to another. Generally speaking, they have in common the introduction, or reintroduction, of a Fregean element, a mode of presentation or possibly simply a notation, which will sit alongside or in place of the reference that the demonstrative secures. In Stalnaker's procedure, the Fregean element appears indirectly, in the form of the specification of the counterfactual situations against which the indexical sentence is evaluated on the diagonal.

Consider again Richard's first example, (17):

(17)  I believe she is in danger.

said by $A$. The semantics sketched in section 10.2 above gives as what the competent speaker of English knows about $A$'s utterance exactly (28) (ignoring the tense):

(28)  If $A$ refers to himself with his utterance of 'I', and to $x$ with his utterance of 'she', and $x$ is female, then his utterance of (17) is true iff $A$ believes the syntactic structure [[$x$] ['is in danger']], understood as $A$ said it.

We know what is going on in the story, enough to know that the consequent of (28) can be detached, with $B$ as value of $x$. For the content of the belief we are left, not with the robust (29), but with the emaciated (30):

(29)  [['the woman across the street from' $A$] ['is in danger']]
(30)  [[$B$] ['is in danger']]

---

[10] Crimmins (1992) uses the substitutional method, but retains the 'singular proposition' (i.e., the truth conditions with respect to the reference) as part of the report.

But it is (30) that we must appreciate, not (29), if we are to grasp the import of *A*'s speech.

Precisely this task, however, is one that we can perform, just because the demonstrative contributes nothing but its reference. The point generalizes, as follows: when $X$ reports the thoughts or speech of $Y$, $X$'s demonstrative does not contribute $Y$'s perspective (which is generally dead and gone anyway), and $X$'s own perspective is foreign to $Y$'s thought. But just for this reason $X$ can use the demonstrative, leaving it open what $Y$'s perspective actually was. So $X$ can intend to convey $Y$'s thought, although $X$ does not (and if a demonstrative mode of reference is to be employed, cannot) express it. Since $X$ and $Y$ as competent speakers both know this, $Y$ can fathom $X$'s intention. Communication then takes place without residue, or guesswork.

If this line of thought is even roughly correct, then Fregean elements need not be imported into indirect discourse and similar contexts, or rather they import themselves. The Fregean elements are not senses, however: they may involve objects intrinsically, and they may be perceptual rather than linguistic (it was for this reason that I used the neutral term of art 'perspective'). They are not, and sometimes cannot be, said. But the rules of use for demonstratives make way for them to be intended, just because the rules deliver only objects.

## 10.7 Concluding remarks

A number of semantic problems have turned upon the fact that indexical and demonstrative reference, made through a perspective such as a rule of use or by other contextual means, including especially perceptual salience, typically takes place in a setting where the perspective gets through to the referent at the particular point where the act of reference from that perspective takes place, and not at other points. It follows that we cannot in indirect speech be faithful to both. We nevertheless convey both, because we can exploit our common knowledge of the general system of demonstrative and indexical reference, and of particular circumstances as they arise. For simple cases such as indexical time reference we succeed because we can correlate egocentric coordinate systems by a simple transformation. For complex cases such as Richard's puzzle, we grasp from the surrounding story what is going on with $A$ and $B$, and we do this by grasping how the demonstrative reference was secured. A semantics for our language—that is, a semantics that aims to express explicitly what we know when we know our language—should incorporate rules of use, and explain how we make use of the surrounding information to arrive at the, now remote, perspective from which the demonstrative reference was made. The relativization of truth to acts of reference, suggested by Burge, is a first step, and the systematic transformations of coordinates perhaps a second. Further reconstructive projects can be envisaged, although questions of theoretical tractability arise here as in other domains. But we may hope as these steps are taken to arrive at a fuller understanding of our linguistic competence.[11]

---

[11] The article on which this chapter is based was written in November 1996, while I was visiting at MIT. It was subsequently lightly revised following presentation and discussion in Oxford in early 1997, and then submitted to Martin Hahn and Bjørn Ramberg for inclusion in a volume they were editing, of essays in honour of Tyler Burge. The volume was published only in 2002, with Burge's reply. I am grateful to James Tomberlin and Blackwell Publishers for allowing it to be reprinted there. Comments and discussion at MIT and Oxford have been useful in shaping the final version, and remarks especially by Philippe Schlenker at USC have helped me the better to see what I was up to.

# 11

# A Plea for Implicit Anaphora

## 11.1 Introduction

The subject matter of binding theory has in recent years been transformed. This theory was originally concerned with the syntactic distribution and the semantic interpretation of the reflexive and reciprocal anaphora of English, and the distribution of anaphoric pronominals, these constituting the 'atoms' of anaphora in the sense of the conference to which a preliminary version of this chapter was presented. The anaphoric forms are observed to be at least very nearly in complementary distribution with ordinary pronominal anaphora, a fact that calls for explanation. Binding theory assumed a greater importance following the theoretical proposal that NP-trace is an anaphor, a proposal that was underwritten by the thesis that NP-trace could not occur in a position from which anaphora were excluded and pronominals permitted; and also following the interpretation of PRO in Chomsky (1981) as a species of 'anaphoric pronominal'. Chomsky (1981) and other work assumed that linguistic structures represented anaphoric dependence explicitly by coindexing, so that the syntactic aspect of binding theory consisted in the conditions, both language-particular and universal, on the distribution of indices that could be assigned to anaphors and antecedents in syntactic structures.

All of the above elements of binding theory have been superseded or challenged in work of the last ten years or so, and the available data, both syntactic and semantic, have expanded in several directions. In this chapter, attending especially to Williams (1994), but also to other work as described below, I consider and promote a further expansion of binding theory, which I believe will preserve it nevertheless as a unified module of syntactic and semantic study. Under the expansion, binding theory is allowed to relate, either as anaphor or as antecedent, open positions in θ-grids, which I here call *implicit anaphora*.

Implicit anaphora contrast with *explicit anaphora*, relating linguistic formatives (including empty categories), and also with *mixed anaphora*, wherein one element is a linguistic formative and the other a θ-position. For a simple example of how control might be understood as implicit anaphora, consider (1):

(1)  John tried [PRO to go to London].

In binding theory as restricted to relations between formatives, the obligatory anaphoric relation between PRO and the matrix subject was established by coindexing these expressions, or as in Higginbotham (1983b) by linking the anaphor, PRO, to its antecedent, 'John'. The semantics interprets the anaphoric relation as inheritance of reference by PRO of the reference of the subject, and so gives the cross-reference that is explicit in (2):

(2)  For $x$=John, $x$ tried [$^\wedge x$ go to London]¹

We can conceive instead, however, that an anaphoric relation is established, as part of the syntax, between the external θ-position of the embedded clause and the external θ-position of the V 'try', so that the cross-referential aspect of interpretation is fixed independently of lexical insertion. Then the formatives need not be linked or coindexed, but the effect on interpretation is as before.

The possibilities for lexical insertion will be influenced, and in the case of the PRO of (1) determined, by the anaphoric relation independently established.

The basis for anaphora just conjectured for (1) applies to cases where there are no formatives at all to bear the anaphoric relations in question. Perhaps the simplest examples, discussed further in section 11.3 below, are those of *anaphor-incorporation*, as in (3):

(3)  self-starting (motor)

In (3) the V 'start' θ-marks neither an internal nor an external argument; nevertheless, the argument positions may stand in an anaphoric relation, since a self-starting motor, on one interpretation, is a motor $x$ such that $x$ starts $x$. In another reading, (3) will apply truly to a motor $x$ such that $x$ starts without the intervention of any cause external to $x$. In either case, we must understand (3) as involving implicit anaphora.

The two cases just given, of control and of anaphor-incorporation, will figure below in my plea for implicit anaphora. A number of examples of mixed anaphora are known, particularly those discussed in Mitchell (1986) and Partee (1989), where a word is understood as containing a θ-position

---

[1] I use the carat '$^\wedge$' for intensional abstraction. Notice that the semantics shown requires PRO to be taken (at least) *de re*; for discussion see Higginbotham (1989a) and references cited there. Following Chapter 12 below, they would all be *de se*.

related to a formative. The simplest are those where the position lies within a relational noun, as in (4):

(4) Every participant had to defeat an enemy.

A salient meaning of (4) is that each participant $x$ had to defeat someone who was an enemy of $x$. Representing the pertinent elements of the θ-grid of *enemy* as <1,2>, with 2 the position for the internal argument, we conceive of the syntax as linking that position to the quantified DP 'every participant' (or, in a bolder step, to the external θ-position of 'defeat', making (4) a case of implicit, rather than mixed, anaphora).

Implicit-anaphora examples go together with cases featuring ordinary pronouns, both showing a weak crossover effect. Thus we have data as in (5):

(5) (a) Every participant had to defeat an enemy (of his).
 (b) ?An enemy (of his) had to defeat every participant.
 (c) How many participants had to defeat an enemy (of theirs).
 (d) ??How many participants did an enemy (of theirs) have to defeat?

It is natural to suggest, therefore, that binding theory should treat these in the same way. As far as (5) goes, it may be proposed that the examples without pronominals arise by some process of deletion. But other examples show that there may be no grammatical source for such deletion:

(6) Every participant had to defeat yesterday's enemy's father.

In (6) we have the interpretation that every participant is an $x$ such that $x$ had to defeat the father of the person who yesterday was an enemy of $x$; but insertion of a pronominal is not possible:

(7) Every participant had to defeat yesterday's enemy (*of his)'s father.

I will therefore assume that (4) and similar examples represent mixed anaphora.

Can mixed anaphora go in the other direction, from formative to θ-position? This question is much harder to answer, since the θ-position will have to be discharged somehow in the semantics (or else the sentence will not be closed), and the means of eliminating it might itself provide an antecedent for the formative. Partee (1989) observes that pronominals cannot in general freely take implicit antecedents. Consider (8):

(8) Many [murderers <1,2>] know them beforehand.

(8) cannot mean: many murderers know their victims beforehand. On the other hand, we have notorious examples such as (9):

(9)  John buttered the toast, but he didn't do it in the bathroom.

Here the antecedent of 'it' is understood to be John's action of buttering the toast, represented by the event-argument or E-position of the head V 'butter'. This position is not discharged by θ-marking, and in standard accounts appears as bound by an existential quantifier. So for the first clause we have the interpretation shown in (10):

(10)  (∃e) butter(John,the toast,e)

However, it could be conjectured that it is the implicit quantification, taking sentential scope, that licenses the pronominal anaphora. In what follows I will leave the mixed cases to one side, with the exception of a brief critical discussion of Culicover and Jackendoff (1995).

My discussion in the sections following will concern control phenomena (section 11.2); anaphor-incorporation (section 11.3); and a mixed-anaphora analysis of the anaphoric character of the word 'else', contrasting it with the views of Culicover and Jackendoff (section 11.4). To the extent that the views defended here are on the right track, they may give substance to the plea that forms my title.

## 11.2 Implicit arguments and control

### 11.2.1 *Preliminary data*

In a terminology familiar from the coinage of Roeper (1987), an 'implicit argument' is seen in an example like (11) (due to M. Rita Manzini), where the understood subject of 'sunk' controls PRO:

(11)  The boat was sunk (in order) [PRO to collect the insurance]

That it is the presence of the implicit argument, and not merely common-sense understanding, that licenses (11) is supported by the contrast between (11) and examples where an element is understood in a discourse, but not present in the thematic structure of the predicative head, and so not available as a controller of PRO. The examples are somewhat delicate, because for me and some other speakers PRO without any controller, explicit or implicit, is acceptable in a dialogue like (12):

(12)  Q: Why is the boat at the bottom of the sea?
      A: To collect the insurance.

where the interpretation is that whoever is responsible for getting the boat to the bottom of the sea intends to collect the insurance.² Still, in (13) such an interpretation is quite marginal:

(13)　?The boat is at the bottom of the sea [PRO to collect the insurance].

Manzini's and similar examples provide evidence that a θ-position discharged merely through existential closure is in some way visible to the syntax, and in particular may be the antecedent of a formative, in this case PRO. Other examples include (14), examined in Epstein (1984):

(14)　[PRO playing chess] is enjoyable.

The unique meaning of (14) is: for $x$ to play chess is enjoyable for $x$ (for any $x$ of the right sort). We conclude, therefore, that the experiencer argument of 'enjoyable' controls PRO, just as it does in (15):

(15)　[PRO playing chess] is enjoyable for me.

But in (13) the experiencer argument of 'enjoyable' is discharged by universal closure, not θ-marking.³

More elaborate cases of the type of (14) include (16):

(16)　Friends are fun [O [PRO to be with $t$]].

which can be interpreted as shown in (17):

(17)　If $x$ is friend of $y$, then it is fun for $y$ for $y$ to be with $x$, for any $x$ and $y$.⁴

---

² The dialogue is perhaps still more nearly acceptable if the respondent himself is the one who intends to collect the insurance, and so supplies the reference for PRO.

³ The interpretation of (14) is necessarily generic, because of the properties of the English bare present in construction with indefinite arguments. In the past tense, as in (i), the interpretation need not be generic (universal):

(i)　PRO playing chess (yesterday) was enjoyable.

But the remarks in the text still apply, since it is the implicit argument of 'enjoyable', anchored in context, that serves as the antecedent of PRO.

⁴ Notice that it is the binary character of the predicate 'friend' that licenses the construction, by revealing two distinct argument positions. Thus it would be wrong to replace '$x$ is friend of $y$' by '$x$ and $y$ are friends' in (7), since that would allow (i) with a meaning like that given for (7), while omitting (ii) in that meaning:

(i)　Lovers are fun to be with.
(ii)　Mothers are fun to be with.

But (i) only means that if $x$ is a lover (or: $x$ and $y$ are lovers), then it is fun for any $z$ for $z$ to be with $x$ (or: with $x$ and $y$); whereas (ii), whose head is a truly relational N, can mean that if $x$ is mother of $y$ then it is fun for $y$ for $y$ to be with $x$. The latter example, incidentally, also shows that we cannot interchange '$x$' and '$y$' in the consequent of (17).

A classical problem in the theory of control and anaphora is that of the understood subject of NP, which can behave as though controlled, and also act as antecedent for other elements. Consider (18):

(18) My instruction [PRO to look at each other] was unheeded.

The unique meaning is as indicated in (19):

(19) The instruction from me to X, that X should look at each other, was unheeded by X.

for whatever people X are in question. The syntax shows PRO as subject of the clause 'to look at each other', and acting as the antecedent of the reciprocal. The controller of PRO is the implicit second object of 'instruction', which is in turn controlled by the implicit argument of 'unheeded', itself derived from the agent argument of the root 'heed'.[5] The chain of control must go as stated. For example, we cannot pass over the understood second object of 'instruction':

(20) *My instruction to Mary [PRO to look at each other] was unheeded (by them).

## 11.2.2 *Conceptions of implicitness*

To this point I have been using the notion 'implicit argument' to mean: an open position (a θ-position) in a θ-grid.[6] But this notion can be used purely descriptively, to signify θ-positions that are not realized overtly by (obvious) θ-marking. (Roeper (1987) seems to me to shift between the descriptive sense and the more technical one.)

The phenomenon of implicit arguments, taken in the purely descriptive sense, is evident from examples like (20) above, and also from what Roberts (1987) calls 'implicit subjects' of verbal passives, illustrated by (21):

(21) The books were thrown away intentionally.

The understood subject of the adverb is linked to the understood agent of the passive form. Assuming that the adverb has exactly the θ-grid of the transitive

---

[5] Thus 'unheeded' is like 'uninhabited' and similar words in allowing a 'by'-phrase, but having no corresponding active form; for discussion see Fiengo (1977).

[6] Not all open positions are θ-positions in the classical sense; i.e., positions that must be discharged by θ-marking, or assigned to arguments, in accordance with the θ-criterion. The E-position, for example, is an open position that is never assigned to an argument, and the open positions of some derived nominals apparently need not be assigned to arguments, their overt realization being in this sense optional. For simplicity, however, I will here use 'open position' and 'θ-position' interchangeably. Note particularly that no substantial account of θ-roles is required for the applications pursued here: it will be enough that open positions are enumerated and distinguished from one another as part of lexical information.

adjective 'intentional', from which is it derived, we may render the semantics schematically as in (22) (see Higginbotham (1989b) for more detail):

(22)  ($\exists x$) ($\exists e$) [threw away($x$,the books,$e$) & $e$ was intentional of $x$]

The θ-position marked by '$x$' in (22) is an implicit argument of the adverb. It does not yet follow, however, that (22) is a case of implicit, rather than mixed, anaphora; indeed, Roberts's view is that the passive affix '-en' may in fact *be* the suppressed external argument of the main V, serving as the antecedent for the adverbial position. Below I shall give some reasons for questioning this analysis; but in principle the case could go either way.

Brody and Manzini (1987) understand implicit arguments in a sense that appears to conform to the technical usage suggested here; i.e., θ-positions not discharged by θ-marking. They defend implicit argument control for cases like (11); but any such defense must consider various problematic examples, to which we now turn.

### 11.2.3 *Contexts disallowing control*

Howard Lasnik (in discussion with the author, from some years back) has observed that a number of cases superficially similar to canonical examples such as (11) nevertheless fail to allow control, giving as a representative example (23):

(23)  *The boat was sunk (in order) [PRO to become a hero].

which contrasts with (24):

(24)  ?The boat was sunk by the sailor (in order) [PRO to become a hero].

These cases are problematic for an account such as Roberts (1987), since on his view an antecedent, namely the passive affix, is equally linguistically present for both (23) and (24). But they are problematic also for an account of control in terms of implicit arguments, unless indeed an appropriate distinction can be made out between cases that do and cases that do not require the syntactic realization of a controller.

Following the typology of Faraci (1974), we distinguish between the *purpose clause* (PC), which may show both control and a 'gap' (assumed syntactically to be a chain consisting of an empty operator and a trace, as proposed in Chomsky (1977)), and the *rationale clause* (RC), optionally preceded by a head like *in order, so as*, etc., which shows control but no gap. The contrast is exemplified in (25)–(26):

(25)  I bought the violin (*in order) [O [PRO to play sonatas on *t*]].

(26)  I bought the violin (in order) [PRO to play sonatas on it].

I will suppose following Whelpton (1995) that in (26) the subject of the adjunct is the event of buying the violin, and the RC is its internal argument, the object of 'in', or 'in order'. The head itself expresses a relation between an event (here, buying the violin) and the content of an intention that its agent tried to fulfill by bringing the event to pass (here, playing sonatas on it). The head may not be overt, but constitutes the 'nexus' in the sense of Jespersen, mediating between the main clause and the RC. For the PC, I assume that the nexus is triadic, expressing a relation between an object (the violin), an event (possessing the violin in consequence of buying it), and the property expressed by the PC by taking the operator $O$ to express $\lambda$-abstraction over the position marked by $t$ (here, $^{\wedge}\lambda x$ (I play sonatas on $x$)); see Whelpton (1995) for further details, not relevant here.

PC, it appears, regularly show control by an implicit argument, as in (27):

(27)  The bones were bought [$O$ [PRO to give $t$ to the dog]].[7]

And in fact we do understand (11) (minus 'in order') as a PC, although it has no syntactic gap: for it is clear that it is the insurance *on the boat* that is to be collected. Inversely, infinitival adjuncts like that in (28), but with a manifest syntactic gap, are more acceptable than (23) itself:

(28)  ?The boat was sunk [$O$ [PRO to become a hero for [PRO having sunk $t$]]]

There is a clear contrast, for instance, between (28) and (29):

(29)  *The boat was sunk [PRO to become a hero for having won the battle]

If so, then we can lay the relative unacceptability of (23) to the difficulty of taking it as a PC, and the relative acceptability of Manzini's original example (11) to the availability, through the internal argument of the derived nominal 'insurance', of an element that makes it construable as a PC.

What can be said about the RC construal, with 'in order'? As a syntactic matter an RC cannot contain a gap; but it certainly can contain a pronominal referring back to an element of the main clause (apart from the agent, which always controls PRO). Thus we may conjecture that an implicit argument in (11) (the object of 'insurance') facilitates the perception of control by removing a potential controller, the surface subject, from consideration.

---

[7] The controller, the understood buyer of the bones, need not be the one who puts them in position for the dog to eat, and in that sense need not be the 'giver' of the bones: I can, at least with license, truly say that the bones were bought by me to give to the dog even if I intend someone else actually to hand them over to the animal. But the same is true where the antecedent of PRO is explicit, as in (i):

(i)  I bought the bones yesterday [$O$ [PRO to give $t$ to the dog]].

We have, then, a partial although incomplete response to Lasnik's observations. PC show control by implicit arguments; but both PC and RC are the more acceptable with implicit argument control in proportion as an implicit argument is supplied whose antecedent is the surface subject, as in (11). Predicates like Lasnik's 'become a hero' are low on the scale, since they do not supply implicit arguments. Hence their use as RC biases control toward the surface subject, semantic absurdity notwithstanding, thus generating typical contrasts such as (30)–(31) and (32)–(33):

(30)  I studied the book [in order [PRO to be well-educated]].

(31)  The book was studied [in order [PRO to be well-educated]].

(32)  The book was put on the shelf [in order [PRO to be consulted $t$ as the need should arise]].

(33)  I put the book on the shelf [in order [PRO to be consulted $t$ as the need should arise]].

In all of these examples, the only accessible controller of PRO is the overt subject.

Supposing now that both controller and controlled may be realized only implicitly, as in the cases we have given, we may consider a theory according to which PRO is a syntactic reflex of control, rather than the controlled element itself; that is, PRO is selected to occur in certain configurations where control has already been established. The syntactic restrictions on the occurrence of PRO remain in force, but anaphora into positions other than those in which PRO can occur can remain at the level of the implicit argument.

In fact we may go farther. Suppose that, control or contextual anchoring of an implicit argument having been established, that argument must be realized, for independent reasons. There are two cases of this, namely (i) where the implicit arguments of the head must be discharged by θ-marking, and (ii) where a position must be syntactically realized on independent grounds. The former case is that of the θ-positions of the head that interact with the θ-criterion; and the latter is that of the subject of a clause, the cases that fall under the Extended Projection Principle. In case (i) PRO is excluded except from an ungoverned subject position, and by (ii) something must be realized in such a position. Hence, if no other expression can fulfill its role, as appears to be the case in English, PRO occurs where, and exactly where, it can. Control itself, however, is indifferent to its occurrence.

Fiengo and Higginbotham (1981) gave examples of control into the external-argument position of N, as in (34):

(34)  Bets against him don't bother John.

Our observation was that anaphora between 'him' and 'John' imply that it is not John who is betting.[8] In (35), where control is obligatory, anaphora are not possible:

(35)  [PRO betting against him] doesn't bother John.

The data suggest that the only difference between the cases stems from the fact that control is not required in (34). As many people have observed, positing PRO in (34) and the like is hard to defend: not only does the subject seem complete by itself, but it can even be supplemented with a genitive (e.g., 'yesterday's bets against John'), without disturbing the control relation. Moreover, if PRO were present in (34) there is no evident reason why control should not be as obligatory, as it is in (35). On the present view, as in Williams (1994), these issues do not arise.

## 11.3 Incorporated anaphora

Consider examples such as: 'self-inflicted (wound)', 'other-regarding (action)', 'different-sounding (syllables)', 'same-looking (cars)'. In these the semantics must be done through communication between implicit arguments. They represent a kind of head-incorporation, but are evidently (in the case of the latter three), or arguably (in the case of 'self-', as discussed below), not themselves capable of discharging a θ-position. The constructions are of variable productivity, partly for elementary semantic reasons, but invite comparison with N-incorporation and an analysis of the general basis for the semantics that they receive.

It has long been observed that some cases of 'self'-incorporation carry the obvious reflexive meaning. Consider again (3), in a full nominal such as 'a self-starting motor'. One can say that a motor $x$ is self-starting if it is such that $x$ starts $x$, and the construction so understood is synonymous with 'motor that starts itself'. The Adjective 'self-starting' combines with the head Noun by unification or θ-identification, and the morpheme 'self' has the effect of identifying the internal with the external implicit argument of 'starting'. I will represent this syntactic transaction and the resulting semantic interpretation as shown in (36):

(36)  a self-starting motor
 a [[self-starting,<1,2>,2=1] [motor <3>],<3>,1=3]
 an $x$ such that motor($x$) & $x$ starts $x$

---

[8] More simply, nominals like 'bets against him' show the same condition B effect as simple sentences 'NP bet against him'.

As above, the θ-positions are shown within angled brackets. Identification of θ-positions is shown by equations whose left side is the modifier and whose right side is the modified, an arbitrary convention to this point. Thus 'self-starting' contains two θ-positions, which are identified, and these in turn are identified, as shown by the annotation '1=3', with the sole θ-position 3 of 'motor'.

Chomsky (1972), in the course of arguing in favor of the lexicalist hypothesis, and against the suggestive evidence for a transformational derivation of constructions like (35), considered a number of cases of 'self'-incorporation. I discuss these examples, and others, below. For the moment, let us consider how the θ-positions in 'self'-incorporation are identified, a question left open by the neutral notation '2=1' in (36) above.

It is straightforward to verify that when an N incorporates into an A=V+-ing, then it fills the internal argument position of V, and that N-incorporation into A=V+-en, formed with the participial affix, fills instead the position that would be external in the active form of V. Thus contrast (37)(a)–(b):

(37) (a) a Wall Street-sustaining enterprise
     (b) a Wall Street-sustained enterprise

These have the interpretations in (38)(a)–(b), respectively:

(38) (a) an enterprise $x$ such that $x$ sustains Wall Street
     (b) an enterprise $x$ such that Wall Street sustains $x$[9]

Taking a cue from these data, we conclude that the 'self' morpheme when incorporated acts in a specific direction, so as to identify an internal θ-position with the external one (in the case of the suffix '-ing'), or to identify the external position with an internal one (the case of '-en'). Let us say that the morpheme *targets* a position $n$, and *identifies* it with position $m$. If so, then we should not regard the direction of θ-identification with indifference, but endow it with a significance reflected in the notation for (36) and other examples.

Our question whether there is a direction of θ-identification arises also for the simpler case of modifier–head relations: are these symmetric or asymmetric? It is natural to suppose that they proceed from the modifier to the head; that is, that θ-identification targets a position of the modifier and

---

[9] Or: $x$ is sustained by Wall Street. With reference to Roberts's hypothesis, notice that the participial affix cannot in this case be the external argument of 'sustain', because the external argument position must be left open for binding by a determiner or quantifier.

identifies it with a position of the head. We shall make this assumption in what follows.

In place of the equations seen in the third line of (36) we now put assignments of target $n$ with identified position $m$, signaled by the notation: '$n \Rightarrow m$'. Thus (36) is replaced by (39):

(39)     a self-starting motor
         a [[self-starting,<1,2>,2⇒1] [motor <3>],<3>,1⇒3]
         an $x$ such that motor($x$) & $x$ starts $x$

Because of the reflexivity of 'self-', we can represent the semantics in (39) without assigning that morpheme any meaning other than that of triggering the anaphora. But consider reciprocal examples, as in (40):

(40)     an other-regarding action
         an $x$ such that action($x$) & the agent of $x$ has regard for some $y \neq x$

or examples with 'different', as in (41):

(41)     different-sounding syllables
         syllables $X$ each one of which is different from the others in $X$

In these cases the semantics must be mediated by the meanings of 'other' and 'different' themselves. For the case of 'other', we shall want a θ-grid [other,<1,2>], which will combine with [regarding,<3,4>], by identifying 1 with 3, and 2 with 4; and similarly for 'different', and for that matter 'same'. Illustrating with reference to (40), we shall have (42):

(42)     an other-regarding action
         an [[[other,<1,2>][regarding,<3,4>],<3,4>,1⇒3,2⇒4]][action, <5>], <3,4,5>]

But now we may propose that 'self', itself, contributes a meaning, namely identity.[10]

In general, the forms 'self'+gerund have quite regular interpretations, as indicated for instance by examples like those in (43):

(43)     (a) self-canning beer
         (b) self-seeking man
         (c) self-breaking chinaware

---

[10] There are of course intimate relations between the conception thus arrived at (itself an old one) and recent discussions of reflexives that have them incorporate into verbal heads.

(43)(a) evidently means: beer that puts itself in a can; (43)(c) refers to chinaware that breaks of its own accord (with inchoative 'break'), or alternatively to chinaware that breaks itself (with causative 'break'); (43)(b) is not generally understood to mean *man who seeks himself*, but rather *selfish man*, or perhaps *man who seeks things (only) for himself*, but it is clear on reflection that it *has* the purely reflexive meaning, usage notwithstanding. The last remark goes also for examples like (44)(a)–(b), of which the first is discussed in Chomsky (1972):

(44)  (a) self-fulfilling prophecy
      (b) self-standing statue

Chomsky (1972: 57–58) writes that (44)(a) 'does not, strictly speaking, mean that the prophecy fulfills the prophecy, which is senseless, but rather that it led to a state of affairs that fulfilled the prophecy.' This characterization of the common meaning can, I think, be improved: (44)(a) is a clever coinage, applying to acts of prophecy having the property that making them causes the fulfillment of their contents. In any case, the crucial question for the status of (44)(a) in the grammar is whether the 'senseless' meaning is in fact available. It seems to me that it is.

The example (44)(b) raises a different set of issues. As illustrated above with respect to (43)(c), inchoatives may allow 'self'-incorporation, and (44)(b) is acceptable with the meaning *statue that stands by itself (without the aid of props)*. The pattern is not, however, generalizeable: thus we do not have *'self-lying rug', *'self-sitting doll', etc., or examples like 'self-walking dog' except with causative 'walk'.

Turning now to the participial and derived nominal forms, we find a regular pattern overlain with special usages, and a possibility that does not obtain with the gerund, of identifying an agent, extraneous to the θ-grid of the head, with a position in the θ-grid. Recall that examples like (37)(b) show that an incorporated N identifies its θ-position with the external argument position of a participle, and that 'self'-incorporation consequently works 'downwards', from the external position to an internal one. Examples such as those (45) then have the expected meanings shown:

(45)  (a) self-canned beer = beer which that beer itself has put in the can
      (b) self-sought man = man who he himself seeks

But (45)(a) has another interpretation as well, namely *beer that is canned by the one who made it*. Similar remarks go for the examples in (46):

(46)  self-addressed envelope, self-decorated house, self-derived conclusion

Finally, examples with derived nominals show both the 'regular' (often silly in practice) interpretations, as well as scattered available readings that reflect the importation of an outside agent, as in (47):

(47)  self-storage facility, self-discovery, self-service machine

Thus a self-storage facility can be a facility where one stores oneself, but (in a non-cryogenic age) is used just to mean a facility where one stores one's belongings by oneself; 'self-discovery' refers to the act of discovering one's 'true self'; and a self-service machine (in British English) is one that serves goods after the insertion of coins (but can be interpreted to mean a machine that serves itself).

Summing up, the 'self'-incorporated forms diverge from what is made available by ordinary reflexive contexts, but contain the meanings given by those contexts as special cases, even where usage assigns them other salient meanings. The gerundives come closest to exhibiting regular behavior; the participles, even where regular, do not follow the lines of syntactic reflexivization, since they target an internal argument, identifying it with the external, whereas syntactic reflexives must follow the reverse pattern; participles and derived nominals allow the importation of agents not given in the θ-grids of the heads; and there is a (limited) variety of special cases. These data are consistent with Chomsky's support for a lexicalist position with respect to 'self-', and more generally anaphor-incorporation, but show at the same time a systematic character that can be expressed only at the level of implicit anaphora.

## 11.4  Else

Culicover and Jackendoff (1995) have discussed anaphora with '(something) else', as seen for instance in (48):

(48)  Everyone loves someone else.

in the meaning: everyone is an *x* such that *x* loves someone other than *x*. Since they regard the expression 'else', or the containing nominal, as itself anaphoric, they conclude on the basis of clause-bound anaphora as in (48) and longer-distance anaphora as in (49) that 'someone else' has the distribution of both anaphors and pronominals.

(49)  Everyone thought that I saw someone else.

In fact, they go so far as to suggest that these anaphora violate condition (C), citing (50):

(50)  Someone else wrote Shakespeare's plays.

Of course, these conclusions are induced only by the assumed formalism of cosubscripting elements as wholes. The consequences for the theory of explicit anaphora are sufficiently drastic that the alternative suggests itself, that these anaphora are triggered by the specific meaning and the argument structure of the anaphoric element 'else', and so engage the semantics at the level of implicit arguments.

Let us return to the point that 'someone else' evidently means *some person y other than person x*, where the value of '*x*' is determined contextually, or else the position it occupies is that of a bound variable; and similarly for 'no one/ anyone/everyone else'. We may take it that 'else', despite its limited distribution, effectively means *other than*, and combines with the head 'one' as illustrated in (51):

(51)   [[one,<1>] [else,<2,3>]],<1,3>,2⇒1]

where 3 is anaphoric, in the case of (50) to 'Shakespeare'.[11]

The alternative just sketched responds at once to the suggestion of Culicover and Jackendoff, that the anaphoric properties of 'else' will have to be specified at some level other than those recognized by customary syntax. They write in (1995: 272) that the construction '*X* else' should be 'decomposed' as '*X* other than α, where α is an anaphoric element', where α is 'not present in the syntax at all'. But thematic structure *is* present in the syntax, and if we allow, as it appears we must on independent grounds, that θ-positions can themselves participate in anaphoric relations, then their conclusion is not warranted.

There are in fact other reasons for supposing that 'else'-anaphora are syntactically represented. Contrary to the judgements of Culicover and Jackendoff (1995: 226–227), I find that 'else'-anaphora obey the crossover conditions:[12]

(52)   It was everyone else that everyone met.

(53)   It was everyone that everyone else met.

(52) can mean that everyone is an *x* such that *x* met everyone *y* other than *x*; but (53) cannot mean that everyone is an *x* such that everyone *y* other than *x* met *x*. The cases are parallel to (54)–(55):

---

[11] The head expression need not be 'one', since, e.g. 'every man else' and similar constructions are attested. On the other hand, the quantifier (in the count system) must apparently be either universal or existential, since we do not have *'many men else' and the like; but for the mass system cf. 'little else', 'much else'.

[12] In fact, Culicover and Jackendoff contradict themselves on this point, since in (1995: 262) they suggest that such conditions are in effect.

(54) It was everyone other than him that everyone met.

(55) ??It was everyone that everyone other than him met.

But no decomposition of anything is called for; rather, we should recognize in the structure of the word 'else' itself the possibility of anaphora, and apply weak crossover conditions to the relation between the position marked 3 in (42) above and the quantificational antecedent 'everyone' in (52)–(53). In support of this hypothesis are the considerations below.

Higginbotham (1989a: 92, 96) advanced the generalization that both PRO and understood subjects always show what was there called *covariance* with their antecedents under association with focus and VP-deletion. Covariance in the latter case ('sloppy identity') shows up with 'else'-anaphora as well. Thus (56), in contrast to (57), does not admit a 'strict' or invariant reading:

(56) Shakespeare liked someone else's plays, but Marlowe didn't.

(57) Shakespeare liked the plays of someone other than him (Shakespeare), but Marlowe didn't.

Similarly, for the case of association with focus, compare (58) to (59):

(58) Only Shakespeare likes someone else's plays.

(59) Only Shakespeare likes plays by someone other than him.

The example (58) is ambiguous in the usual way, between the invariant (60) and the covariant (61):

(60) Only Shakespeare is an $x$ such that $x$ likes plays by someone other than Shakespeare.

(61) Only Shakespeare is an $x$ such that $x$ likes plays by someone other than $x$.

But the invariant or strict interpretation is unavailable for (58). These data suggest that Culicover and Jackendoff's recourse to decomposition is not only unnecessary but as it stands misleading, since the result of restoring an argument for 'else' cannot, unlike pronominals, show strict identity interpretations.

I have suggested that 'else' means *other than*, and carries two implicit arguments. This thesis is supported independently by the free occurrence of 'else' with disjunction. The addition of 'else' forces an extra dimension of interpretation in (62):

(62) You must go, or (else) you will be late.

(62) invites a conditional interpretation, 'If you do not go', i.e., 'if you do otherwise than go, you will be late', for the second disjunct. In one natural interpretation of (63), the 'free-choice' interpretation discussed in Higginbotham (1991c), the addition of 'else' implicates that one and only one alternative is permitted:

(63)   You are allowed to play chess or (else) checkers here.

Furthermore, in contexts that escape tautology through Gricean implicature, as in (64) said in response to the question whether one will be at the party, the addition of 'else' creates anomaly:

(64)   I may go, or I may not.

(65)   ?I may go, or else I may not.

We thus have, from within the contemporary language, ample evidence that 'else' involves the concept *other than* as part of its thematic structure.

## 11.5 Concluding remarks

The selected cases discussed here are evidence that the general theory of anaphoric relations in syntax should be extended to include implicit anaphora, not at a hypothetical level of the representation of full discourse and communication, but at the classic level, where syntactic structures and the form and meaning of lexical items impose their own conditions on possible interpretations. Besides these cases there are a number of others, including for example tense-agreement phenomena and sequence of tense, which limitations of space have precluded discussing here. If so, then the question arises what lexical items are permitted to bear the anaphoric relations in question. It can be no accident, for example, that the incorporated anaphora over and over employ the notions of identity and non-identity, or that words like 'else', 'another', and 'different' appear in this connection. But for this point a wider cross-linguistic survey is needed.[13]

---

[13] Material from which this chapter is excerpted was presented at the Leiden Workshop 1996, and subsequently at the LF Reading Group, MIT; the University of Arizona; and the University of Oxford. I am grateful to the audiences for comments and suggestions, and to Mario Montalbetti and Andrew Barss for substantial discussion. I am also indebted to Robert Fiengo for extensive comments.

# 12

# Remembering, Imagining, and the First Person

## 12.1 Introduction

It is widely supposed that certain uses of anaphoric forms (pronouns, reflexives, and others to be discussed below) give rise to peculiarly 'first-personal' interpretations, and it has become customary following David Lewis (1979) to call these interpretations *de se*. Assuming that *de se* interpretations do indeed contrast with interpretations along the familiar, if not necessarily pellucid, *de dicto–de re* axis, there are then four questions about the *de se*, the first two more philosophical and the latter two more linguistic: (i) what is the nature of *de se* interpretations? (ii) what relation do they bear to ordinary uses of the first-person pronoun? (iii) why are they triggered by the particular linguistic items that trigger them? and (iv) are they universal in human language, and what relation, if any, do they bear to logophoric phenomena in languages having special logophoric forms?[1] Here I consider almost exclusively the first question, hazarding only a few remarks about the second and third; and I omit the fourth, most properly linguistic, question entirely. I believe that questions (iii) and (iv) in particular are more deserving of philosophical attention than it might at first seem; but that discussion will have to await another occasion.

Constructions such as those in (1)–(3) below, stretching back to the original work of Castañeda (1966) and (1967), have been discussed at length over the years:

(1) John/Each man expects (that) he will win.

(2) John/Each man expects (that) he himself will win.

(3) John/Each man expects himself to win.

---

[1] The logophors are special anaphors, said to refer to 'centers of consciousness'. The term has been extended to cases including some English reflexives. For discussion of the syntax and semantics of logophoric forms, see Huang (2000), Schlenker (1999) and (2003), and references cited there.

To these constructions must be added the case where the subject of the infinitival complement is understood, as in 'John/Each man expects to win'. Throughout this chapter, I represent the understood subject by the element PRO, as in Chomsky (1981). PRO is an expression having an interpretation (in fact, necessarily anaphoric to the main clause subject), but no phonetic realization. Alternative views of the understood subject are possible. My choice may not ultimately affect the semantic question (i) above, but it will have consequences for (ii)–(iv).² Given PRO as the understood subject, to the examples (1)–(3) we may add (4):

(4)  John/Each man expects PRO to win.

The datum to be considered, then, is that there is something first-personal about the contents of the complements in (2)–(4) that need not obtain in (1); that is, that there are contexts in which the assertion (1) is true (with 'he' anaphoric to the subject, 'John' or 'each man') that are not first-personal, but no such contexts for the assertion of any of (2)–(4). I do not give a preliminary rehearsal of the familiar scenarios given in support of this view; see below for discussion of examples.³

The contrast to be considered is between the ways in which (2)–(4) must be understood, and (1) need not be understood, so that (1) possesses an ambiguity that (2)–(4) lack.⁴ There would appear to be three, and only three, modes of explanation of the observed contrast.

First (as in Higginbotham (1989a) and (1991a), for example) it may be suggested that the contexts in which (1) is not first-personal are concealed *de dicto* contexts, where some Fregean 'mode of presentation' attends the bound pronoun *he*. Consider Castañeda's example of the amnesiac war hero, who is reading about himself and his heroic exploits, all unaware, indeed disbelieving, that it is he himself that he is reading about. We are licensed to say truly (5):

(5)  The war hero thinks that he is a hero.

---

² For recent critical discussion, see Landau (2000), esp. ch. 5.
³ The scenarios are of two basic kinds: (a) those in which a subject knows (or believes, etc.) something about herself that it is questionable whether others know, as when I know in the ordinary way that I am standing; and (b) those where a subject knows something about himself, but does not have the knowledge that would be required in order to justify the use of locutions with reflexive, emphatic reflexive, or PRO (understood subject) arguments, as when he knows (as we say) that he was elected, because he knows that the candidate with the largest war chest was elected, but does not know that he himself was elected, having failed to realize that he himself was the candidate with the largest war chest. Again, see Castañeda for persuasive examples.
⁴ The case of (4) was already observed in Fodor (1975), as noted below. Chierchia (1990) provided a more systematic taxonomy, concentrating however on propositional attitudes.

but not (6):

(6)   The war hero thinks that he himself is a hero.

How can these be distinguished? According to the first method, they are distinguished in that, while the pronoun in (5) need not be taken as a mere variable, having for its antecedent the expression 'the war hero', the emphatic reflexive must be so taken. Suppose that we understand the ordinary pronoun as if, while referring to the war hero, it presented him as, say, *the person that he (the war hero) is reading about.* Then we have a sense in which (5) can be true although (6), being for whatever reason strictly *de re*, is false. So the interpretations of (2)–(4) must be, and that of (1) can be, first-personal simply because *de re*.

The above view is rejected in Lewis (1979) for substantially theoretical reasons. It may also be questioned on the ground that it doesn't reveal what is peculiarly first-personal about, say, John's or each man's expectations in (3). The latter point will chiefly occupy us here.

Second, following the path taken by Lewis, and in a simplified form by Chierchia (1990), it may be proposed that the complements of the *de se* constructions are of a higher logical type, properties instead of propositions. Thus, according to Chierchia, (2) has it that, for John or each man=$x$, $x$ expects the property of being a thing $y$ such that $y$ wins; or, to put it perhaps more naturally, $x$ expects of $x$ that property. If $x$'s expectations come to pass, then $x$ has the property, and so $x$ wins. Likewise, when the war hero thinks he is a hero, but not that he himself is a hero, then for him=$x$, $x$ thinks that $x$ is a hero, but it is not the case that for him=$x$, $x$ thinks, or ascribes to $x$, the property of being a thing $y$ such that $y$ is a hero.

I shall elaborate somewhat upon this second proposal, and what I will argue is its chief shortcoming, in what follows. For the moment, I note that Stalnaker (1981) responded to Lewis in such a way as to defend a variant of the first view above, albeit from a different angle. For Stalnaker, the modes of presentation relevant to (5) do not figure in the logical form of the examples, but rather in setting up the possible worlds in which John has expectations about himself, but doesn't realize that it is himself he has expectations about. I discuss this view in section 12.7 below.

Third, there is a possibility, sympathetically elucidated in Perry (1983) (but leading in the end to a sceptical conclusion), and notoriously having roots in Frege's (1918) discussion of the first person, as well as in Castañeda's work: it may be that there is a *special*, first-personal interpretation of the emphatic reflexive as in (2), of the reflexive as in (3), and of PRO as in (4), contributing its meaning to the propositional complement; and perhaps this special interpretation is also involved in the first-person forms themselves. The special interpretation would be available for (1), but not obligatory. The problem then is to elucidate what this interpretation is.

In this chapter I will argue that the third view is correct, and I will offer a particular way of understanding it. If it is correct, then *de se* interpretations of embedded clauses, obligatory in (4) and (6), optional in (1) and (5) above, are neither the result of suppressing a conceptualized constituent in favor of the bare object, as in the first view, nor do they call for a reconstrual of clauses as expressions of properties, as in the second, but rather they have their own conceptualized constituents (analogous to Fregean senses, but only analogous, since they may, and in the view I advance, will, contain objects that are not senses), whose properties explain why they are different from *de re* contexts.

One approach to what is special about first-person contexts is already illustrated in Peacocke (1981) as well as Perry (1983), cited above. I use Peacocke's exposition: suppose that there is a special mode of presentation *self* that a thinker $x$ can employ in thinking about himself, and no one else, and others cannot therefore employ in thinking about $x$. A particular first-person thought will employ a token $[self_x]$, indexed by $x$. The problem will now be to elucidate the empirical as well as the formal content of *self* and $[self_x]$.

The view that I advance in section 12.6 below will not be Peacocke's, for reasons having to do with some empirical peculiarities of first-personal embedded constructions that I outline in earlier sections. Like his, however, it may be thought of as sympathetic to a latter-day Fregean perspective; and there are some direct points of contact, as well as room for differences. My remarks will in any case cash out some promissory notes from Chapters 3 and 4.

## 12.2 Gerundive complements

I have outlined a general view, that there is something distinctive in the beliefs or expectations about oneself that are alleged in assertions of examples such as (2)–(4), or (6). The phenomena may be illustrated with other types of examples, where the anaphora having distinctive interpretations appear within complement clauses, and so on a classical view occur as constituents of linguistic elements referring to propositions. The linguistic contexts hosting these examples would include predicates expressing epistemic states, as in knowing oneself to be so and so; indirect discourse; and other predicates involving states, conditions, or activities, such as dreaming, fantasizing, or pretending. Here, however, I turn to a different domain, that of the contexts of remembering, imagining, and the like, where the anaphor is the subject of a verbal gerundive complement, as in (7)–(10):

(7)   John/Each man remembered/imagined [his going to the movies].
(8)   John/Each man remembered/imagined [him, himself going to the movies].
(9)   John/Each man remembered/imagined [himself going to the movies].
(10)  John/Each man remembered/imagined [PRO going to the movies].

The above examples are parallel, or as parallel as can be, to (1)–(4) above.[5] I call particular attention to (10).

The first-personal character of such reports as (10) is foreshadowed in the notorious example (11), which arose some years ago in discussion between Jerry Fodor and Judith Thomson:

(11)  Only Churchill remembers giving the speech (about blood, toil, tears, and sweat).

As Fodor (1975: 133 ff.) remarks, (11) is true provided that (a) only Churchill gave the speech, and (b) he remembers doing so. Thus (12) is a valid argument (with PRO explicit in the premises and conclusion):

(12)  Only Churchill gave the speech;
      Churchill remembers [PRO giving the speech]; therefore,
      Only Churchill remembers [PRO giving the speech].[6]

Compare the conclusion of (12) to (13):

(13)  Only Churchill remembers his giving the speech.

The latter is, at first sight, obviously false, and is therefore not implied by the premises of (12). Indeed, it appears that, for the simple reason that those people who listened to Churchill's speech (in person, or on the radio) at the time he gave it, were aware in the ordinary way of what was going on, and

---

[5] In English, the ordinary pronominal 'him' as in

John remembered/imagined [him going to the movies]

cannot be anaphoric to 'John', just as it cannot be anaphoric in simple clauses such as 'John remembered him'. Hence I use the possessive form 'his' in (7). The emphatic reflexive 'him, himself' in (8) seems to me acceptable and interpretable, if unnatural in comparison, say, to (9) and (10).

[6] Fodor used the validity of (12), in conjunction with the Katz-Postal hypothesis, that optional grammatical transformations did not change meaning, to argue against 'pronominalization'; that is, against the view that the understood subject represents deletion of an anaphoric pronominal or reflexive element in the course of the syntactic derivation of (11). His thesis translates into the present syntactic system as: PRO is not semantically equivalent to any anaphoric pronominal or reflexive form. I will argue below that the thesis is correct.

subsequently remembered it, are all of them counterexamples to the truth of (13). If so, (13) is not true on any interpretation.

Now, Fodor's observation does not, and should not, show that what Churchill remembers when he remembers giving the speech is different from what he or others remember when they remember his giving it. We shall, however, accumulate evidence that there is indeed something special about Churchill's memorial state.

Before returning to Fodor's and similar cases, I endeavor in the next two sections to establish two points: first, that the gerundive complements in (7)–(10) have an event-like (in a sense to be explained) rather than a proposition-like reference; and second, that those with PRO subjects exhibit the phenomenon of 'immunity to error through misidentification' in the sense of Shoemaker (1968), and as refined in Pryor (1999).

## 12.3 The interpretation of (certain) gerundive complements

It is obvious that we remember events, and that we can speak of ourselves as engaged in remembering them. Furthermore, to remember an event—the Vietnam War, for example, or a birthday party—one must have had appropriate perceptual and other experience of it. The memory of an event may 'fade', as we say, and in particular one may know that one used to remember something one no longer remembers. Using these facts, we can swiftly show that the verbal gerundive complements to 'remember' fall on the event side of things, and in this way are sharply to be distinguished from the finite complements *that so and so*.

(i) My father's father died before I was born. I remember that he was called 'Rufus'. But I do not remember his being called 'Rufus', because I was not alive when he was called that. Thus the complement

> my grandfather's being called 'Rufus'

does not refer to the proposition (or fact) that he was called 'Rufus'; for if it did, then (14) and (15) would be true or false together, whereas in fact (14) is true and (15) false:

(14)   I remember that my grandfather was called 'Rufus'.

(15)   I remember my grandfather's being called 'Rufus'.

(ii) Expressions involving propositional attitudes or epistemic states resist the English progressive. Thus the examples in (16) are simply ungrammatical:

(16)   *I am believing/knowing/remembering that I walked to school in the fifth grade.

However, if someone comes across me looking pensive, and I am asked, 'What are you doing?' I can well respond with (17):

(17)  I am remembering walking to school in the fifth grade.

as indeed I could respond with, 'I am remembering the birthday party', where the direct object of 'remember' obviously refers to an event. We conclude that the complement in (17) so refers.[7]

(iii) Finite complements contrast with the gerundive in that, whereas (18) is reminiscent of the 'Moore Paradox', the anomaly of asserting that one does not believe something that one has just asserted, (19) may be an ordinary truth:

(18)  I used to remember that I walked to school in the fifth grade, but I no longer remember it.

(19)  I used to remember walking to school in the fifth grade, but I no longer remember it.

The above diagnostics show that the gerundive complements to 'remember' speak of memory of events, rather than remembering facts, or remembering, or remembering-true, propositions.

Throughout the above, I have assumed that 'remember', in all uses, is factive: one can only remember true propositions; and when one speaks of remembering, say, walking to school, then there was indeed an event of one's walking to school. Whether factivity can be safely assumed or not, 'remember' conspicuously contrasts with the non-factive 'imagine', and indeed with most other contexts in which the analogues of the above diagnostics can be carried out. There must, then, be a general perspective, abstracting away from factivity, from which gerundive and finite complements are put into semantic contrast. Our task in bringing it out is somewhat complicated by the fact that gerundive complements do not always contrast with finite or other complements in the stark way we have just illustrated, using 'remember'. Passing over the complexities of the linguistic taxonomy, I outline a way that I would favor of making the semantic contrast where it obtains.

---

[7] The 'success verbs', as Gilbert Ryle called them, do not generally admit the progressive: thus I cannot say that I am seeing (as opposed to looking at) my watch. When the same verbs are used without a 'success' connotation, however, the progressive becomes possible, as when I say that I am seeing spots before my eyes. Individual dialects diverge here: thus Christopher Peacocke finds the progressive of *see* acceptable where it involves making something out, or discernment, as in 'I am not seeing the third letter', said during an eye test. In my speech, however, this is a far fetch. It is useful, though not of itself enlightening, to put the divergence down to a distinction between expressions ranging over processes and those ranging over momentary transitions, or *achievements* in a common terminology, with my dialect admitting only the latter for epistemic or 'success' expressions, including *see*.

I will assume, as in the familiar story derived from Davidson, and exploited by myself and many others, that the basic argument structure of a natural language predicate P will have, besides some number $n$ of slots for the overt arguments that appear with it, also a slot for a variable $e$ that ranges over events, thus:

$$P(x_1,\ldots,x_n,e)$$

(We abstract as usual from considerations of time and tense, as well as from the details of English morphology.) Supposing the arguments apart from the position marked by $e$ filled in, we derive a predicate $\varphi(e)$ true only of events, as it might be *love(John,Mary,e)*.[8] An assertion of the sentence 'John loves Mary' is an assertion:

$$(\exists e)\ \text{love}(\text{John},\text{Mary},e)$$

to the effect that there is at least one event of (as we may say) John loving Mary. Any sentence that may be asserted may occur also as a finite complement (hosted by a complementizer such as 'that'), in which case it will refer to a proposition. Following Richard Montague's (1960) notation, the reference of the finite complement is

$$^{\wedge}(\exists e)\ \text{love}(\text{John},\text{Mary},e)$$

where the circumflex '$^{\wedge}$' represents $\lambda$-abstraction over possible worlds. If $\psi(p)$ is a factive predicate with respect to a propositional argument $p$, then its factivity is expressed by adopting the postulate:

$$\psi(p) \rightarrow {}^{\vee}p$$

where '$^{\vee}p$' refers to the extension, in this case the truth value, of $p$ in the actual world. If $\psi(p)$ is so to speak anti-factive, implying the falsehood of its propositional argument (as is plausibly the case, for instance, with the propositional argument in 'He fancies that p'), then the postulate to be adopted is

$$\psi(p) \rightarrow {}^{\vee}\neg p$$

The above familiar apparatus may now be modified so as to apply to the case of event-like reference, as in the gerundive complements. Consider a predicate $\varphi(e)$ of events. This predicate yields a term $(\lambda e)\varphi(e)$ by $\lambda$-abstraction,

---

[8] In these last sentences and in what follows I suppress some distinctions between use and mention. I use single quotes for mentioned English words throughout, but do not further mark elements already italicized.

hence a term $^\wedge(\lambda e)\varphi(e)$ referring (in Montague's terminology) to properties of events. We propose that a predicate $\Gamma$ with respect to an event-like argument (as established through the above diagnostics) takes arguments $\alpha$ of the type of $^\wedge(\lambda e)\varphi(e)$: thus 'John remembers/imagines Mary singing the song' would be

$$(\exists e')\,[\text{remembers/imagines}(\text{John},{}^\wedge\lambda e\,\text{sing}(\text{Mary, the song},e),e')]$$

If $\Gamma(\alpha)$ is a factive predicate with respect to arguments $\alpha$, then we adopt the postulate

$$\Gamma(\alpha) \rightarrow (\exists e^*)\,[(^\vee\alpha)\,e^*]$$

and if $\Gamma(\alpha)$ is anti-factive (as is plausibly the case for the gerundive complement in 'He feigned taking offense at that remark', for example) then the postulate to be adopted is

$$\Gamma(\alpha) \rightarrow \neg(\exists e^*)\,[(^\vee\alpha)\,e^*]$$

An easy calculation now confirms that 'John remembers Mary singing the song', together with the factive postulate governing 'remember', implies

$$(\exists e^*)\,\text{sing}(\text{Mary},\text{the song},\,e^*)$$

We have thus, following in effect Montague's strategy of ascending to the worst-case scenario, found a uniform way to give the semantics of gerundive complements in our target contexts, while accommodating, via postulates, the intuitions governing the factive and anti-factive cases.

Suppose now that in place of gerundive complements we have ordinary nominal objects, as in (20):

(20) Mary remembered/imagined the party for her thirty-third birthday/a tree.

We can suppose that the remembered objects are ordinary things: birthday parties, trees. But Mary may imagine the party that (as we say) she will never have, and she may imagine a tree without imagining any particular tree. Evidently, we can bring these cases under our wing by supposing that when Mary imagines, or remembers, the party for her thirty-third birthday, she imagines, or remembers $^\wedge(\lambda e)e=$the party for her thirty-third birthday, and that when she imagines a tree (but no particular tree), she imagines $^\wedge(\lambda x)(\exists y)$ tree$(y)$ & $y=x$; that is, the property of being a thing $x$ that is identical to some tree. It does not seem possible to remember a tree without there being a tree that one remembers (even if one does not remember what tree it was). But the factive postulate, applied to this case, has only the consequence that if Mary remembers a tree, then there are trees, and not also the consequence that there is a tree of which her memory is a memory. But I leave this further matter aside for the present discussion.

## 12.4 Immunity to error through misidentification: A characteristic of PRO

The phenomenon of immunity to error through misidentification is widely appreciated, following Shoemaker (1968) and subsequent work. Recent discussions to which I will advert include Pryor (1999) and Campbell (1999). In this section I will sketch the phenomenon, and show that it applies to the contexts that we have been considering, of memory, imagination, and others, with respect to the positions marked by the understood subject PRO; but also, and more tendentiously, I will show that it does *not* apply to other subjects, including the reflexive, the emphatic reflexive, and even the first-person pronoun itself. A closer examination of the phenomenon follows in section 12.5.

Put in terms of language, the phenomenon of immunity to error through misidentification arises for certain circumstantial reports of experience in which one cannot sensibly wonder whether it is oneself that plays a given role in what is reported. Suppose (to use an example of John Campbell's) it seems to me, on the basis of present perceptual experience, that I hear trumpets. I might be mistaken. It may not be trumpets that I hear. If I am mistaken, I have made an error due to misidentification; misidentification, that is, of the object that is the source of my experience. I might ask myself whether I am so mistaken. But I cannot sensibly ask myself whether I am mistaken *just* in thinking that it is *I* who hear trumpets. In this sense, there is immunity to error through misidentification.

Similarly, as in a famous discussion of Wittgenstein's, if I feel that I am in pain, although I might conceivably ask whether it is really pain that I am in (perhaps others would consider it merely mild discomfort), I can't ask whether it is *I* who am in pain if anybody is, or think correctly that somebody is in pain, and wonder whether it is me.

What I have just put in terms of language may also be put in terms of the properties of occurrent thoughts; indeed there would seem to be nothing to distinguish these descriptions of the phenomenon except for the manner of presentation; or so I shall assume in what follows.

What is the reason for immunity to error through misidentification in the case of thinking, on the basis of a present perception, 'I hear trumpets?' I will assume it is this: that when I am in the relevant perceptual state, what I think is *that the subject of that state hears trumpets*. Hence, there can be no question of my *identifying* myself as the subject of the state. I enlarge upon this thesis below.

There are, as Pryor notes, two distinguishable cases of error through misidentification, and correlatively of immunity to error. In the first, or as I shall call it the simple case of immunity, one is immune from the following error in believing $F(a)$: that, knowing that $F(b)$ and believing, mistakenly, that $a=b$, one believes on those grounds that $F(a)$. In the second, or as I shall call it the generalized case, one is immune from the error, in believing $F(a)$: that, knowing that something is $F$, and believing, mistakenly, that it is $a$'s being $F$ that is responsible for its being the case that something is $F$, one therefore believes that $F(a)$.

Illustration of the simple case: John sees a woman at some distance, and sees that she is smoking a cigarette. Identifying the woman as Mary, he comes to believe that Mary is smoking a cigarette. The identification is mistaken, and so there is an error due to misidentification, even if, unbeknownst to John, Mary is indeed off somewhere smoking a cigarette. Illustration of the generalized case (from Pryor): John smells the smell of skunk in his back yard. Going outside, he sees a skunk, and concludes that it is that skunk that is (wholly or partly) responsible for the smell; but in fact the source is (entirely) another skunk.

The above characterizations of errors of identification, and of immunity to error, are rough in various ways. For one thing, they leave the notion of identification itself obscure. We often pass from the knowledge that $F(b)$ to the belief that $F(a)$ on the basis of the just-acquired belief that $a=b$; but only some such cases are cases of identifying $b$ as $a$. Knowing as I do that Fischer played the best move in position P, and having on the basis of my own analysis concluded that P-K6 is the best move, I come to believe that Fischer played P-K6 in P; but I do not thereby identify P-K6 as Fischer's move. Not all occasions in which one comes to believe an identity are identificatory of anything. Furthermore, although it is natural, as in the core cases of perceptual identification, to think of identification as identification of objects pure and simple, and therefore of the belief $F(b)$ that one has prior to identification as being *de re*, as a general rule this is too restrictive, I think: when, looking out of the airplane window, I identify yonder snowy expanse as Mont Blanc, no doubt I have beliefs about Mont Blanc itself; but it is also crucial to my so identifying it that it was presented to me as a snowy expanse glimpsed from an airplane window.

Passing over the further subtleties that would be required precisely to delimit errors due to misidentification, and even with the limited apparatus sketched to this point, we can now ask, as Shoemaker (1970) asked, whether immunity to error through misidentification arises in the case of ordinary memory, as it does in perception. That memory of events is subject to errors of misidentification is evident. Suppose that it seems to me that I remember Mary walking through the streets of Oxford. I describe the scene: certain buildings, cobblestones, etc., and Mary walking along. You observe, however, that the buildings and streets I am remembering are obviously in Cambridge, not Oxford, and from my description you recognize that it is Alice I am talking about, not Mary. I stand corrected. As you might say to me: you remember something all right, but it is not Mary walking through the streets of Oxford, but Alice walking through the streets of Cambridge that you remember. I have made a (double) error of misidentification: everything is in place for knowledge by memory of past events, except that certain objects have been misidentified.

Suppose I seem to remember walking through the streets of some city or another. I might again be corrected about which city I am remembering walking through, or informed that the city I am remembering walking through is in fact Cambridge, not Oxford: but can I be mistaken just in thinking that it is *my* walking through the streets of Cambridge that I remember, or remember someone's walking through the streets of Cambridge, and wonder whether it is me?

Such errors do not at first appear credible: but Shoemaker considers the possibility that some sort of 'false memory' has been implanted in me, so that it seems to me that I remember walking through the streets of Oxford, whereas the experience that is responsible for the memory is either nonexistent, or the experience of someone else, functional bits of whose brain have been somehow transplanted into mine. In my state, I experience what Shoemaker calls 'quasi-memories'; that is, what appear to me to be genuine memories of mine (and might actually have originated in the memories of someone else) but which are not memories of mine anyway, even if they could by a stretch be called memories, deriving as they did from someone else's experience.

Suppose that it seems to me that I remember falling downstairs (I am having an experience as of remembering falling downstairs); but, having been for all I know subjected to a partial brain transplant, I am aware that there may have been no such past episode in my life. Am I therefore subject to error through misidentification? Certainly, I (at least) quasi-remember falling downstairs, and there is no question of error due to misidentification there. Indeed, question whether I am in error is just the question whether what I am doing is *remembering*, as opposed to quasi-remembering. It is not as if I misidentified as myself a memorial subject that was not me (even though my experience has its origin in someone else's episodic memory); the question who is the subject of what is quasi-remembered does not even arise. Rather, if

I am in error in thinking that I remember falling downstairs, it is because I take for a memory what was only a quasi-memory (as I might take for a memory what I only imagine having happened to me in the past). If so, then immunity to error through misidentification, at least as I intend this notion, is not called into question. (Compare the discussion in Recanati (2007: 156 ff.) of different kinds of immunity.)

With the above understanding, we appear to have immunity to error through misidentification in the case described, of seeming to remember walking through the streets of Oxford. But I am now going to observe that, when it comes to the gerundive complements that we have been considering, the problem of their first-personal character shows up when we contrast PRO subjects with the first person itself.

## 12.5 Ways of remembering and imagining

Suppose that we form a small party, agreeing that we will call on John and encourage him to finish his thesis by July. Having cornered John, we explain how he should really be prudent given his scholastic and financial circumstances, and so forth. After the session, I try to remember whether we merely hinted around the subject, or whether it was explicitly said to John that he should finish his thesis by July. After a time, I might remember someone saying to John that he should finish his thesis by July; but I don't remember whether it was I who said it. Your memory for the occasion is better than mine, and you do remember my saying it; and you tell me so. I draw an inference as follows:

(21)   I remember someone saying John should finish his thesis by July;

   In fact, as I am now assured, it was I who said it; therefore,

   I remember my saying John should finish his thesis by July.

The reasoning seems to me impeccable. But (22) does not follow from the premises of (21), and is indeed obviously false:

(22)   I remember saying John should finish his thesis by July.

However, the only difference between (22) and the true conclusion of (21) is that the first-person pronoun has been replaced by PRO.

A certain intuition about this case seems clear enough. When I remember (what turns out to be) my saying that John should finish his thesis by July, I remember this through my recollection of the words in the air, which turn out to have been put there by me, though I don't remember that. When I fail to remember saying that John should finish his thesis by July, that is a failure that would be remedied if I remembered my saying that as an act of mine.

But suppose I do come to remember saying that John should finish his thesis by July. It cannot (and should not) be inferred that the event that I then remember is different from the event that I remembered earlier, through remembering hearing the words in the air. There is just one event in question, namely my saying John should finish his thesis by July. I might remember this event (as indeed I remember people, cities, and other things) in any of various ways; but these different ways do not translate into different remembered events in the complements of the conclusion of (21), on the one hand, and (22) on the other.

And, finally, there is this case: I remember a certain person's (my) saying that John should finish his thesis by July, but not saying it; that is, I remember hearing the words that, given that I recognize my own voice, I know could only have come from me, but I do not remember their having done so. Again there is just one event. But it can be remembered in either of two ways, namely as an action that I performed, or as an event that I witnessed. The latter sits well with pronouns, but the former is required of PRO.

Imagination goes along with memory here. Thus (an example modeled on Peacocke (1998: 212)) I can imagine my playing *Three Blind Mice* on the piano, but (since I do not play the piano) I cannot imagine playing *Three Blind Mice*; and that is because I cannot imagine it as an action that I myself perform.

As Michael Martin pointed out at the Sheffield conference, the above characteristic of PRO shows up in many contexts. There is, for instance, a difference in the intentions I may have when I intend to stop smoking (i.e., PRO to stop smoking), and when I intend merely that I should stop smoking. The latter intention might be fulfilled, say, by paying someone forcibly to remove cigarettes from my person whenever I am caught with them; but that is not fulfillment of an intention to stop smoking, which can only be done through willful refusal to put a cigarette to my lips and light up.

I have concentrated on remembering and imagining actions, or events that could be actions; but the peculiarities of PRO appear in matters that befall one, as well as what one does. Thus for me to remember falling downstairs, or crying, is to remember those events as processes that I underwent; whereas I might remember my falling downstairs by remembering how I felt as I picked myself up, or remember my crying by remembering how the tears felt rolling down my cheeks.

Pryor (1999) alludes to remembering things 'from the inside', as he puts it, setting aside other ways of remembering. This is a useful label to put on the problem, which might be translated into the present setting by saying that if in reports of remembering events, as indicated by gerundive complements, there is no semantic difference between the first-person pronoun and the understood subject PRO, then there can be no semantic difference between (22) and the conclusion of (21), contrary to fact. Indeed, there is more: the conclusion of (21) seems to be subject to errors of misidentification, at least given the right context. Remembering as I do someone saying John should finish his thesis by July, I might, in virtue of remembering the tone of voice that I heard, ascribe authorship of this event to you by mistake, or to myself by mistake; but that scenario seems impossible with (22).

In the connection with immunity to error through misidentification I have spoken thus far of memory; but examples with imagination come to mind as well. There is an intuitive difference between (23) and (24):

(23) Mary imagined herself flying through space (although she didn't realize it was she herself who was flying through space).

(24) Mary imagined [PRO flying through space] (although she didn't realize it was she herself who was flying through space).

(23) is possibly true; (24) is contradictory, or so it would appear.

If the above is correct, then we have isolated a case wherein PRO is, so to speak, more first-personal than the reflexive forms, and even more first-personal than the first-person pronoun itself. It is more first-personal in two respects: (i) unlike the first-personal forms, it is immune from error through misidentification; and (ii) the use of PRO always brings in an 'internal' dimension to the way what is remembered or imagined is apprehended. These phenomena point up the reality of the *de se* phenomenon more radically than the ordinary contexts of propositional attitude, or epistemic states. In the next section, I offer a way of understanding them.

## 12.6 The semantic contribution of PRO

A solution to the problems posed thus far in our discussion should have the following properties:

(a) It should state what is peculiar about the semantic contribution of the understood subject PRO;
(b) This contribution should be such as immediately to characterize the distinction between *de se* and *de re* interpretations;
(c) It should likewise imply immunity to error through misidentification;
(d) It should do this in such a way that immunity to error through misidentification in the classification of ordinary perceptual experience follows along as a special case; and

(e) It should explain the distinction between the 'internal' dimension signalled by PRO, and the possibly only 'external' dimension expressed by ordinary pronouns and reflexive forms.

In short, as I see it, the problems of the *de se*, immunity to error through misidentification, and the rest, call for a solution in terms of logical form. The solution, moreover, should explain the *grounds* upon which *de se* interpretation, and immunity to error through misidentification, arise.

Now, it is obvious that immunity to error through misidentification must arise, not because identification is infallible, but because there is no question of identification at all. If we ask what it is for a position, call it π, in a construction

$$\ldots \pi \ldots$$

not to require identification within that construction, there is a case that at once presents itself, namely the case where π is a variable, free within the context ... π ..., but bound from outside it; and more generally where π is a functional context $f(\pi')$, $\pi'$ a variable free inside but bound outside the context, and $f$ interpreted by a function that is given once the context surrounding ... π ... is given.

In Chapter 3 above it was argued that contexts of the above shape were crucially involved in locating events with respect to one's own position in time. So in saying (or thinking), as in A.N. Prior's famous example, 'Well, *that's over*', the event of which one is thinking that it is over is thought of as coming before one's thinking that. Thoughts of this type were called *reflexive*, the general form being

$$\varphi(e) \;\&\; R(e,e')$$

where φ is some condition on $e$, and $R$ expresses a temporal relation between $e$ and the episode $e'$ of thinking or saying. Suppose, for instance, I think, or say on the basis of perception, that a dog just barked. The logical form is then (25):

(25) $(\exists e')$ think/say[I,$e'$, $^\wedge(\exists e)(\exists x)$ (dog($x$) & bark($x,e$) & $e$ just before $e'$)]

I cannot then ask whether I am right in having located in the near past any barking that would make my belief or utterance true; for it is given in the thought itself that it belongs to *my* near past; i.e., just before my thinking or saying.[9]

---

[9] Thus the experience $e'$ has been 'loaded' into the proposition expressed. But isn't the truth of the proposition independent of that connection, and indeed of whether there was any experience at all? An analogous problem was discussed in Chapter 3, inconclusively; however, I would maintain that the

Perhaps my last statement is somewhat too strong. Perhaps, even with the alleged barking still ringing in my ears, I have misestimated the lapse of time between my perception and my thought; and how much before is 'just before' anyway? However this may be, I cannot ask myself whether I am mistaken just in thinking that it was in *my* past that a dog barked.

Following the analogy of reflexive thoughts with respect to time, suppose that we identify as the peculiar semantic contribution of PRO that it presents the subject as *the subject (or experiencer) of the event or state e* as given in the higher clause, or $\sigma(e)$ for short. This conjecture immediately gives for (4), repeated here, the logical form (26):

(4)  John/Each man expects PRO to win.

(26)  (For John/each man=$x$) ($\exists e$) expect[$x, e,$ $^{\wedge}(\exists e')$ win($\sigma(e), e'$)].

The intended contrast is with (27):

(27)  (For John/each man=$x$) ($\exists e$) expect[$x, e,$ $^{\wedge}(\exists e')$ win($x, e'$)].

The complement of the latter is one interpretation of (1), repeated here:

(1)  John/Each man expects (that) he will win.

an interpretation that, on the hypothesis under consideration, is not available for (4). But this complement is not immune to error through misidentification. For suppose that I expect, indeed know, that the contestant who trained hardest will win the competition I have entered; but I do not know, and I know that I do not know, whether I myself am that contestant. Then, for all I know, it is I myself whom I expect to win. But I also know that it is not true that I expect to win. Later, but still before the competition, I come on the basis of certain evidence to identify myself as the person who trained hardest. Holding fast to my previous knowledge, I now come to believe that I myself will win, and therefore to expect that I will win, and to expect to win. My first expectation, that I will win, is subject to error through misidentification: if the person who trained hardest turns out, despite my evidence, to be other than me, then I have made such an error. But my second expectation, namely my expectation of winning, is not subject to such an error, despite the fact that I have this expectation only because I expect that I will win, an expectation that involves the possibility of error.

The informal considerations just given are decisive against construing (4) as merely having the logical form (27), provided indeed that we take it that the

---

interpretation of the speaker's word, or thought-constituent, marked by 'just' does carry the temporal anchoring expressed in (25).

reflexive pronoun *myself* can only be taken up as a bound variable, which is precisely what the proposal that there will be an intervening mode of presentation denies. However, the premiss that the complement of (1) on some construal is not immune to error through misidentification still stands. The situation as I conceive it is the following. When I expect that I, or I myself, will be F, my expectation is subject to error through misidentification if my grounds for it are the possibly mistaken belief that I am the G, and the knowledge merely that the G will be F. Thus the complement of (1) is subject to such error, where taken up as shown in (27). Knowing as I do that I am the experiencer of the state $e$ of that expectation, when I expect that I myself will be F, I also expect to be F; hence anything that supports or undermines the first expectation will support or undermine the second. However, whereas I can sensibly ask myself whether, after all, I have identified myself correctly in expecting that I will win, I cannot ask myself whether I have identified myself correctly in expecting to win.

The considerations just given are intuitive. Indeed, so long as we hold to the thesis that the subject or experiencer $\sigma(e)$ of a state $e$ cannot fail to be known as the thing $x$ that is that subject or experiencer, the link between, for instance, (28) and (29) cannot be broken:

(28)  I expect that I (myself) will win.

(29)  I expect to win.

There is, nevertheless, a difference between them. The thought

$$^\wedge(\exists e')\ \text{win}(\sigma(e), e')$$

is distinct from

$$^\wedge(\exists e')\ \text{win}(x, e')$$

(for given values of $x$ and $e$), even if they are not intensionally different; or so I would submit. The peculiar contribution of PRO, an optional contribution of pronouns and (depending upon the context) perhaps of reflexive forms as well, is that it picks up the subject, the 'controller' in familiar linguistic terminology, through the role that it plays with respect to the superordinate or matrix predicate, in this case 'expect'.

Consider the application of the above view to the classic case, Castañeda's amnesiac war hero, where the data are that (5) but not (6) may be said truly:

(5)   The war hero thinks that he is a hero.

(6)   The war hero thinks that he himself is a hero.

Suppose we allow that (5) is true, with the logical form (30):

(30)  (For the war hero=x) ($\exists e$) think[$x,e,{}^\wedge(\exists e')$ hero($x,e'$)]

but take (6) as false, with the logical form (31):

(31)  (For the war hero=x) ($\exists e$) think[$x,e,{}^\wedge(\exists e')$ hero($\sigma(e),e'$)]

Are the thoughts attributed in the two cases intensionally different? In other words, could anyone other than the war hero have been the subject or experiencer of that war hero's individual state? This is not a trivial question; but I shall proceed here on the assumption that the answer is negative.[10] If that is so, then there are no grounds upon which the intensionally individuated contents of (30) and (31) may be distinguished: they will coincide in truth value in any actual or counterfactual situation. Even if they do coincide, it does not follow that they are the same thought (but for a construal that would make them intensionally different, see section 12.8 below.)

Thus far I have concentrated upon one aspect of PRO, namely its immunity to error through misidentification. But there is also the 'internal' aspect of PRO to be considered, an aspect that is not brought out on the view given thus far.

In the picture that we have been using throughout this discussion, the bare predicates of a language are to be thought of as classifiers of events, and their arguments are selected as participants in the events so classified. The relation of a given participant to an event—agent, or patient, or whatever it is exactly—is, to use a terminology that is common to a variety of perspectives, and even conceptions of semantics, the *thematic role* that the participant bears to that event. Now, without delving into the variety of linguistic and metaphysical questions that have been raised about thematic roles, we may distinguish: (i) the case where an object $\alpha$ in a predication $\varphi(e,\alpha)$ is given through some description external to its participation in $e$; and (ii) the case where $\alpha$ is given simply as $\theta(e)$, where $\theta$ expresses the thematic role that $\alpha$ bears to $e$.

I suggest that the 'internal' aspect of PRO results from that element's being considered, either exclusively or in conjunction with its value as given by its antecedent, as the bearer of some thematic role that its syntactic position selects for the bare predicate with which it is in construction. On this hypothesis, for example, the interpretation of the subject in

PRO falling downstairs

---

[10] Plainly, however, a full treatment must take a view on the very general question, what properties of events (taken as objects of some sort, following Davidson) are contingent, and what necessary. (In Chapter 3 it was suggested that the spatiotemporal location of at least some events was a contingent matter.)

is as in

$$\text{falling downstairs}(\theta(e), e)$$

where $\theta(e)$ expresses the relation, something like *undergoer*, that a thing falling downstairs bears to an event of so falling.

The above suggestion accords with Michael Martin's observation. When I intend to stop smoking, I intend that I am the agent of my stopping smoking; but when I merely intend that I stop smoking there is no implication of my agency in the stopping, any more than there would be on the part of the automobile in 'the car stopped moving'.

In Martin's case and others, it will be a primitive property of PRO that it is construed as the bearer of one or another relation to events as classified by the predicate it appears with. Supposing this property given, we can express the difference between (22), repeated here, and the conclusion of (21), here given as (32):

(22) I remember saying that John should finish his thesis by July.

(32) I remember my saying that John should finish his thesis by July.

For (22) to be true I must remember the event in question *as* something of which I was the agent; that is, the property of events that I remember puts me in the picture as *agent of e*. That requirement does not obtain in (32).[11] Likewise we can distinguish, I believe, minimal pairs such as those in (33)–(34):

(33) I remember/imagine [PRO/myself falling downstairs].

(34) I remember/imagine [PRO/myself crying].

We can now join Martin's observation together with the suggested explanation for immunity to error through misidentification, as follows. When one remembers or imagines *PRO being F*, then the linguistic element PRO is distinguished in two ways: (i) by being understood as the thing

---

[11] As Stephen Parkinson has made me aware, there is at least one case where contexts such as (22) and (32) are not to be discriminated, namely the case where the question is not merely what one remembers, but more stringently what one remembers out of one's own memory, or of one's own knowledge. Thus suppose I am to testify as to what was said to John. I remember someone's saying that he should finish his thesis, but not that it was I who said it. In that case, even if I have become convinced on other grounds that it must have been I who spoke, I cannot agree with an inquisitor's assertion that I do after all remember my saying it; for in the setting of testimony I am supposed to state what I remember without reliance upon external evidence. Cases of this sort are of course not confined to memory of oneself: if I remember the blue Ford at the scene of the crime, and have only since become convinced (rightly) that it was the getaway car, I still cannot respond 'Yes' to the question put at trial whether I remember the getaway car at the scene of the crime.

σ(e) that is in the state *e* of remembering or imagining itself; and (ii) by being at the same time understood as the bearer of the thematic role θ(e′) as determined through the selection for the subject of the predicate F(e′) (so in general that σ(e)=θ(e′) is presupposed). I shall abbreviate this dual role of PRO by 'σ(e) & θ(e′)'. With PRO so understood, (22) for instance comes out as (35):

(35)  (∃e) Remember{I,e,^λ(e′) [say(σ(e) & θ(e′),that John should finish his thesis by July,e′)]}.

We thus bring out both the fact that, if (22) is true, then the subject cannot make an error of misidentification, and that what is remembered is remembered *as* an action performed.

In concluding this section, I show how the Fodor-Thomson example comes out on the view advanced here. We are given the premises (36) and (37):

(36)  Only Churchill gave the speech.

(37)  Churchill remembers PRO giving the speech.

And we aim to derive (38):

(38)  Only Churchill remembers PRO giving the speech.

The proper name 'Churchill' may be rendered as a quantifier, 'for x=Churchill', with obvious semantics, and the subject 'only Churchill' of (36) and (38) is understood as quantificational as well, where in general 'Only x such that A are B' is true if and only if all B are A. We need also to assume, perhaps as a matter of presupposition, that 'Only Churchill is F' warrants 'Churchill is F'.

With these assumptions, (36) will have a logical form equivalent to (39):

(39)  (∃e) give(Churchill,the speech,e) & (∀x≠Churchill) ¬(∃e′) give(x,the speech,e′)

For (37), taking PRO as merely a bound variable, we have (40):

(40)  (For x=Churchill)(∃e) Remember[x,e,^(λe′) give(x,the speech,e′)]

and it will be sufficient to derive (41):

(41)  (∀x≠Churchill) ¬(∃e) Remember[x,e,^(λe′) give(x,the speech,e′)]

Supposing on the contrary

        x≠Churchill & Remember[x,e,^(λe′) give(x,the speech,e′)]

we have, by the factivity of 'remember', the consequence

$$x{\neq}\text{Churchill} \ \& \ (\exists e') \ \text{give}(x,\text{the speech},e')$$

contradicting (39).

The assumption crucial to the above derivation of (38) is that PRO be 'captured' by the quasi-quantifier 'only Churchill'. Because, as remarked above, it is not true that the premisses (36)–(37) lead to the conclusion (42), we must say something about the interpretation of the pronoun 'his', even where it is anaphoric to 'Churchill':

(42)  Only Churchill remembers his [Churchill's] giving the speech.

It is sufficient to suggest that the pronoun, unlike PRO, can simply go proxy for the name, that being enough to block the implication.

The simple treatment of PRO as obligatorily a bound variable is sufficient to explain the Fodor-Thomson observation. On the more complex treatment suggested in this section, the premiss (39) is replaced by (43), and the desired conclusion (41) by (44):

(43)  (For $x=$Churchill)$(\exists e)$ Remember$[x,e,^\wedge(\lambda e')$ give$(\sigma(e) \ \& \ \theta(e'),$the speech,$e')]$

(44)  $(\forall x{\neq}\text{Churchill}) \ \neg(\exists e)$ Remember$[x,e,^\wedge(\lambda e')$ give$(\sigma(e) \ \& \ \theta(e'),$the speech,$e')]$

The derivation of this conclusion is only marginally more complex, requiring as it does just the added point that, where $e$ is a state of Churchill's remembering, and $e'$ is any event of giving the speech, Churchill himself is indeed $\sigma(e)$ and $\theta(e')$.

But could a person $x$ be in a state $e$ of imagining being $F$ without *recognizing* that $x=\sigma(e)$, the subject of the property of events being imagined? If this can happen then perhaps, as tentatively suggested in Campbell (1999), $x$ would have thoughts of which he did not seem to himself to be the author—in this case, the thought that someone $y$ was in a state $e$ of imagining some property of events befalling the subject of $e$, without recognizing that $x$ himself was the subject of $e$. In any case, it seems safe to assume that any such condition would be pathological.[12]

---

[12] I have profited here from the criticism of my original discussion in Recanati (2007: 183 ff.), and I have tried in the present revision to clarify the example. The reflexive interpretation of the contents of certain thoughts, or properties of events, concerning oneself aims to explain (a) how they are different from *de re* thought and (b) why they are not subject to error through misidentification, in the sense that the question cannot arise whether the subject of such thoughts is identical to the thinker of them; similarly, *mutatis mutandis*, for certain thoughts about one's own past, present, or future, as in

These remarks conclude my discussion of the contribution of PRO, and the perspective that the account given here affords upon the semantic data that suggest it. If the account is correct, then PRO, and, I will assume, at least some reflexive and emphatic reflexive elements, are distinguished by having special interpretations, as in the third of the three options that I presented in section 12.1 above. In the next section I take up the question of the other options directly.

## 12.7 Alternatives explored

As we know from the story surrounding (5), repeated here, in any situation in which the war hero's beliefs are true, he is not reading about himself.

(5)  The war hero thinks that he is a hero.

In the world according to the war hero, as we might say, there is on the one hand him, and on the other the person whose exploits he is reading about. It is this reflection that encourages the idea, expressed in the first hypothesis of section 12.1 above, that the apparent existence of contexts that are simply and strictly *de re*, but not first-personal, is after all an illusion: in all such cases, there is an intervening 'mode of presentation', which would in the present instance be brought out in the logical form (45):

(45)  (For the war hero$=x$) ($\exists e$) think[$x,e$, $^\wedge(\exists e')$ hero(the person $x$ is reading about,$e'$)]

---

Chapters 3 and 4, or *de se* memories (or quasi-memories), or imaginative episodes. Nothing in that interpretation implies (and nothing in any interpretation should imply) that a person who is having a *de se* thought, a thought about her own past, or a *de se* imaginative or memorial experience must recognize it as such. Thus pathological *x* in my example *is* imagining *de se* being *F*, but fails to recognize that he himself is the one doing so. Recanati supposes, I think, that *de se* imagining requires such recognition, else immunity to error through misidentification will not be satisfied. But that is not so: pathological *x* cannot and does not ask himself whether *the subject of imagination* is really the same as *the subject of the imagining F*: that question is already settled. Pathological *x*'s error is not with respect to the identity of these elements, but in his failure to recognize that he is either.

In Chapter 4 above, I allowed in response to Richard that the feeling of relief that accompanied the reflexive thought that *x* believed that such-and-such painful episode was over (as of the time of so thinking) was not of itself sufficient to bring about the feeling of relief. For that feeling to ensue, it was required also that the affirmation of the belief be located temporally within the belief state. (The corresponding requirement in the case of speech, for the time of utterance to be located within the time of the belief state, is trivially satisfied, because speech is necessarily self-conscious.) My response to Richard was not a concession, except in the sense of acknowledging the need to recognize that what goes without saying for speech must in the case of silent thought be mentioned.

Finally, I note that Recanati's worries about self-knowledge do not tell one way or another concerning the nature of *de se* thoughts, at least with respect to the options that I consider here: see further note 15 below.

This mode of presentation contains the war hero himself as value of $x$, and in that sense is *de re*. But if all that is going on in the example is that the thought attributed in the complement of *He thinks he is a hero* has a structure that is not revealed in the linguistic material alone, then it would seem that the first-personal or *de se* thought has no peculiar status to be explained, being simply the *de re* case unadorned.

As I understand it, Stalnaker's (1981) discussion of indexical belief could lead to a similar conclusion, transposed, as it were, into a different key. For Stalnaker, the background story (and its presuppositions, including the presupposition, if it is present, that the war hero is in fact reading about himself) serves, not to fix a mode of presentation, but rather to determine which alternative situations of utterance of 'He (the war hero) is a hero' are to be taken into account. So consider all of those situations $w$ such that the war hero is in $w$ reading about a person other than himself. In those situations, the speaker's embedded subject 'he' refers, not to the war hero, but to that other person. Moreover, only such situations are consistent with what the war hero believes (assuming that the speaker's presuppositions are satisfied, as they would be if the war hero thinks that the person he is reading about is not himself). The content that the speaker attributes to the war hero's beliefs is then just the content

$$^\wedge(\exists e')\ \text{hero}(\text{the person } x \text{ is reading about}, e')]$$

for the war hero as value of $x$, with the presuppositions mentioned. This content is constructed, not by first filling in a mode of presentation and then taking the expression so filled in around the counterfactual situations $w$, but rather by taking what Stalnaker calls the *diagonal* proposition, obtained by determining, for each $w$, what the truth value of 'He (the war hero) is a hero' would be as said by the speaker in $w$.

It is pretty clear that, for any *particular* way of filling in the notion of a situation consistent with what the war hero believes, we can construct a mode of presentation that will, when supplanted for $x$ in the complement clause, deliver along the horizontal just what the diagonal proposition delivers along the diagonal. In the case under consideration, we supplant '$x$' with 'the person $x$ is reading about', for instance. We can also proceed in the other direction, supplanting 'the person x is reading about' with the simple variable, but taking along the diagonal the worlds $w$ and the utterances, 'He is a hero', where the pronoun refers to whoever it is would have been meant by its utterance in $w$. There are perhaps differences between these approaches, centering on the point that in the method of supplementation we ascribe a mode of presentation for which, in effect, we regard what is said as elliptical, whereas in Stalnaker's diagonal method we supply instead a conception of what is merely implicated by the speaker; but I shall not dwell on these differences here. In either case, we are taking those *de re* attributions that are not *de se* (that is, those that would sustain a use of the bare pronoun, but not of the emphatic reflexive, or of PRO) as not meant literally. And indeed, how could they be? For, after all, we know that the amnesiac war hero believes he is not the person whom he is reading about, and that he is ready to say as much, and in the first person. Yet his beliefs cannot be internally faulted, or rectified by mere cogitation. So if we are to have a conception of how the world would be if his beliefs were true, we cannot found it upon a combination of the literal interpretation of what he is reported to believe, on the one hand, and his own avowals on the other.

I suggest that the considerations just rehearsed do show, either through Stalnaker's route or through that suggested by invoking modes of presentation, that so long as we wish to have a conception of 'how the world would be' if a believer's beliefs were true (assuming of course that there *is* such a way); or, to put it only slightly differently, but to the same effect, so long as we need to have a conception of what the notation we use to ascribe thoughts to ourselves or to others is a notation *for*, we should regard the true report in (5), as it might be called a report of a true belief in the absence of proper identification (in this case of the person the war hero is reading about with himself), as expressing something other than just what is given on its face (taking the proposition expressed in the usual way, and not 'on the diagonal').

The tempting conclusion is that (6), repeated here, is the true *de re* report:

(6)   The war hero believes that he himself is a hero.

The difference between (5) and (6) cannot be left just at that, however; for we need also to explain why (6) cannot be asserted under the same circumstances as (5), or why PRO should contrast even with the emphatic reflexive in the contexts of imagining, for example.[13]

For these reasons also in part, the constructions of Lewis (1979) and Chierchia (1990) don't appear to satisfy the demands of the case. Recall that

---

[13] There are important comparative-linguistic questions here. To take one example, note that in English 'believe', unlike 'expect', does not take controlled complements, so that we do not have *'John believes [PRO to be a hero]'. The corresponding construction in Italian, namely 'Gianni crede [PRO di essere un eroe]' is, however, fully grammatical, and (I am informed) unambiguously *de se*. Corresponding to English 'John believes that he himself is a hero' Italian has the construction 'Gianni crede che lei stesso è un eroe'; but this, as again I am told, is not necessarily *de se*. From these facts we might draw the cross-linguistic conclusion that it is the understood subject (which, as pointed out for instance in Chierchia (1990), must for languages like Italian be distinguished from the null subject pronoun of a finite clause) that is crucially involved in the *de se* phenomena.

on Chierchia's view the positions critical for *de se* interpretation are abstracted over, so that the object of the thought that one is oneself a hero is: $^\wedge(\lambda x)$ hero $(x)$. There is no evident reason why immunity to error through misidentification should be associated with the abstracted position, or why, to use Pryor's term, true reports of imagining and remembering with understood, PRO, subjects should always indicate imagining and remembering 'from the inside'. Furthermore, as suggested by David Kaplan in his Bielefeld Lecture, 1995, and subsequently in a Gareth Evans Memorial Lecture at Oxford (1995), Lewis's strategy would generalize, implausibly, to other embedded indexicals, words like *now*, *here*, *today*, and the like. Finally, as noted in Landau (2000: ch. 2), the account faces difficulties in accounting for the phenomenon he calls *partial control*, where the understood subject is plural, but its antecedent is singular; I give one example of this phenomenon below.

Granting that the understood subject must be a real subject in the logical form, it may be asked whether the unadorned *de re* already exhibits the property of immunity to error through misidentification; that is, whether the recourse to $\sigma(e)$ exploited above is really necessary. The question arises, because the apparent cases of *de re* that were not *de se* all seem upon closer examination, either through the invocation of hidden modes of presentation or through Stalnaker's suggestion, to be understandable as carrying more semantic baggage than the simple *de re* would suggest. This diagnosis applies even to cases of the embedded first person, as we saw above: when I remembered (what, from my point of view, turned out to be) my saying that John should finish his thesis by July, I remembered it through a conception of the subject of that action *as* some producer of words in the air, the bearer of a certain tone of voice, or something similar. Thus when the *de se* is missing, there is always, so to speak, a fallback to some underlying content that is not strictly *de re*.

Now, this last reflection, assuming it is correct, of course does not show that the *de re* thought is not there, but only that, if it is there, it is there in virtue of something else, something that is not purely *de re*. But this phenomenon holds quite generally for embedded indexicals. If I wonder, now, quite out of the blue, whether it was sunny yesterday in Los Angeles, there is no question of my misidentifying yesterday, that day being given as *the day before my wondering this*. But if I wonder whether it was sunny yesterday in Los Angeles because I wonder whether it was sunny on 27 May, believing, mistakenly, that the 27th was two days ago rather than yesterday, then I make an error due to misidentification (I have not properly grasped what I am wondering about). That fact alone does not show that I am not wondering about yesterday, the day itself. Likewise, in the setting due to Castañeda, the war hero's belief that he is a hero can be a belief about himself, purely *de re*, despite his misidentification or lack of identification. That attribution need not be withdrawn just because another stands behind it. Our question therefore remains.

For the purposes of this chapter, I shall leave that question unanswered. In any case, it seems to me that immunity to error through misidentification calls for a thing's being given through material supplied from a higher context, as in the example just presented of wondering whether yesterday was sunny in Los Angeles. But I must leave this matter for another occasion.

## 12.8 Links to formalization

Much of the recent literature on the *de se* has taken as its point of departure the account of demonstrative and indexical expressions developed originally in Kaplan (1977). Schlenker (2003) proposes a modification of Kaplan's Logic of Demonstratives that is designed to incorporate the *de se* by admitting context-sensitivities of the type that Kaplan dubs 'monsters'. Assuming the account of the *de se* advanced above, I examine the extent to which it can be seen, within the formal perspective of that modification, as a further specification of it.

Recall that in Kaplan (1977), truth in a model is defined relative to pairs $(c,w)$, where $c$ is a context and $w$ a possible world, and that the content of a sentence in a context $c$ is the set of possible worlds in which it is true. Contexts, whatever they are, are anyway such that one can pull from them a speaker, a time, and a world of the context, namely the world in which the speaker is conceived of as saying the sentence at the time in question. The system thus involves double-indexing with respect to the possible worlds, as in two-dimensional modal logic, and it therefore permits, in principle, operators that generalize over context worlds as well as worlds of evaluation. Such operators are 'monsters', and Kaplan urged that, although they are definable, they could not exist in our language (or, presumably, human languages generally).

Schlenker (2003) develops a formal account of the *de se* that allows manipulation of the context parameter, specifically the agent of the context (a suggestion to similar effect is found in Israel and Perry (1996)). This allows Schlenker to distinguish, for example, the content of the complement in '$x$ hopes $x$ is elected', namely the one true in those worlds in which $x$ is elected (independently of the agent), from that of '$x$ hopes [PRO to be elected]', which comprises those $(a,w)$ in which $a$ is the agent of the context, and $a$ is elected. Assuming as Schlenker does the modal account of the propositional attitudes, '$x$ hopes that $p$' will be true in a context $c$ in a world $w$ just in case every *context* (not: possible world) compatible with what *x* hopes is one in which *p*, where the context comes with a world of evaluation and also an agent. Thus a context is compatible with what *x* hopes in hoping that *x* is elected if and only if it is one in which *x* is elected; but it is compatible with what *x* hopes in hoping to be elected if and only if it is one in which the agent of that context is elected, independently of whether that agent is *x*.[14]

Assuming the account developed in this article, we can see it as a further specification of Schlenker's method. Supposing as above that the content of the complement subject position in '*x* hopes [PRO to be elected]' is the conjunction '$\sigma(e)$ & $\theta(e)$', where *e* is the situation of *x*'s hoping, we may suppose that, although the individual situation *e* belongs essentially to *x*, the *kind* of situation that *e* is could belong to anybody. If, therefore, we allow the instance *e* of that kind to vary independently, and make it part of the context, we arrive at an account that specifies more precisely, but in the same manner as the parameter of the agent of the context, what it will be for a context to be compatible with what *x* hopes. Thus, whatever the advantages and uses, or the disadvantages and abuses, of the modal theory of the attitudes, the empirical material given here, if I am right, will supplement the purely formal move that Schlenker suggests.

## 12.9 Concluding examples and extensions

The above discussion of PRO has developed a point of view according to which two rather sophisticated concepts are involved in its correct employment: (a) the concept of being an agent that thinks thoughts, expressed by '$\sigma(e)$', and (b) the concept of being an undergoer or agent of experience, expressed by '$\theta(e)$'. It follows that those who use this form, or the relevant constructions, correctly, or have thoughts that are properly reported using them, must be able to deploy both concepts. But is that really essential to first-person thoughts?

I leave aside the question of reports of the thoughts of creatures for which the question how to take our very expression of the thoughts that we attribute to them, or in what sense they have thoughts, is itself an issue. The problem is whether there are notions of the self, more primitive or anyway different from those that I have recruited, namely of oneself as a thinker of thoughts and undergoer of experiences, that, whether or not they answer to English PRO or anything else, deserve to be brought into the realm of first-person thoughts.

---

[14] Schlenker's formal theory involves an extensionalization of Kaplan's Logic of Demonstratives, in which the relevant parameters occupy quantifiable places.

Recall the general suggestion of Peacocke (1981), that first-person thoughts by $x$ contain a constituent $[self_x]$ a token of a type *self* available to all. I am proposing, to use Peacocke's terminology, that one such type is that expressed by '$\sigma(e)$ & $\theta(e)$', where $e$ is some particular event, so that the tokens are instantiations of $e$, where $x=\sigma(e)=\theta(e)$. That does not exclude the existence of other types. At the same time, the phenomena of memory 'from the inside', and of complements necessarily interpreted as denoting particular ways of remembering and imagining things, appear to show that these types are not included in our most basic system of speech; unsurprisingly, since we all do conceive of ourselves in the ways required for the account.

In concluding, I consider three points, the first two of which have appeared in the literature, and the third of which will likely have occurred to the reader in passing. The first point is the problem of like belief, as discussed by Lewis, and the second concerns a question raised early on for Castañeda, whether or to what extent first-personal knowledge can be shared. The third point addresses briefly the peculiarities of the distribution of the understood subject, whose semantics has chiefly occupied us.

Lewis (1979) discusses Perry's (1977) case of crazy Heimson, who believes that he—he himself—is David Hume. He is ready to say, 'I am David Hume', 'I wrote the *Treatise*', 'I served my King in France, and was denied a chair in Edinburgh', and so forth, and to behave accordingly, whatever that may come to exactly. In Lewis's view, there should be a sense in which Heimson and Hume believe alike; that is, a sense in which it is not merely true that each conceives himself to be an $x$ such that: $x$ is David Hume (for this would give them different beliefs, a false one for $x$=Heimson, and a true one for $x$=Hume), but rather, or anyway also, that each has numerically the same belief as the other. Lewis presented several considerations in favor of this view.[15] Abstracting from these, and from the critical discussion in Stalnaker (1981) and Higginbotham (1991a),

---

[15] For Lewis, using the full apparatus of counterpart theory, Heimson=$x$ is in the following state (i):

(i) $x$ ascribes to $x$ the property of being a $y$ such that $y$ inhabits a possible world in which $y$=David Hume.

Nothing in this formulation prevents it from being the case that Heimson is in such a state without realizing it, or even in error in thinking that it is not to *himself* that he ascribes the property; that is, nothing prevents Heimson=$x$ from being also as in (ii):

(ii) $x$ does not ascribe to $x$ the property of being a $y$ such that $y$ ascribes to $y$ the property of being a $z$ such that $z$ inhabits a possible world in which $z$=David Hume.

From this point of view, Lewis's exposition takes for granted (as does my recapitulation, intended to be faithful to Lewis) that Heimson is indeed aware that he believes that he himself is David Hume (as Lewis writes, Heimson is ready to say, 'I am David Hume', 'I wrote the *Treatise*', etc.).

I consider the question, on the view of beliefs about oneself advanced here, to what extent Lewis's view can be sustained.

It cannot, if I am right, be literally sustained. For the anaphoric possibilities for an element in a complement structure, whether (in the terminology developed here) event-like or proposition-like, are limited to these:

(i) The anaphoric element inherits the reference of its antecedent, giving for

Heimson believes that he (himself) is Hume

I mention this matter because it might be supposed (and appears to be supposed in Recanati (2007: 182)) that thoughts about oneself must involve a kind of overarching or fully transparent self-knowledge, whereby one not only has thoughts about oneself, but recognizes that they are about oneself, recognizes one's own recognition, and so on. But this extra dimension of the first person is in addition to the question of the nature of *de se* thought, at least insofar as, for instance, Lewis's view and (or versus) the view taken here are concerned.

At the same time, in raising the issue of self-knowledge Recanati advances an important question. Consider a reflexive attitude $A$ with respect to a complement $F$ as in (i):

(i)  $(\exists e)\ A[x, {}^\wedge(\exists e')\ F(\text{subject of } e, e'), e]$

Suppose (i) is true of $\alpha$. Then, or so we have said, pathological $\alpha$ may fail to recognize $e$ as his own experience, and in that sense may have a *de se* attitude that he conceives to be the *de se* attitude of someone else. He may even come to believe that whoever-that-is believes *de se* the whole of (i), with '$x$' replaced by 'subject of $e^*$', without recognizing that $e^*$ is his own state of belief, as in (ii):

(ii)  $(\exists e^*)\ \text{Believes}\{x, (\exists e)\ A[\text{subject of } e^*, (\exists e')\ F(\text{subject of } e, e'), e], e^*\}$

Obviously, the construction iterates. So long as $\alpha$ fails to recognize the relevant states as his, he will remain pathological.

However, pathological $\alpha$ believes, with respect to a certain experience $e$, the existentially general (iii), or perhaps believes with respect to some other thing $\beta$ and the experience $e$ the particular (iv):

(iii)  $(\exists y)\ A[y, {}^\wedge(\exists e')\ F(\text{subject of } e, e'), e]$

(iv)  $A[y, {}^\wedge(\exists e')\ F(\text{subject of } e, e'), e]$

Taking (iv) for simplicity, $\alpha$ will believe (v) of $\beta$ and $\mathbf{e}$:

(v)  $y=$subject of $e$

But he fails to realize that (v) is true of $\alpha$ and $e$. I take it that this failure, in Recanati's view, disqualifies (iv), or (i), with $\alpha$ assigned to '$x$', as a true *de se* thought.

Still, there are two separate questions to be considered. First, what is it for an attitude or other experiential state, in whose object the bearer $\alpha$ of that attitude or state figures, to be immune from error through misidentification? Second, what is it for such an attitude or state, in whose object the thing $\alpha$ that has that attitude or state figures, to constitute knowledge by $\alpha$, insofar as $\alpha$ herself figures in it, that it is about $\alpha$? The answer suggested to the first question is: there can be no misidentification when $\alpha$ is given as just the subject of the attitude or state. It can be that where $\alpha$ believes $F(\alpha)$, $\alpha$ does not recognize that the belief is about herself (because she has not identified the subject of the belief as herself). But insofar as $\alpha$ believes $F$(subject of belief state), and knows that the belief state is hers, she recognizes the subject of belief as herself. Pathological $\alpha$ can indeed fail to recognize that the belief state is hers, but only because her state is one that he does not construe as her own, and not because she has not recognized that its object concerns the one holding the belief. We attribute *de se* beliefs to others; but pathological $\alpha$ attributes a *de se* belief to herself without recognizing that it is herself to the logical form

> For Heimson=x, (∃e) believes[x,e,^(∃e′) identical(x,Hume,e′)]

(ii) The anaphoric element takes on the same reference, but now given as σ(e), expressing the relation of the subject to the state that it is in, giving

> For Heimson=x, (∃e) believes[x,e,^(∃e′) identical(σ(e),Hume,e′)]

(iii) Besides taking on the reference as σ(e), the anaphoric element expresses the thematic relation θ(e′) determined by the events classified by the subordinate predicate, in this case identity. Then we have

> For Heimson=x, (∃e) believes[x,e,^(∃e′) identical(σ(e)&θ(e′),Hume,e′)]

In none of these cases will Heimson and Hume believe numerically alike.

On the other hand, I suggest, there is a sense in (ii), and therefore in (iii), in which Heimson and Hume do believe alike. Let α and β be two belief states satisfying

> ^(∃e′) identical(σ(e),Hume,e′)

Does α=β? Well, we know that α=β if and only if σ(α)=σ(β); but there is as it were nothing *within* α and β to distinguish them: they are states of believing that one is David Hume, possibly the same, possibly different, depending upon whether the bearers σ(α) and σ(β) of those states are the same or different. In this sense, they are alike.

For an analogy, consider two collapses of bridges. Are they the same collapse, or different collapses? Ignoring time, we may say that they are the same if the bridges are the same, otherwise different. But insofar as they are given merely as collapses of bridges, there is nothing to tell them apart. It is not just a matter of one-to-one correspondences. It is true that two squares of natural numbers are identical just in case the numbers of which they are the squares are identical; but the numbers are already given as the same or different independently of this consideration. With events and states, I am suggesting, this is not so (and perhaps this counts in some degree against thinking of events as objects). Events of the same kind are discriminated

---

whom she is attributing it. The answer to the second question would then be: α's knowledge of her own attitudes or other experiential states requires not only that their objects involve the bearers of those attitudes or states, but also the recognition that their bearer is α.

The two questions above can become intertwined if we take for granted that we recognize ourselves as the bearers of our experiences (and of course 'pathological α' is not offered as a clinical possibility (let alone reality), but rather as a logical exercise); but their coming apart should not, I think, detract from the interpretation of immunity to error through misidentification in terms of reflexive attitudes and states.

through their participants, rather than intrinsically. I conclude, then, that we have a strong sense in which Heimson and Hume believe alike.

In this chapter I have been defending a version of Castañeda's original view, that there is something special about first-personal reports of thoughts. An issue for this view that was raised early on, in Kretzmann (1966), was: could anyone other than $x$ know what $x$ knows when $x$ knows something first-personal about $x$? Could even God know it? Reviewing the discussion, Perry (1983) cites Castañeda's response (Castañeda (1968)), which I paraphrase as follows.

Suppose that John is in the hospital, and he knows in the ordinary way that he himself is in the hospital. What he knows is a fact or true proposition, $p$ say. Evidently, many others may know, and God in particular is bound to know, that John knows $p$. But $p$ itself is a consequence, and a pretty trivial one at that, of what they then know. We would be, to put it mildly, surprised to learn that whereas $x$ knows that John knows $p$, $x$ does not know $p$; and such incapacity is out of the question where God is concerned. So we may assume that $x$ knows $p$, and it follows in particular that God knows $p$.

The above reasoning is all very well; but it does not apply to the construction of first-person knowledge given here. Suppose we had taken up 'John knows that he is in the hospital' merely as the proposition expressed by (46):

(46)  For John=$x$ ($\exists e$) knows[$x,e,{}^{\wedge}(\exists e')$ in-hospital($x,e'$)]

From (46) there follows, knowledge being knowledge of truth, (47), where $\alpha$ is the person John:

(47)  ($\exists e'$) in-hospital($\alpha,e'$)

Thus Castañeda's response to Kretzmann would be vindicated. But we are supposing that the peculiarly first-personal reading of our target sentence is given by (48):

(48)  For John=$x$ ($\exists e$) knows[$x,e,{}^{\wedge}(\exists e')$ in-hospital($\sigma(e)$ & $\theta(e'),e'$)]

and from knowledge of what (48) expresses we would have to be able to infer (49):

(49)  ($\exists e'$) in-hospital($\sigma(\beta),e'$)

where $\beta$ is the state of knowledge that John is in. But this is too much to ask: from the fact that I know that there is some state $e$ or other such that John knows that its subject (he, John) is in the hospital, I can't derive the knowledge, with respect to any state $\beta$ at all, that the subject of that state is in the hospital; to suppose otherwise would be as wrong as to suppose that merely by knowing that someone or other knows that he is in the hospital I could come to know, with respect to a particular person, that that person is in the hospital.[16]

I suppose we should concede that it would be different with God. For (49) expresses one of the things that there is to be known; and God knows everything. That case apart, we have a further dividend of the account suggested here: for John, being himself *in* the state β, can be expected to know what (49) expresses; but others in general will not, even if they know what is expressed by (48).

Of course, it does not follow that no one other than John and God can know what is expressed by (49). On the contrary, there is at least so far no intrinsic reason that one cannot have knowledge of John's state of knowledge as one has knowledge of other events and states. Events and states, I have suggested, have their participants essentially, so that no one other than John can *be* in the state β; but nothing about knowledge of β follows from that.

We have at this point bumped up against some familiar philosophical questions of privacy, even perhaps 'privileged access', and so forth, which I will not consider here. However, it may be observed that the construction lends credence both to the thesis that there is a special way in which one is given to oneself when one knows in a first-personal way that one is in the hospital (or driving a car, or looking around the room, etc.), *and* that this special way is, *mutatis mutandis*, available to all.

A final example. In this discussion I have concentrated upon the properties of understood subjects, construed here as PRO. It happens that this particular element occurs only in one place in English and other languages, namely as the subject of a clausal or nominal complex lacking a tense.[17] We can, however, so to speak tease the effects of PRO into another position by taking it as the antecedent of a reciprocal construction, as in (50):

(50)    *a* and *b* remembered/imagined [PRO kissing each other]

where we are interested in the interpretation according to which each remembered or imagined the reciprocal kissing (and not the one where each merely remembered or imagined kissing the other).[18] Even if the events remembered

---

[16] Compare the discussion in Perry (1983: 88).

[17] There has been a lengthy debate in the linguistics literature about whether PRO occurs as the subject of nominals as well as clauses, a matter from which I abstract in the present discussion.

[18] The example is a case of 'partial control' in the sense of Landau (2000: ch. 2), in the sense that the subject position of what each remembers includes the other as well as herself. As remarked briefly above, partial control, which brings the *de se* in its wake, threatens the Lewis-Chierchia picture of the subject as disappearing under abstraction.

by $a$ and $b$ are the same, they are given to them in different ways. For, on the account suggested here, $a$'s memory is given to $a$ as of concurrent events $e'$ and $e''$, and through a memorial state $e$ such that

$$\text{kiss}(\sigma(e)\ \&\ \theta_1(e'), b, e')\ \&\ \text{kiss}(b, \sigma(e)\ \&\ \theta_2(e''), e'')$$

where $\theta_1$ expresses agency, and $\theta_2$, say, the 'undergoing' relation, whereas not only is $b$'s memorial state different, but also the roles are reversed, as in

$$\text{kiss}(\sigma(e)\ \&\ \theta_1(e'), a, e')\ \&\ \text{kiss}(a, \sigma(e)\ \&\ \theta_2(e''), e'')$$

I believe that these consequences are in accord with intuition. If so, then we can so to speak push the properties of PRO into the direct object position, as we can in verbal passives, such as '*a* remembers PRO being kissed by b'. That language, or English anyway, provides us with only a small window for the direct expression of the peculiarities of certain first-person thoughts is not, therefore, of itself a reason to doubt their existence.[19]

---

[19] A first draft of this chapter was presented at the Sheffield conference Epistemology of Language, July 2000, Michael Martin commenting. That draft was itself based upon earlier presentations at the University of Oxford, at the University of Michigan, and at the tenth conference on Semantics and Linguistic Theory, Cornell University, March 2000. Presentations subsequent to the Sheffield draft include talks at the University of Siena, the University of London, and the University of California, Davis. I am grateful to my various audiences for their comments, and especially to Carl Ginet, Allen Gibbard, Alessandra Giorgi, Stephen Parkinson, Christopher Peacocke, Philippe Schlenker, Gabriel Segal, and Orsolya Schreiner. Alex Barber and Christopher Peacocke provided very useful comments on earlier drafts; and discussion with Philippe Schlenker and members of the audience at the European Summer School for Logic, Language, and Information in Trento in 2002 helped me to draw the connections between my discussion and certain revisionist movements in intensional logic.

# References

Abusch, D. (1988). 'Sequence of Tense, Intensionality, and Scope', in H. Borer (ed.), *Proceedings of the Seventh West Coast Conference on Formal Linguistics*. Stanford, CA: CSLI Publications, distributed by the University of Chicago Press, 1–14.
—— (1991). 'The Present Under Past as *De Re* Interpretation', in D. Bates (ed.), *Proceedings of the Tenth West Coast Conference on Formal Linguistics*. Stanford, CA: CSLI Publications, distributed by the University of Chicago Press, 1–12.
—— (1994). 'Sequence of Tense Revisited: Two Semantic Accounts of Tense in Intensional Contexts', in H. Kamp (ed.), *Ellipsis, Tense, and Questions*. DYANA deliverable, University of Amsterdam, 87–139.
—— (1997). 'Sequence of Tense and Temporal *De Re*', *Linguistics and Philosophy* 20: 1–50.
Bach, E. (1982). 'Purpose Clauses and Control', in P. Jacobson and G.K. Pullum (eds.), *The Nature of Syntactic Representation*. Dordrecht, Holland: D. Reidel, 35–57.
—— (1986). 'The Algebra of Events'. *Linguistics and Philosophy* 9: 5–16.
Balaguer, M. (1997). 'Indexical Senses', ms., CA State University, Los Angeles.
Bar-Hillel, Y. (1954). 'Indexical Expressions'. *Mind* 63: 359–379.
Bhatt, R. (2001). *Covert Modality in Non-Finite Contexts*. Unpub. Ph.D. thesis, University of Pennsylvania.
Bonomi, A. (1997). 'The Progressive and the Structure of Events'. *Journal of Semantics* 14: 173–205.
—— (1998). 'Semantical Remarks on the Progressive Reading of the Imperfective', ms., University of Milan.
Boogaart, R. (1999). *Aspect and Temporal Ordering: A Contrastive Analysis of Dutch and English*. Ph.D. thesis, University of Amsterdam.
Bowers, J. (1993). 'The Syntax of Predication'. *Linguistic Inquiry* 24: 591–656.
Brody, Michael, and Manzini, M. Rita (1987). 'On Implicit Arguments', in R.M. Kempson (ed.), *Mental Representations: The Interface Between Language and Reality*. Cambridge: Cambridge University Press, 105–130.
Burge, T. (1974). 'Demonstrative Constructions, Reference, and Truth'. *Journal of Philosophy* 71: 205–223.
—— (1978). 'Self-Reference and Translation', in F. Guenthner and M. Guenthner-Reutter (eds.), *Meaning and Translation*. New York: NYU Press, 137–153.
Byun, H. (2006). 'Sequence of Tense in Korean and Japanese', ms., University of Southern California.
Campbell, J. (1999). 'Immunity to Error Through Misidentification and the Meaning of a Referring Term'. *Philosophical Topics* 26: 89–104.
Carlson, G. (1980). *Reference to Kinds in English*. New York: Garland Publishing.

—— (1989). 'Truth Conditions of Generic Sentences: Two Contrasting Views', in G. Carlson and F.J. Pelletier (eds.) (1995), 224–237.
—— and Pelletier, F.J. (eds.) (1995). *The Generic Book*. Chicago: University of Chicago Press.
Castañeda, H.-N. (1966). 'He*: A Study in the Logic of Self-Consciousness'. *Ratio* 8: 130–157.
—— (1967). 'Indicators and Quasi-Indicators'. *American Philosophical Quarterly* 4: 85–100.
—— (1968). 'On the Logic of Attributions of Self-Knowledge to Others'. *Journal of Philosophy* 65: 439–456.
Chierchia, G. (1990). 'Anaphora and Attitudes *De Se*', in R. Bartsch *et al.* (eds.), *Language in Action*. Dordrecht, Holland: Foris Publications, 1–31.
—— (1995). 'Individual-Level Predicates as Inherent Generics', in G. Carlson and F.J. Pelletier (eds.) (1995), 176–223.
Chomsky, N. (1957). *Syntactic Structures*. The Hague: Mouton.
—— (1972). 'Remarks on Nominalization', in Chomsky, *Studies on Semantics in Generative Grammar*. The Hague: Mouton, 11–61.
—— (1977). 'On WH-Movement', in P.W. Culicover, T. Wasow, and A. Akmajian (eds.), *Formal Syntax*. New York: Academic Press, 71–132.
—— (1981). *Lectures on Government and Binding*. Dordrecht, Holland: Foris.
Cinque, G. (1999). *Adverbs and Functional Heads: A Cross-Linguistic Perspective*. New York and Oxford: Oxford University Press.
Cresswell, M.J. (1990). *Entities and Indices*. Dordrecht, Holland: Kluwer.
Crimmins, M. (1992). *Talk About Beliefs*. Cambridge, MA: MIT Press.
Culicover, P.W. and Jackendoff, R. (1995). '*Something Else* for the Binding Theory'. *Linguistic Inquiry* 26: 249–276.
Davidson, D. (1967). 'The Logical Form of Action Sentences', in N. Rescher (ed.), *The Logic of Decision and Action*. Pittsburgh, PA: University of Pittsburgh Press. Repr. in Davidson (1980), 105–148.
—— (1979). 'Moods and Performances', in A. Margalit (ed.), *Meaning and Use*. Dordrecht, Holland: D. Reidel. Repr. in Davidson (1984), 109–121.
—— (1980). *Essays on Actions and Events*. Oxford: Clarendon Press.
—— (1984). *Inquiries into Truth and Interpretation*. Oxford: Clarendon Press.
Dowty, D. (1977). 'Toward a Semantic Analysis of Verb Aspect and the English "Imperfective" Progressive'. *Linguistics and Philosophy* 1: 45–77.
—— (1979). *Word Meaning and Montague Grammar*. Dordrecht, Holland: D. Reidel.
—— (1982). 'Tenses, Time Adverbs, and Compositional Semantic Theory'. *Linguistics and Philosophy* 5: 23–53.
Enç, M. (1987). 'Anchoring Conditions for Tense'. *Linguistic Inquiry* 18: 1–26.
—— (1991). 'On the Absence of the Present Tense Morpheme in English', ms., University of Wisconsin, Madison.

Epstein, S. (1984). 'Quantifier PRO and the LF-Representation of PRO$_{ARB}$'. *Linguistic Inquiry* 15: 499–505.

Evans, G. (1981). 'Understanding Demonstratives', in H. Parret and J. Bouveresse (eds.), *Meaning and Understanding*. Berlin: Walter de Gruyter. Repr. in Evans, *Collected Papers*. Oxford: Clarendon Press, 1985, 291–321.

—— (1982). *The Varieties of Reference*. Oxford: Clarendon Press.

Faraci, R. (1974). *Aspects of the Grammar of Infinitives and For-Phrases*. Unpub. PhD. thesis, MA Institute of Technology, Cambridge, MA.

Fiengo, R. (1977). 'On Trace Theory'. *Linguistic Inquiry* 8: 35–61.

—— and Higginbotham, J. (1981). 'Opacity in NP'. *Linguistic Analysis* 7: 395–421.

Fodor, J. (1975). *The Language of Thought*. New York: Crowell.

—— and Lepore, E. (1998). 'Lexical Decomposition; or, Please Don't Play That *Again*, Sam', ms., Rutgers University.

Folli, R. (2002). *Constructing Telicity in English and Italian*. D.Phil. thesis, University of Oxford.

Frege, G. (1918). 'The Thought: A Logical Inquiry', trans. A.M. and M. Quinton, in P.F. Strawson (ed.), *Philosophical Logic*. Oxford: Oxford University Press, 1967, 17–38.

Giorgi, A. (2005). 'Perspectives on Tense', ms., University of Venice.

—— and Pianesi, F. (1997). *Tense and Aspect: From Semantics to Morphosyntax*. New York: Oxford University Press.

———— (1998a). 'Present Tense, Perfectivity, and the Anchoring Conditions', in A. Wyner (ed.), *Proceedings of the 13th Conference of the Israeli Association for Theoretical Linguistics (IATL-5)*. Bar-Ilan University, Ramat-Gan, Israel, 75–95.

———— (1998b). 'The Generalized Double-Access Reading', ms., University of Bergamo, Italy.

———— (2000). 'Sequence of Tense Phenomena in Italian'. *Probus* 12: 1–32.

———— (2001). 'Tense, Attitudes, and Subjects', in R. Hastings, B. Jackson, and Z. Zvolensky (eds.), *Proceedings, SALT XI*. Cornell University: CLC Publications, 212–230.

Grimshaw, J. (1991). *Argument Structure*. Cambridge, MA: MIT Press.

Hale, K. and Keyser, S.J. (1998). 'Conflation', ms., MIT, Cambridge, MA.

Higginbotham, J. (1983a). 'The Logic of Perceptual Reports: An Extensional Alternative to Situation Semantics'. *Journal of Philosophy* 80: 100–127.

—— (1983b). 'Logical Form, Binding, and Nominals'. *Linguistic Inquiry* 14: 395–420.

—— (1985). 'On Semantics'. *Linguistic Inquiry* 16: 547–593.

—— (1986). 'Linguistic Theory and Davidson's Program in Semantics', in E. LePore (ed.), *Truth and Interpretation: Perspectives on the Philosophy of Donald Davidson*. Oxford: Basil Blackwell, 29–48.

—— (1988). 'Contexts, Models, and Meanings: A Note on the Data of Semantics', in R. Kempson (ed.), *Mental Representations: The Interface Between Language and Reality*. Cambridge: Cambridge University Press, 29–48.

—— (1989a). 'Reference and Control'. *Rivista di Linguistica* 1. Repr. with minor revisions in R. Larson, S. Iatridou, U. Lahiri, and J. Higginbotham (eds.), *Control and Grammar*. Dordrecht, Holland: Kluwer, 1990, 79–108.

—— (1989b). 'Elucidations of Meaning'. *Linguistics and Philosophy* 12: 465–517.

—— (1991a). 'Belief and Logical Form'. *Mind and Language* 6: 344–369.

—— (1991b). 'Truth and Understanding'. *Iyyun* 40: 271–288.

—— (1991c). 'Either/Or'. *NELS XXI Proceedings*. GLSA, University of MA, Amherst, 143–155.

—— (1993a). 'Notes on Sequence of Tense', ms., University of Oxford.

—— (1993b). Review of M.J. Cresswell, *Entities and Indices*. *Journal of Symbolic Logic* 58: 723–725.

—— (1993c). 'Remarks on Aspect'. Invited lecture, SALT III, University of CA, Irvine. Ms., University of Southern CA.

—— (1994a). 'Priorities in the Philosophy of Thought'. *Proceedings of the Aristotelian Society Supplementary Volume*: 85–106.

—— (1994b). 'Mass and Count Quantifiers'. *Linguistics and Philosophy* 17: 447–480. Repr. in E. Bach, E. Jelinek, A. Kratzer, and B.H. Partee (eds.), *Quantification in Natural Language*, Dordrecht, Holland: Kluwer, 1995, 383–419.

—— (1995a). *Sense and Syntax*. Inaugural lecture, University of Oxford. Oxford: Clarendon Press.

—— (1995b). 'Tensed Thoughts'. *Mind and Language* 10: 226–249. Repr. in W. Künne, A. Newen, and M. Anduschus (eds.), *Direct Reference, Indexicality, and Propositional Attitudes*. Stanford, CA: CSLI Publications, 1997, 21–48.

—— (1996). 'Competence with Demonstratives', ms., University of Oxford. Pub. in *Philosophical Perspectives* 16 (2002): 3–18. Also in B. Ramberg and M. Hahn (eds.), *Reflections and Replies: Essays on the Philosophy of Tyler Burge*. Cambridge, MA: MIT Press, 2003, 101–115.

—— (1997). 'A Plea for Implicit Anaphora', in H. Bennis, P. Pica, and J. Rooryck (eds.), *Atomism and Binding*. Amsterdam: Foris, 183–203.

—— (2000a). 'On Events in Linguistic Semantics', in J. Higginbotham, F. Pianesi, and A. Varzi (eds.), *Speaking of Events*. New York: Oxford University Press, 49–79.

—— (2000b). 'Accomplishments'. *Proceedings of Glow in Asia II*. Nagoya, Japan: Nanzan University, 72–82.

—— (2002a). 'Why is Sequence of Tense Obligatory?', in G. Preyer and G. Peter (eds.), *Logical Form and Language*. Oxford: Clarendon Press, 207–227.

—— (2002b). 'Competence with Demonstratives'. *Philosophical Perspectives* 16: 3–18.

—— (2003a). 'Tensed Second Thoughts: Comments on Richard', in A. Jokič and Q. Smith (eds.), *Time, Tense, and Reference*. Cambridge, MA: MIT Press, 191–197.

Higginbotham, J. (2003b). 'Remembering, Imagining, and the First Person', in A. Barber (ed.), *Epistemology of Language*. Oxford: Oxford University Press, 496–533.

—— (2005). 'Event Positions: Suppression and Emergence'. *Theoretical Linguistics* 31: 349–358.

—— (2006a). 'The Anaphoric Theory of Tense', in M. Gibson and J. Howell (eds.), *Proceedings from Semantics and Linguistic Theory 16*. CLC Publications, Cornell University, Ithaca, NY, 59–76.

—— (2006b). 'Sententialism: The Thesis that Complement Clauses Refer to Themselves', in E. Sosa and E. Villanueva (eds.), *Philosophical Issues 16: Philosophy of Language* (a supplementary volume to *Noûs*). Oxford: Blackwell Publishing, 101–119.

—— (2007). 'Remarks on Compositionality'. G. Ramchand and C. Reiss (eds.), *The Oxford Handbook of Linguistic Interfaces*. Oxford: Oxford University Press, 425–444.

—— (2008). 'The English Perfect and the Metaphysics of Events', in J. Lecarme and J. Guéron (eds.), *Time and Modality*. Berlin: Springer Verlag, 173–193.

—— and Ramchand, G. (1997). 'The Stage-Level/Individual-Level Distinction and the Mapping Hypothesis'. *Oxford Working Papers in Linguistics, Philology, and Phonetics* 2: 53–83.

Hoekstra, T. (1992). 'Aspect and Theta Theory', in I. Roca (ed.), *Thematic Structure: Its Role in Grammar*. Amsterdam: Foris, 145–174.

Huang, Y. (2000). *Anaphora: A Cross-Linguistic Study*. Oxford: Oxford University Press.

Iatridou, S., Anagnostopoulou, E., and Izvorski, R. (2005). 'Observations About the Form and Meaning of the Perfect', in M. Kenstowicz (ed.), *Ken Hale: A Life in Language*. Cambridge, MA: MIT Press, 189–238.

Ippolito, M. (1996). *Tense and Aspect in English and Italian*. M.Phil. thesis, University of Oxford.

—— (1998). 'Reference Time and Tense Anaphora', ms., MIT, Cambridge, MA.

—— (1999). 'The Imperfect and Modality', ms., MIT, Cambridge, MA.

Israel, D. and Perry, J. (1996). 'Where Monsters Dwell', in J. Seligman and D. Westerståhl (eds.), *Logic, Language, and Computation*, vol. 1. Stanford, CA: CSLI Publications, 1–14.

Jespersen, O. (1924). *The Philosophy of Grammar*. New York: Norton.

Jones, C. (1991). *Purpose Clauses: Syntax, Thematics, and Semantics of English Purpose Constructions*. Dordrecht, Holland: Kluwer.

Kamp, J.A.W. (1971). 'Formal Properties of "Now"'. *Theoria* 37: 227–273.

—— (1981). 'A Theory of Truth and Semantic Representation', in J. Groenendijk *et al.* (eds.), *Formal Methods in the Study of Language*. Amsterdam: Mathematical Centre, 277–322.

—— and Reyle, U. (1993). *From Discourse to Logic*. Dordrecht, Holland: Kluwer.

Kaplan, D. (1977). 'Demonstratives'. Pub. with afterthoughts in J. Almog *et al.* (eds.), *Themes From Kaplan*. Oxford: Oxford University Press, 1989, 481–614.

—— (1995). 'Meaning and Use'. Gareth Evans Memorial Lecture, University of Oxford.

Kayne, R. (1985). 'Principles of Particle Constructions', in H. Obenauer et al. (eds.), *Levels of Syntactic Representation.* Amsterdam: Foris, 101–140.

—— (1994). *The Antisymmetry of Syntax.* Cambridge, MA: MIT Press.

Kiparsky, P. (1996). 'Remarks on Denominal Verbs', in A. Alsina et al. (eds.), *Complex Predicates.* Stanford, CA: CSLI Publications.

—— (2002). 'Event Structure and the Perfect', in D.I. Beaver, L.D. Casillas Martínez, B.Z. Clark, and S. Kaufmann (eds.), *The Construction of Meaning.* Stanford, CA: CSLI Publications, 1–20.

Kratzer, A. (1995). 'Stage-Level and Individual-Level Predicates', in G. Carlson and F.J. Pelletier (eds.) (1995), 125–175.

Kretzmann, N. (1966). 'Omniscience and Immutability'. *Journal of Philosophy* 63: 409–421.

Krifka, M. (1992). 'Thematic Relations as Links between Nominal Reference and Temporal Constitution', in I. Sag and A. Szabolcsi (eds.), *Lexical Matters.* Stanford, CA: CSLI Publications, 29–53.

Ladusaw, W. (1977). 'Some Problems with Tense in PTQ'. *Texas Linguistic Forum* 6: 89–102.

Landau, I. (2000). *Elements of Control: Structure and Meaning in Infinitival Constructions.* Dordrecht, Holland: Kluwer.

Landman, F. (1992). 'The Progressive'. *Natural Language Semantics* 1: 1–32.

Lewis, D. (1970). 'General Semantics'. *Synthèse* 22. Reprinted in Lewis (1983), 189–232.

—— (1973). *Counterfactuals.* Cambridge, MA: Harvard University Press.

—— (1979) 'Attitudes *de dicto* and *de se*'. *Philosophical Review* 88: 513–543. Repr. in Lewis (1983), 133–159.

—— (1980). 'Index, Context, and Content', in S. Kanger and S. Öhman (eds.), *Philosophy and Grammar.* Dordrecht, Holland: D. Reidel. Repr. in Lewis (1998), 21–44.

—— (1983). *Philosophical Papers, Vol. I.* Oxford: Oxford University Press.

—— (1998). *Papers in Philosophical Logic.* Cambridge: Cambridge University Press.

McTaggart, E. (1908). 'The Unreality of Time'. *Mind* 17: 456–473.

Mitchell, J. (1986). *The Formal Semantics Point of View.* Unpub. Ph.D. thesis, University of MA, Amherst MA.

Mittwoch, A. (1988). 'Aspects of English Aspect: On the Interaction of Perfect, Progressive, and Durational Phrases'. *Linguistics and Philosophy* 11: 203–254.

Montague, R. (1960). 'On the Nature of Certain Philosophical Entities'. *The Monist* 53. Repr. in Montague (1974), 148–187.

—— (1968). 'Pragmatics', in R. Klibansky (ed.), *Contemporary Philosophy.* Florence, Italy: La Nuova Italia Editrice, 102–121. Repr. in Montague (1974), 95–118.

—— (1974). *Formal Philosophy*, ed. R. Thomason. New Haven: Yale University Press.

Moore, G.E. (1927). 'Facts and Propositions'. *Aristotelian Society Supplementary Vol. VII* (Symposium with F.P. Ramsey.) Repr. in Moore, *Philosophical Papers.* London: George, Allen and Unwin, 1959, 60–88.

Ogihara, T. (1989). *Temporal Reference in English and Japanese.* Unpub. Ph.D. thesis, University of Texas at Austin.

—— (1994). 'Adverbs of Quantification and Sequence-of-Tense Phenomena', in M. Harvey and L. Santelmann (eds.), *Proceedings of Semantics and Linguistic Theory IV.* Cornell University, Ithaca, NY: DMLL Publications, 251–267.

—— (1995). *Tense, Attitudes, and Scope.* Dordrecht, Holland: Kluwer.

Pancheva, R. (2004). 'Another Perfect Puzzle', in V. Chand *et al.* (eds.), *Proceedings, WCCFL 23.* Somerville, MA: Cascadilla Press, 621–634.

—— and Stechow, A. von (2004). 'On the Present Perfect Puzzle', in K. Moulton and M. Wolf (eds.), *Proceedings NELS 34.* University of MA, Amherst, 469–483.

Parsons, T. (1989). 'The Progressive in English: Events, States, and Processes'. *Linguistics and Philosophy* 12: 213–241.

—— (1990). *Events in the Semantics of English: A Study in Subatomic Semantics.* Cambridge, MA: MIT Press.

Partee, B. (1989). 'Binding Implicit Variables in Quantified Contexts'. *Chicago Linguistics Society* 25, University of Chicago: 342–365.

Peacocke, C. (1981). 'Demonstrative Thought and Psychological Explanation'. *Synthèse* 49: 187–217.

—— (1998). *Being Known.* Oxford: Oxford University Press.

Perry, J. (1979). 'The Problem of the Essential Indexical'. *Noûs* 13: 3–21. Repr. with a postscript in Perry (2000), 27–44.

—— (1983). 'Castañeda on *He* and *I*', (ed.) J.E. Tomberlin, *Agent, Language, and the Structure of the World: Essays Presented to Hector-Neri Castañeda With His Replies.* Indianapolis: Hackett Publishing Company. Repr. in Perry (2000), 77–100.

—— (1993). Postscript to 'Frege on Demonstratives'. *The Problem of the Essential Indexical and Other Essays.* Oxford: Oxford University Press. Repr. in Perry (2000), 21–26.

—— (2000). *The Problem of the Essential Indexical and Other Essays.* Expanded edn. Stanford: CSLI Publications.

Portner, P. (2003). 'The (Temporal) Semantics and the (Modal) Pragmatics of the Perfect'. *Linguistics and Philosophy* 26: 459–510.

Prior, A.N. (1957). *Time and Modality.* Oxford: Oxford University Press.

—— (1967). *Past, Present, and Future.* Oxford: Oxford University Press.

Pryor, J. (1999). 'Immunity to Error Through Misidentification'. *Philosophical Topics* 26: 271–304.

Quine, W.V. (1960). *Word and Object.* Cambridge, MA: MIT Press.

Recanati, F. (2007). *Perspectival Thought.* Oxford: Oxford University Press.

Reichenbach, H. (1947). *Elements of Symbolic Logic.* New York: Macmillan.

Richard, M. (1983). 'Direct Reference and Ascriptions of Belief'. *Journal of Philosophical Logic* 12: 425–452.
—— (1990). *Propositional Attitudes: An Essay on Thoughts and How We Ascribe Them.* Cambridge: Cambridge University Press.
—— (2003). 'Objects of Relief', in A. Jokič and Q. Smith (eds.), *Time, Tense, and Reference.* Cambridge, MA: MIT Press, 157–189.
Roberts, I. (1987). *The Representation of Implicit and Dethematized Subjects.* Dordrecht, Holland: Foris.
Roeper, T. (1987). 'Implicit Arguments and the Head–Complement Relation'. *Linguistic Inquiry* 18: 267–310.
Rothstein, S. (2000). 'Progressive Accomplishments', ms., Bar-Ilan University, Tel-Aviv, Israel.
Salmon, N. (1986). *Frege's Puzzle.* Cambridge, MA: MIT Press.
Schein, B. (1993). *Plurals and Events.* Cambridge, MA: MIT Press.
Schiffer, S. (1977). 'Naming and Knowing', in P. French, T. Uehling, Jr., and H. Wettstein (eds.), *Contemporary Perspectives in the Philosophy of Language.* Minneapolis: University of Minnesota Press, 61–74.
—— (1987). 'The "Fido"-Fido Theory of Belief', in J.E. Tomberlin (ed.), *Philosophical Perspectives 1: Metaphysics.* Altascadero, CA: Ridgeview Publishing Company, 457–480.
Schlenker, P. (1999). *Propositional Attitudes and Indexicality: A Cross-Categorial Approach.* Unpub. Ph.D. thesis, MA Institute of Technology, Cambridge, MA.
—— (2003). 'A Plea for Monsters'. *Linguistics and Philosophy* 26: 29–120.
Segerberg, K. (1973). 'Two Dimensional Modal Logic'. *Journal of Philosophical Logic* 2: 77–101.
Shoemaker, S. (1968). 'Self-Reference and Self-Awareness'. *Journal of Philosophy* 65: 555–567.
—— (1970). 'Persons and Their Pasts'. *American Philosophical Quarterly* 7: 269–285.
Smith, C. (1978). 'The Syntax and Interpretation of Temporal Expressions in English'. *Linguistics and Philosophy* 2: 43–99.
—— (1991). *The Parameter of Aspect.* Dordrecht, Holland: Kluwer.
Stalnaker, R. (1981). 'Indexical Belief'. *Synthèse* 49: 129–151. Repr. in Stalnaker (1999), 130–149.
—— (1984). *Inquiry.* Cambridge, MA: MIT Press.
—— (1987). 'Semantics for Belief'. *Philosophical Topics* 15: 177–190. Repr. in Stalnaker (1999), 117–130.
—— (1999). *Context and Content.* Oxford: Oxford University Press.
Stechow, A. von (1995). 'On the Proper Treatment of Tense'. Paper presented at SALT V.
—— (2001). 'Temporally Opaque Arguments in Verbs of Creation', in C. Cecchetto, G. Chierchia, and M.T. Guasti (eds.), *Semantic Interfaces: Reference, Anaphora, and Aspect.* Stanford, CA: CSLI Publications, 278–319.
—— (2002). 'Tense in Intensional Contexts: Two Semantic Accounts of Abusch's Theory of Tense', ms., University of Tübingen.

Stowell, T. (1993). 'Syntax and Tense', ms., University of CA, Los Angeles.

Strawson, P. (1950). 'On Referring'. *Mind* 59: 320–344.

Talmy, Leonard (1985). 'Lexicalization Patterns: Semantic Structure in Lexical Forms', in T. Shopen (ed.), *Language Typology and Syntactic Description III: Grammatical Categories and the Lexicon*. Cambridge: Cambridge University Press.

Tenny, C. (1994). *Aspectual Roles and the Syntax–Semantics Interface*. Dordrecht, Holland: Kluwer.

Tortora, C.M. (1998). 'Verbs of Inherently Directed Motion are Compatible with Resultative Phrases'. *Linguistic Inquiry* 29: 338–345.

Verkuyl, H. (1993). *Aspectuality*. Cambridge: Cambridge University Press.

Vlach, F. (1981). 'The Semantics of the Progressive', in P. Tedeschi and A. Zaenen (eds.), *Tense and Aspect (Syntax and Semantics, Vol. 14)*. New York: Academic Press, 271–292.

Weinstein, S. (1974). 'Truth and Demonstratives'. *Nous* 8: 179–184.

Whelpton, M. (1993). *The Syntax and Semantics of Infinitives of Result in English*. Unpub. M.Phil. thesis, University of Oxford.

—— (1995). *Syntactic and Semantic Functions in Control Theory*. Unpub. D.Phil. thesis, University of Oxford.

Williams, E. (1994). *Thematic Structure in Syntax*. Cambridge, MA: MIT Press.

Wurmbrand, S. (2001). 'Back to the Future'. *Snippets* 3: 15–16.

Zagona, K. (1992). 'Tense Binding and the Construal of Present Tense', in C. Laeufer and T. Morgan (eds.), *Theoretical Analyses in Romance Linguistics*. Amsterdam: John Benjamins.

—— (2000). 'Tense Construal in Complement Clauses: Verbs of Communication and the Double Access Reading', ms., University of Washington, Seattle.

Zubizarretta, M.-L. (1982). *On the Relationship of the Lexicon to Syntax*. Unpub. Ph.D. thesis, MA Institute of Technology, Cambridge, MA.

Zucchi, A. (1997). 'Incomplete Events, Intensionality, and Imperfective Aspect'. *Natural Language Semantics* 7: 179–215.

# Index

Abusch, D. 5 n. 4, 61, 89, 101 n. 1, 102, 109–110
Adverbs, types of interpretation 28–36
Aspect:
  Perfect 157–178
  Progressive 126–156
  Telic pairs 116–125
  Vendler classes 128, 129

Bach, E. 40, 45
Balaguer, M. 79
Bar-Hillel, Y. 83
Bhatt, R. 120
Bonomi, A. 133, 142 n. 4, 147 n. 9, 156 n. 10
Boogaart, R. 159 n. 2
Bowers, J. 32
Brody, M. and Manzini, M. 201
Burge, T. 8, 88, 112, 182, 185 n. 5
Byun, H. 112–113

Campbell, J. 221, 233
Carlson, G. 18–19, 22
Castañeda, H.-N. 212, 243
Causative 120–125
Chierchia, G. 27 n. 5, 213 n. 4, 214, 236–237
Chomsky, N. 45, 126, 195, 201, 205, 207–208, 213
Cinque, G. 32 n. 8
Competence, semantic 18–19, 69–70
  with demonstratives 179–194
Complements, interpretation of 88, 185–186
Compositionality, local 32 n. 8
Cresswell, M. 3
Crimmins, M. 189, 192 n. 10
Culicover, P. and Jackendoff, R. 198, 208–210, 209 n. 12

Davidson, D. 5, 18–23, 30, 59, 85, 103, 111, 112, 163–164, 184
Declerk, R. 169
Decomposition, lexical 121–125
Demonstratives 179–194
  and normal forms 182–184
*De se* see First person

Diagonal Proposition 66–67, 191–192, 235–236
Dowty, D. 3, 41 n. 15, 85, 126, 130–133, 131 n. 2, 141, 150–151, 152, 156 n. 10

Enč, M. 5 n. 4, 14, 16 n. 12, 61, 88,
Epstein, S. 199
Evans, G. 75, 187
E-positions 19, 160–165
Events and Event Reference:
  Davidson's account 5–6, 18–19
  Montague's account 18–27
  through an E-position 18–27
  and nominalization 20–21
  and kinds of events 22–23
  and quantification 28
  and negation 48–51
  and telicity 116
  and purpose clauses 45–48
  generic 19–23

Faraci, R. 201
Fiengo, R. 200 n. 5
Fiengo, R. and Higginbotham, J. 203–204
First person 190 n. 8, 212–245
Fodor, J. 213 n. 4, 216, 216 n. 6
Fodor, J. and Lepore, E. 116, 121
Folli, R. 128, 141
Frege, G. 214

Gerundive complements and events 217–221
Giorgi, A. 101 n. 1, 112
Giorgi, A. and Pianesi, F. 17 n. 13, 92, 94, 99, 104, 135–136, 156, 171, 174
Grimshaw, J. 21, n. 2
Guéron, J. 145

Hale, K. and Keyser, S. 116, 121–122
Hamburger, R. 163
Heim, I. 16 n. 12
Higginbotham, J. 3, 5 n. 4, 5 n. 5, 8, 32 n. 8, 36, 42, 43 n. 16, 44 n. 17, 49, 59, 90, 103, 116, 134, 157, 163, 183 n. 3, 185, 187, 196, 210, 211, 213, 240

# Index

Higginbotham, J. and Ramchand, G. 27 n. 5
Hoekstra, T. 118
Huang, Y. 212 n. 1

Iatridou, S. 168
Immunity to error through misidentification 74, 221–224
and PRO 224–234
Imperfective paradox 148
Implicit Arguments 86–87, 185–211
and control 198–200
and purpose clauses 201–204
and incorporated anaphora 204–208
Indexicals:
and modality 80–81
and perspective 112–114
and rules of use 179–185
and "monsters" 238–239
mismatch with tense 111–113, 178
Ippolito, M. 6, 7 n. 6, 87, 88, 101 n. 1, 133
Israel, D. and Perry, J. 238

Jespersen, O. 110–111, 157–158
Jones, C. 45

Kamp, J.A.W. 3, 7
Kamp, J.A.W. and Reyle, U. 3, 85
Kant, I. 115
Kaplan, D. 5 n. 3, 12, 15, 15 n. 10, 54, 56, 66, 71, 112, 183, 185, 237, 238–239
Kayne, R. 32 n. 7, 118
Kiparsky, P. 116, 122–123, 169
Kratzer, A. 27, 27 n. 5, 145
Kretzmann, N. 243
Krifka, M. 40 n. 11, 43

Ladusaw, W. 3, 4, 84
Landau, I. 213, n. 2, 237, 244 n. 18
Landman, F. 127, 133, 137, 138–139, 148–149, 156 n. 10
Lasnik, H. 201
Lewis, D. 147 n. 9, 182, 190 n. 8, 212, 214, 236–237, 240
Location and locatum verbs 122–125
Logophor 212

McTaggart, E. 172
Manzini, M. 198
Martin, M. 225, 231, 245 n. 19
Measure phrases 42
Mitchell, J. 196

Mittwoch, A. 138
Montague, R. 18–27, 50, 103–104, 182, 219
Moore, G.E. 11

Ogihara, T. 5 n. 4, 8 n. 8, 16, 85, 88, 89, 90, 92, 100, 101 n.1, 102, 106, 168

Pancheva, R. 112
Pancheva, R. and von Stechow, A. 170–171, 173–174 n. 8
Parameters, aspectual:
for arguments 38–45
for accomplishment predicate formation 119
Parkinson, S. 231 n. 11
Parsons, T. 28, 101 n. 1, 110–111, 123 n. 3, 127, 128, 133–138, 154, 156 n. 10, 157–158
Partee, B. 196–197
Peacocke, C. 215, 218 n. 7, 225, 240
Perfect 110–111, 157–178
and sequence of tense 165–169
and result/resultant states 128
Perry, J. 57, 64 n. 3, 187, 214–215, 240, 243, 244 n. 16
Portner, P. 164 n. 5, 169, 173
Preposition, accomplishment 119
Present perfect puzzle 169–171
shifted 175–177
Prior, A.N. 3, 53–54, 85
Progressive 126–157
and counterfactuals 130–133, 138–139, 146–147
and telicity 138, 139–142
and causation 151–154
and agency 36
in Chinese 155–156
in Italian 135–136
Pryor, J. 217, 221–224, 225
Pustejovsky, J. 116

Quine, W.V. 1

Recanati, F. 224, 233–234 n. 12, 240–242 n. 15
Reflexive thought (state) 53–63, 76–82
Reichenbach, H. 57, 103
Resultative 118–120, 128–129
Richard, M. 76–80, 188–189, 234 n. 12
Roberts, I. 201, 205 n. 9
Roeper, T. 87, 198, 200
Rothstein, S. 141
Ryle, G. 218 n. 7

Salmon, N. 189
Schein, B. 42, 143, 144 n. 6
Schiffer, S. 189
Schlenker, P. 212 n. 1, 238–239
Segerberg, K. 7
Shoemaker, S. 74, 78, 217, 221, 222
Smith, C. 100, 155
Stalnaker, R. 66–67, 191, 214, 235–236, 240
Stowell, T. 5 n. 4, 61, 93
Strawson, P. 9

Talmy, L. 117–118
Telicity 36–37
Tenny, C. 39
Tenses:
    and logical consequence 8–12
    as operators 3–7
    as relations 2–8, 83–101
    and anaphora 12–16, 102–115
    and sequence of tense 83–101, 102–115
    and double access 14, 90–99, 104–105, 166–167
    and subjective time 114–115
Thomason, R. 150–151
Thomson, J. 122 n. 2
Tortora, C. 120
Truth conditions, conditional 9–10

Verkuyl, H. 38
Vlach, F. 131–133
von Stechow, A. 102, 106–109, 145, 170–171

Weinstein, S. 8, 182
Williams, E. 87, 195, 204
Whelpton, M. 46–47, 202
Wurmbrand, S. 112

Zagona, K. 5 n. 4, 94
Zubizarreta, M. 35
Zucchi, A. 127, 134, 136, 137, 142, 156 n. 10

# OXFORD STUDIES IN THEORETICAL LINGUISTICS

PUBLISHED

1. The Syntax of Silence
   Sluicing, Islands, and the Theory of Ellipsis
   *by* Jason Merchant
2. Questions and Answers in Embedded Contexts
   *by* Utpal Lahiri
3. Phonetics, Phonology, and Cognition
   *edited by* Jacques Durand and Bernard Laks
4. At the Syntax-Pragmatics Interface
   Concept Formation and Verbal Underspecification in Dynamic Syntax
   *by* Lutz Marten
5. The Unaccusativity Puzzle
   Explorations of the Syntax-Lexicon Interface
   *edited by* Artemis Alexiadou, Elena Anagnostopoulou, and Martin Everaert
6. Beyond Morphology
   Interface Conditions on Word Formation
   *by* Peter Ackema and Ad Neeleman
7. The Logic of Conventional Implicatures
   *by* Christopher Potts
8. Paradigms of Phonological Theory
   *edited by* Laura Downing, T. Alan Hall, and Renate Raffelsiefen
9. The Verbal Complex in Romance
   *by* Paola Monachesi
10. The Syntax of Aspect
    Deriving Thematic and Aspectual Interpretation
    *Edited by* Nomi Erteschik-Shir and Tova Rapoport
11. Aspects of the Theory of Clitics
    *by* Stephen Anderson
12. Canonical Forms in Prosodic Morphology
    *by* Laura J. Downing
13. Aspect and Reference Time
    *by* Olga Borik
14. Direct Compositionality
    *edited by* Chris Barker and Pauline Jacobson
15. A Natural History of Infixation
    *by* Alan C. L. Yu
16. Phi-Theory
    Phi-Features Across Interfaces and Modules
    *edited by* Daniel Harbour, David Adger, and Susana Béjar
17. French Dislocation: Interpretation, Syntax, Acquisition
    *by* Cécile De Cat
18. Inflectional Identity
    *edited by* Asaf Bachrach and Andrew Nevins
19. Lexical Plurals
    *by* Paolo Acquaviva
20. Adjectives and Adverbs
    Syntax, Semantics, and Discourse
    *Edited by* Louise McNally and Christopher Kennedy
21. InterPhases
    Phase-Theoretic Investigations of Linguistic Interfaces
    *edited by* Kleanthes Grohmann
22. Negation in Gapping
    *by* Sophie Repp
23. A Derivational Syntax for Information Structure
    *by* Luis López
24. Quantification, Definiteness, and Nominalization
    *edited by* Anastasia Giannakidou and Monika Rathert
25. The Syntax of Sentential Stress
    *by* Arsalan Kahnemuyipour
26. Tense, Aspect, and Indexicality
    *by* James Higginbotham
27. Lexical Semantics, Syntax and Event Structure
    *edited by* Malka Rappaport Hovav, Edit Doron and Ivy Sichel
28. About the Speaker
    Towards a Syntax of Indexicality
    *by* Alessandra Giorgi
29. The Sound Patterns of Syntax
    *edited by* Nomi Erteschik-Shir and Lisa Rochman

PUBLISHED IN ASSOCIATION WITH THE SERIES
The Oxford Handbook of Linguistic Interfaces
*edited by* Gillian Ramchand and Charles Reiss

IN PREPARATION
External Arguments in Transitivity Alternations
*by* Artemis Alexiadou, Elena Anagnostopoulou, and Florian Schäfer

The Logic of Pronominal Resumption
*by* Ash Asudeh

Phi Syntax: A Theory of Agreement
*by* Susana Béjar

Stratal Optimality Theory
*by* Ricardo Bermúdez Otero

Phonology in Phonetics
*by* Abigail Cohn

Interfaces in Linguistics
New Research Perspectives
*edited by* Raffaella Folli and Christiane Ulbrich

Conditionals
*by* Angelika Kratzer

The Complementizer Phase
*edited by* Phoevos Panagiotidis

Negative Indefinites
*by* Doris Penka

Computing Optimality
*by* Jason Riggle

Nonverbal Predications
*by* Isabelle Roy

Null Subject Languages
*by* Evi Sifaki and Ioanna Sitaridou

Gradience in Split Intransitivity
*by* Antonella Sorace

The Morphology and Phonology of Exponence
*edited by* Jochen Trommer

Events, Phrases, and Questions
*by* Robert Truswell